ON RECORD
1978-1997

MARTIN POPOFF

BEHIND THE LINES

ON RECORD
1978-1997

MARTIN POPOFF

WYMER
PUBLISHING
Bedford, England

First published in 2024 by Wymer Publishing, Bedford, England
www.wymerpublishing.co.uk Tel: 01234 326691.
Wymer Publishing is a trading name of Wymer (UK) Ltd.

Copyright © 2024 Martin Popoff / Wymer Publishing.

Print edition (fully illustrated): **ISBN: 978-1-915246-64-6**

Edited by Agustin Garcia de Paredes.

The Author hereby asserts his rights to be identified
as the author of this work in accordance with sections
77 to 78 of the Copyright, Designs & Patents Act 1988.

All rights reserved. No part of this publication may be
reproduced or transmitted in any form or by any means,
electronic or mechanical, including photocopying, or any
information storage and retrieval system, without written
permission from the publisher.

This publication is sold subject to the condition that it shall not,
by way of trade or otherwise, be lent, re-sold, hired out or
otherwise circulated without the publisher's prior consent in any
form of binding or cover other than that in which it is published
and without a similar condition including this condition
being imposed on the subsequent purchaser.

Printed and bound in Great Britain by CMP, Dorset.
A catalogue record for this book is available from the British Library.

Typeset/Design by Andy Bishop / Tusseheia Creative.
Cover design by Tusseheia Creative.
Cover photos © Alan Perry Photography.

TABLE OF CONTENTS

Introduction	7
And Then There Were Three	9
Duke	45
Abacab	81
Genesis	109
Invisible Touch	143
We Can't Dance	177
Calling All Stations	219
Contributor Biographies	245
Special Thanks	248
About the Author	248
A Complete Martin Popoff Bibliography	249

BEHIND THE LINES

GENESIS ON RECORD 1978-1997

MARTIN POPOFF

INTRODUCTION

As you may have gathered, there's a sister book to the tome you now hold in your hands. It's called *Entangled: Genesis on Record 1969 – 1976* and it takes us from the band's inception up to *Wind & Wuthering*, the last album with Steve Hackett. *Behind the Lines: Genesis on Record 1978 – 1997* picks up with *And Then There Were Three* and takes us through to the end, namely *Calling All Stations*, the notorious, arguably airless Ray Wilson album that crashed in flames, even though it did not mark the end of band activities.

The nutty thing about this "part two" book is that it excels in one area over and above every book in this series (check out similar reads on Blue Öyster Cult, The Cure, Robert Plant, Thin Lizzy and Rainbow), and that is taking super-seriously albums that are regularly abused by critics and even the Genesis fan base. And what I love about that is that the uncommonly detailed defences of these maligned records sent me scurrying back to check out deep album tracks on the likes of *We Can't Dance* and the aforementioned *Calling All Stations* to get inside the minds of the music-makers and, most rewardingly, the lyric-writers.

Of course there's mostly well-loved Genesis music across this expanse of seven albums, and that goes for long-time Genesis watchers as well as the millions who came on board and shot the band stratospheric, beginning with *Abacab* and most pertinently, through *Genesis* and *Invisible Touch*, four times platinum and six times platinum respectively. In fact, *We Can't Dance* also currently sits at four times platinum, even though it's a record somewhat forgotten by time, rectified here given the eloquent oration upon it by my esteemed panel of wise music swamis. In fact, I'm on record calling *Abacab* my favourite Genesis album, while *And Then There Were Three* and *Duke* aren't far behind, although those are entangled for me with many from the first half of the career and, thusly, the first book of this purposeful and percussive pairing.

But yes, for those unfamiliar with the format, the idea is to talk to some smart classic rock scholars about each and every studio album by a given band, with me as moderator, hammering these guys track by track until you, the reader, is in the same position I was in with *Behind the Lines*, saying to myself, as soon as we're done here, I gotta go reread those lyrics plus listen to what Tony's doing at 4:14 or how Phil is produced for that drum fill at 2:12. At other times, it's more about how does this record fit with what's happening in the '80s, or with synthesizers in the late '70s, or with what Peter Gabriel is doing on a parallel path?

But mostly it was about the lyrics, with some interesting allusions to what Phil was doing as a solo artist, totally killing it in parallel to the mothership in the '80s. The conceptual *Duke* talk was also interesting from a lyric standpoint, as were the subject matter choices across the final, somewhat stranded Ray Wilson proposal. Bottom line, even when Genesis busied themselves with sounding ostentatious and even corporate, they did the hard graft on the lyrics, eloquently exploring the human condition.

In any event, circling back, I'd have to say that *Behind the Lines: Genesis on Record 1978 – 1997* just might have inspired me to look at some other bands with a bunch of albums that are pretty much dismissed. Not that we came up with this concept, but albums like *We Can't Dance* and *Calling All Stations* are dark horses, as we call them on our YouTube channel, *The Contrarians* (you can see some of this book's guest speakers there). I bring that up because we've had a regular series of episodes dealing with these types of records, and it's usually an illuminating conversation, in part because, again, these records rarely get talked about in such detail. So yes, that's what I love about this particular one of my panel books above all others, and I hope, upon reading, that same spirit of discovery enters your body as it did mine.

Martin Popoff
martinp@inforamp.net; martinpopoff.com

AND THEN THERE WERE THREE

March 31, 1978
Charisma CDS 4010
Produced by David Hentschel and Genesis
Engineered by David Hentschel; assisted by Pierre Geofroy Chateau
Recorded at Relight Studios, Hilvarenbeek, Netherlands
Personnel: Phil Collins – drums, voices; Tony Banks – keyboards; Mike Rutherford – guitars, basses

Side 1
1. Down and Out (Collins, Banks, Rutherford) 5:25
2. Undertow (Banks) 4:47
3. Ballad of Big (Collins, Banks, Rutherford) 4:47
4. Snowbound (Rutherford) 4:30
5. Burning Rope (Banks) 7:07

Behind The Lines: Genesis on Record 1978-1997

Side 2
1. Deep in the Motherlode (Rutherford) 5:14
2. Many Too Many (Banks) 3:30
3. Scenes from a Night's Dream (Collins, Banks) 3:30
4. Say It's Alright Joe (Rutherford) 4:18
5. The Lady Lies (Banks) 6:05
6. Follow You Follow Me (Rutherford, Banks, Collins) 3:58

Behind The Lines: Genesis on Record 1978-1997

An *And Then There Were Three* Timeline

September – October 1977. Genesis work at Relight Studios in Hilvarenbeek, The Netherlands on tracks slated for their first album without Steve Hackett. Producing for a third album in a row is David Hentschel.

February 24, 1978. Genesis issue as an advance single, "Follow You Follow Me" backed with album track "Ballad of Big" in the UK and the non-LP "Inside and Out" in the US. The song reaches No.7 on the UK charts and No.23 in the US, becoming the newly minted trio's first Top 40 hit stateside. The single certifies silver in the UK.

Early 1978. Guitarist Daryl Stuermer auditions with Mike Rutherford, in New York City, to become the band's new supporting live guitarist. He is instantly hired.

March 26 – April 22, 1978. Genesis support the new *And Then There Were Three* album with a North American tour.

March 31, 1978. Genesis issue their ninth album, entitled *And Then There Were Three*. The album reaches No.3 on the UK charts and No.14 on Billboard and eventually goes gold in the UK and platinum in the US.

April 1978. Steve Hackett issues a second solo album. For *Please Don't Touch!*, he's still on Genesis' label Charisma. Drumming on most of the album is Genesis live drummer Chester Thompson.

May 14 – June 24, 1978. Genesis conduct European tour dates. The June 24 stop at Knebworth constitutes the tour's only UK show.

May 31, 1978. *And Then There Were Three* is certified gold.

June 2, 1978. Peter Gabriel issues a second untitled solo album, known as "scratch." Two albums on now, there are no ties to Genesis, other than the label of issue, Charisma.

June 16, 1978. "Many Too Many," backed with "The Day the Light Went Out" and "Vancouver," is issued as a single. The A-side reaches No.43 on the UK charts. Also on this day, a horror movie called *The Shout* is released to theatres. The music is by Mike Rutherford and Tony Banks, with "From the Undertow" from Tony's solo album featured.

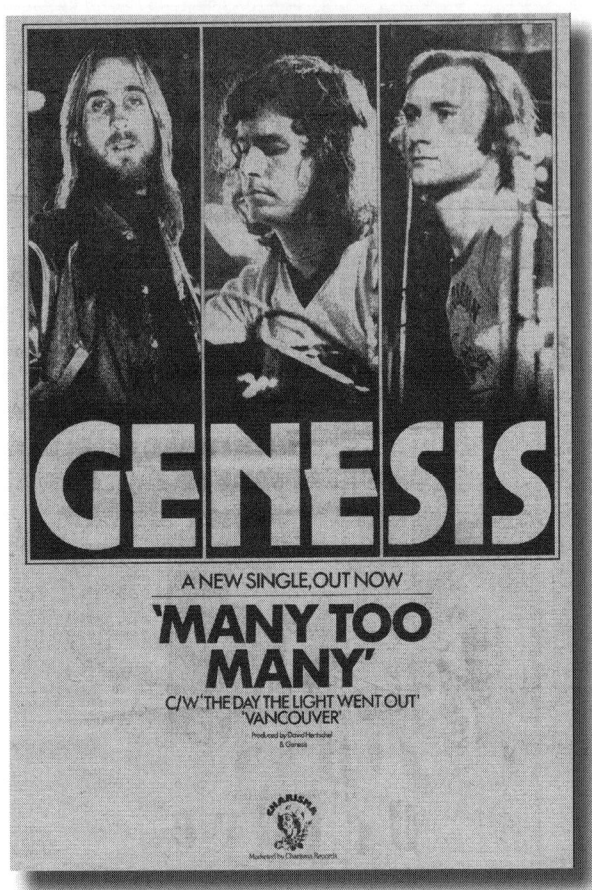

July 1978. "Deep in the Motherlode," backed with "Scenes from a Night's Dream," is issued as a single.

July 10 – 31, 1978. The band return for a second North American tour leg.

August 26 – September 9, 1978. The band return to Europe for additional dates.

September 8, 1978. Brand X issue a third studio album, called *Masques*. Phil Collins is not on it.

September 29 – October 22, 1978. The band return for additional US shows.

November 27 – December 3, 1978. The band conduct a tour of Japan.

Late 1978. Phil's wife Andrea and the kids move to Vancouver, BC, Canada.

April 1979. Phil Collins returns from Vancouver, where attempts to save his marriage with Andrea had failed.

May 1979. Steve Hackett, still recording for Charisma, issues a third solo album, entitled *Spectral Mornings*.

June – December 1979. The band work on tracks slated for inclusion on their next album. First there are writing and rehearsal sessions at Phil's place in Shalford, followed by recording sessions at Polar Studios in Sweden, commencing November 12. Producing once again is David Hentschel.

September 14, 1979. Brand X issue their fourth album, *Product*, and Phil Collins is back, drumming on seven tracks and singing on three.

October 8, 1979. Tony Banks issues his first solo album, entitled *A Curious Feeling*. Producing is David Hentschel and on drums is Chester Thompson.

February 2, 1980. Phil and Andrea divorce.

February 15, 1980. Mike Rutherford issues his debut solo album, entitled *Smallcreep's Day*. Producing the record is David Hentschel and guesting is early-days Genesis member Anthony Phillips.

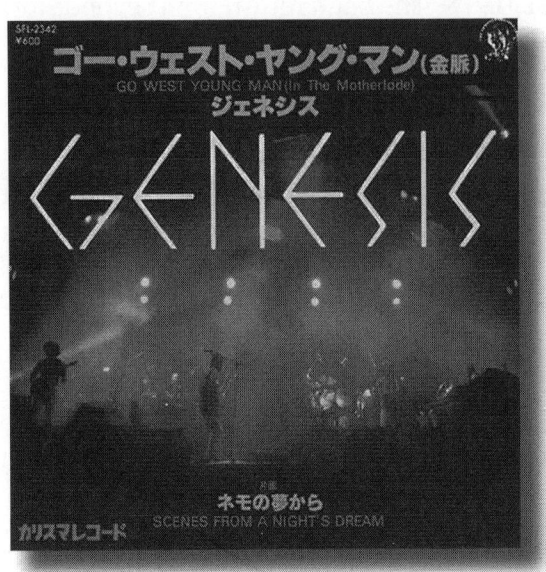

Martin talks to Tate Davis, Rand Kelly, Pontus Norshammar and Pete Pardo about *And Then There Were Three*.

Martin Popoff: All right, welcome gents. We kick off this book with the shedding of Steve Hackett from the Genesis roster. In a general sense, what kind of album do Phil Collins, Tony Banks and Mike Rutherford come up with to start this new phase of the band?

Pete Pardo: Well, it's a band that has a lot to prove. They have to show the world that they can do this on their own as a three-piece, the three main guys. I suppose two of them are family from back in the Charterhouse school days, and then of course Phil is crucial and key to the band, as an addition to the fold back on *Nursery Cryme,* so 1971. Fans would have been thinking, how are they going to do this? They lost Peter Gabriel three years and two records ago and they obviously kept on going very successfully with Phil taking over the vocals.

But once you lose Steve Hackett, people were like well, he's such a tremendous guitar player, how can you make it work? And they're basically like, we're gonna do it. Mike is going to play all the guitars and the bass. He's not really much of a lead guitarist, but he's going to kind of make it work. So the mission is to show the world that they could still be a viable band and a successful band, doing it all themselves and not bringing anybody else into the band.

As for losing Steve, I know they had issues. Or maybe Steve Hackett had more of an issue. But they were very hesitant to use a lot of Steve's songwriting in the band. Not accepting a lot of the material he brought to the table is one of the main reasons why he left. You have to wonder if not bringing anyone new in was a case of these three wanting to keep a tight grip on the songwriting, if the satisfaction in moving forward as a trio came from being able to have more than enough of each of their songs make the albums. So they're like, we're going to do this all on our own.

They got David Hentschel, who already had done *A Trick of the Tail* and *Wind & Wuthering* for them, to produce the album. Whether that's the reason or not, the resulting album still sounds very much like the Genesis we know well, from every album, really, except maybe the debut and *The Lamb Lies Down on Broadway.* I'll get into some things that I think we're kind of lacking here, but overall, it was a sort of stable and moderate progression. We're talking 1978, right? So they're moving away from their heavy prog and folk beginnings into an increasing amount of pop-based material. As the '70s is winding down, music is changing. You've had disco and punk and now new wave and all manner of pop. They needed to prove that they were still viable, but also prove that they were willing to try new things. Arguably, they lean toward the status quo, but nonetheless, *And Then There Were Three* represents at least an evolution.

Tate Davis: I tend to agree with that. Any progression or change in direction we get with *And Then There Were Three* is in terms of commercial viability and commercial appeal. It feels like they were oriented toward that goal. As discussed, Steve Hackett is gone. He's been fed up with having his songs rejected for these albums, and he's gonna go off and do a solo thing. The three of them are left to write the kind of material that they want to do and find a touring guitar player that is willing to put up with this sort of thing and they find that guy in Daryl Stuermer. Overall, there's still a healthy degree of old-school prog here. But sure, it's prog with pop overlays. Lyrically, it's even more of a pop vibe, but they still find ways to keep things interesting. And this combination would continue, I'd say, up until the self-titled Genesis album, because *Invisible Touch* is pretty much straightforward pop.

Rand Kelly: *And Then There Were Three* is a transitional album. It's also Mike Rutherford deciding to take on the duties as the band's guitar player because Steve left. We all know that Steve left because when they were mixing the *Seconds Out* live album, he felt like they kept mixing his solos too low. He kept saying, "I can't hear myself, I can't hear myself," so during the mixing session, Steve quits the band.

Okay, so when this album comes up, Mike Rutherford bought himself a little toy. It's called the Roland GR-500 guitar synthesizer. And you hear that all throughout the album, especially on "Burning Rope," which is one of my favourite songs. I've actually seen him do that live and it's an amazing song. But that's that sound. A lot of people think that's Tony Banks on his synthesizers and stuff—no, that's Mike Rutherford.

Martin: How does that thing work?

Rand: There's a plug-in; like a 13-point plug or something. You plug it into the guitar and then that goes into the unit on the floor, which then goes into the amp. It's into the amp and then also out of the amp so that when he plays, you can mix it. You can add guitar to it or take the guitar all the way out and just have the sounds that are in the instrument.

But the one drawback of these things is you can't play fast. But that worked to Mike's advantage because he's not a fast lead player. He's not like Steve Hackett, who can sort of shred. Mike's playing long David Gilmour-type lines on this whole album. They sound great. They've got kind of a brass sound to them. So my feeling is that he mixed the guitar completely out and just used the synthesizer.

I'll tell you another thing. I remember when I first bought this album, I bought it on LP and I had a bass booster on my amp, but I had to be careful how I used it because I could blow the speakers out if I wasn't careful. So I put this on without the bass booster and the first thing I noticed was there's no bass. You just can't hear it; it's not there. So I had to use the bass booster for it and it worked out perfect. But that's the one thing I have a problem with, is that it isn't bassy enough.

Martin: Do you feel like the personality or complexion of this album is greatly influenced by Steve leaving?

Rand: Not really, because if you listen to *Wind & Wuthering*, and even *A Trick of the Tail*, you'll see how Steve Hackett is already being mixed out, especially on *Wind & Wuthering*. Tony Banks is playing lead lines on the synthesizer that should have been his lines. Or that's what most people would have thought, and probably Steve would have thought. Even on "One for the Vine" you hardly hear Steve Hackett. It's all keyboards, keyboards, keyboards. So I don't blame him. I mean, he did "Blood on the Rooftops" and the only thing that's particularly accentuated about that song is the beautiful acoustic guitar, the classical guitar intro. They needed him to do that, because there was nobody else that could play like that. But on "Eleventh Earl of Mar," which is probably my favourite song on that album, and "All in a Mouse's Night" and all that, you hardly hear Steve Hackett at all.

Martin: Is Tony Banks, then, kind of like the boss of the band. Is he running the show?

Rand: At that point it really feels like it. Phil's doing the vocals and he's playing the drums, but it seems like he has kind of a hands-off attitude about this album. I mean, Mike Rutherford and Tony Banks have always been the heart of this band from day one. They're the only ones that were there from the beginning.

Martin: What is the influence of Brand X in all of this? Was there ever any areas of conflict?

Rand: Good question. So they first got together in 1974. And I think Phil just got together with Percy Jones, John Goodsall—may he rest in peace—and Robin Lumley, who actually also has passed on, in 2023. But he just got together with those guys somehow, and nobody had ever heard of them. And all sudden, this album comes out, *Unorthodox Behaviour*, in 1976.

But he always did them when Genesis was taking a break. He never said, "No, I can't, man, 'cos I gotta go with Brand X." Phil did Brand X because he wanted to play jazz. He was already doing this stuff with Genesis, but nobody really knew that. I mean, listen to "Wot Gorilla?" on *Wind & Wuthering*—if that's not Brand X, I don't know what is. And it's actually the same lead line that they took out of "One for the Vine," if you haven't noticed. But that busy playing, they actually started with "Los Endos." I think that's where it begins. And that heavy rhythm work, they're doing it again here on "The Lady Lies." That's why it's my favourite on this album, because it just rips. We used to call that going balls-out.

Pontus Norshammar: When you told me where you thought you were putting the cut-off for the first book from the second, I thought you could call the first one *From Dusk to Afterglow*, and somehow get *The Trio Years* into the second title. Because, I agree, it's the big shift. I mean, *Wind & Wuthering* and *Seconds Out* are the big shift because Steve Hackett leaves and we're down to the trio.

Going into *And Then There Were Three*. a lot of things are happening. This album signals a new beginning, in a sense. The elephant in the room is the fact that Mike Rutherford is a rhythm guitarist and a great bassist, but he was never a lead guitarist. If he had been a lead guitarist, Steve Hackett would have never entered the band. They would have recruited a bassist instead. Because it was the Charterhouse boys' band, right? It was their band. So they had to simplify in order to get him to play the parts. So this is the big secret with this album, although I think it serves them well, because they do it in the right sort of rock 'n' roll era. There's Dire Straits and Patti Smith and still some punk and the huge band at the time is Fleetwood Mac, who are an incredibly bare-bones band. And in that environment, Genesis want to be popular and they want to have a hit single.

So they streamlined, most notably in the guitar area, but they don't discuss it that much. But Mike couldn't play those old Steve Hackett-type parts and as a result, this album is very hard for me to listen to. It's a record that... you know those records where the songs actually disappear from you when you listen to them? You listen to a song once and you listen to it twice. You almost know the song, but it sort of fades into the background. You don't remember how it goes. This is my experience with most of this record.

But yes, stylistically, it's the beginning of the band's pop years but it's also the beginning of what we now call neo-prog, right? This sort of extending a pop song by adding a flavour of progressive rock into it. Because every sort of imaginative step beginning with *Trespass*, where the acoustic stuff led to another variation on a theme and all that, that's now simplified into straight songs. I think the *Duke* album works better, because it's more varied. The problem here is that everything sounds the same. Tony's put all this sort of Yamaha piano all over the record and then there are some other synthesizers he uses, but there's nothing that ever really sticks out above the foxhole, except maybe "Follow You Follow Me" because it's simpler and it's a poppy.

But in general it's a ballad-based album and oddly, quite wintery, in terms of imagery. Collins does his job, but they say that he had problems with his divorce and wasn't too focussed on the album. They also said that it was done very quickly and sat on the shelf for a while. I think the big mistake they made was not to ask Daryl Stuermer, who had played with them live, to come in and put some guitars on it and beef it up a bit. Because that is missing, that variation of light and shade. When *Duke* comes along, they've managed to sort of work around what they have, right? They know how to make variations on different themes. And of course, they had the *Duke* suite and all that and chopped it up. But you also get "Turn It On Again." There's nothing like that on here.

Martin: Concerning the album cover and the title, first I made a judgment call with the title for purposes of presentation in the book and violently lopped off the ellipses at both ends, along with converting it into standard U/L, uppercase and lowercase. Of course, given this is the rock 'n' roll business, they couldn't even keep it consistent right from the first issue of the album, where the title is presented in all capitals on the spine and label. Anyway, my irritation at the title aside, anybody have any comment on the cover art? Which, putting the text aside, I actually love!

Tate: I think it's perfectly acceptable for Genesis fans to reject the all-lowercase title with front and back ellipses—man! It's not blasphemy on your part to do that, so don't worry (laughs). In fact, I sometimes call it *Then There Were Three* when talking about this album with other people, or if I'm being formal, with a slight "n" sound at the front. So it's perfectly acceptable for that. You know why? Because I'm a Genesis fan and I don't like it. I get where they're coming from with it. I think the title is clever, but it's poorly executed, and yes, hard to say in a sentence but even more of a pain to type. As for the cover, I don't know what to think of it. There's just this sort of black background. I don't really get what it has to do with *And Then There Were Three*.

Martin: What I envision is that Steve's been bumped off and he's in the trunk of the car. You've got these criminals hanging around, clearly up to no good. It was a gang of four, and then there were three. One guy's got the flashlight out looking at some directions or something, showing where they're supposed to dump the body.

Tate: Yeah, well, if it has to do with Steve Hackett leaving, I could probably see that (laughs). That's pretty cool. I obviously get that's what the title is about, but yeah, I like your story. At least with *A Trick of the Tail*, you get this parade of characters and it goes along with the music. This cover is good, even solid, but not awesome. It's not one of my favourite Hipgnosis covers.

Martin: Plus it's got those green and yellow splotches on that sweet logo of theirs.

Tate: Yeah, you know, at least with Roger Dean, you're gonna get a great album cover. Roger Dean is like Neon Park and Paul Whitehead, where you get these wild illustrations. With Hipgnosis, there are some really terrific album covers, some pretty good ones, some mediocre ones, and then there's what the hell am I looking at?

Pontus: It's a dark and moody album and the cover strikes the perfect tone for the album. It's shadowy and gloomy, with those three figures. It's also very British, right? (laughs). It's quintessential British humour, like Hipgnosis doing *Monty Python*. But, again, the music, to me, sounds like it's in those colours.

Pete: You've got the storm clouds overhead, the three guys who look like spies or like you say, criminals. It's lonely and desolate. To me it's saying that despite storm clouds, despite everything that's going on, we're kind of united here. So despite all the storm clouds happening around us and all this change and fury and darkness, we're gonna make a go of it. I like your theory though. I never thought about that. Because they do look like gangsters. So that is possible. But even gangsters are notorious for saying we're all in this together and it's us against the world, type of thing. So whatever the story, there's a defiance there. It's like, we're going to do this, the three of us, and there's nobody that's going to stop us.

And you're right, it's annoying how only the G and part of the E in Genesis are filled in with colour. And then the title, it would be more correct as *Genesis... and then there were three*. You need the Genesis as part of the title to make a phrase, and then it's a period at the end. That end ellipses is worse than unnecessary; it's not even right.

Martin: Yes, perfectly put (laughs). Not to get too deep, but I also look at that scene and think, as grown-ups, we have to put on our big boy shoes more and more as life throws curves at us. You see those guys, and you think, man, they've done some living; they've been through a lot. You lose some friends. Maybe you even have to kill somebody along the way. Or worse, somebody leaves the band (laughs). Whatever though, it's classic Hipgnosis. Even that slow exposure light effect is one of their things. All right, before we move on, I also wanted to remark, it's another long album on a single piece of vinyl, isn't it?

Tate: Yeah, that's why I needed a full week of prep work (laughs). Because these albums are long and you want to be able to prepare accordingly. But they figured it out. There weren't many bands that were pushing it like this, but Genesis made it work. Most bands around this time were following the 30- to 43-minute album length for vinyl. I can't name another band who were routinely putting out albums this long. I think of UFO's second album, *Flying*, which came out and told you that it was "One Hour Space Rock" or something like that. Yeah, 27 minutes a side is almost like a whole Van Halen album. One side of a Genesis album is the entire length of *Diver Down*.

Martin: Which is a nice segue into the tracks, because the first song is called "Down and Out." What are your thoughts on the opening track?

Tate: "Down and Out" is a great song, and it shows you that Mike Rutherford is able to come up with guitar riffs—and different from Steve Hackett's style—that are engaging and actually quite heavy.

Martin: Exactly. This is my candidate for the heaviest song Genesis ever did. I think "The Knife" gets too much credit for that.

Tate: Yeah, I can see that. Phil's drumming on this song and throughout the entire album is very Neil Peart-sounding, meaning that there's a lot of highly-pitched rack toms, where he's just going around the world in a descending order as he's completing the fill or the drum stanza that he's doing. It's almost like Steve never left, with this song. Or it's like, I know Steve Hackett is gone, but I entrust Mike to come up with a good riff and to come up with a good solo as well. More on the solo situation as we get later into the album. And Tony Banks gives us a really cool synth solo. Lyrically it hints at Genesis' future commercial direction; it's more real world and very straightforward. So "Down and Out" is a great beginning to an album that is a shift in direction for Genesis.

Rand: Man, "Down and Out" is relentless, even though it's in 5/8—1,2,3,4,5, 1,2,3,4,5—just pounding and such a huge sound. It's about living life on the road. He's describing what it's like. You know, "It's good to be here! How've you been?/Check my bags boy! Where's my room?" So he's going into a room but he's burned-out and just wants to relax. They're talking about how they're tired of the games that are played in the music business and you gotta be honest with him face-to-face. You never know who you can trust. That seems to be what the song's about.

Pontus: Yeah, "Down and Out" is the most explicit song here lyrically, and also the liveliest song on the album, with that sort of weird drum beat that almost falls over itself. Apparently it was very hard to play live. They played it a few times, but dropped it from the set. But it's a very good opener, with a great vocal melody, both in the verses and the pre-chorus, the middle eight. There's lots of production and Banks shines. It's the best "trio" track on the album.

Pete: "Down and Out" is one of my favourite songs from this late '70s period. I hate to call it heavy, Martin, because it's not really. It's not metal, it's not hard rock, but for Genesis, sure, this is pretty dark and heavy. If you read the lyrics, it's like a jab at the record labels, signing and dropping bands on a whim and the repercussions that are left, along with just the grind of touring.

There's nice use of synth and organ from Banks and there's that big, meaty bass and, I guess, guitar riff thing that Rutherford's doing, along the busy drums. It certainly rocks. Maybe it's because of the lack of guitar presence generally across this record, but I really focus on Phil's drumming on most of these songs. He's produced masterfully on this record. There's lots of rolling tom fills all over the place and especially on this song. Plus you've got that wild synth from Banks, which ebbs and flows and is really dramatic. Phil's vocals are killer and the chorus is really memorable. It's one of the liveliest songs in their catalogue and easily my favourite song here. It starts this album out with a bang. Whether you think the rest of the album lives up to it or not is up for debate.

Martin: I suppose this is an odd thing to say, but even though the next track, "Undertow," is a ballad, given Phil powering his way through it, there's a sense that the energy from "Down and Out" is somewhat maintained.

Tate: Yes, for a ballad, it's very noisy (laugh). I feel like it could have been a single. It's like a cousin to "Your Own Special Way." My favourite part, there's a great roll on the floor tom before the chorus, which I think adds a lot. So yeah, cool ballad with great drumming by Phil.

Martin: Compared to Neil Peart, Phil's sound on this album is so alive and vibrant, right? Neil is snappy and scientific, but this is splashy.

Tate: Yeah, it's more going back to the City Boy drum sound that we discussed with *Wind & Wuthering* in the early-days book. There's more of that on here. It's still not the gated drum sound he'd become famous for. The toms are a lot more airy and polished, like you say, vibrant, or maybe analogue and live-sounding.

Rand: "Undertow" is a beautiful song. One of the highlights or features of the song is that Mike Rutherford is playing fretless bass for the first time. Tony Banks wrote the song, and I can't really tell you what it's about, but I just enjoy listening to it. It's another one of these where they demonstrate their ability to build things up, kind of like "Stairway to Heaven." They start out real mellow, and without changing the speed of the song, they add in instruments and layers and power. By the end it's a wall of sound. There are parts on "Undertow" that are so intense, but nothing's really changed. It's just that they've layered sound on sound on sound. You know, a two-by-four is one thing, but then when you put three two-by-fours together, you've got a six-by-four. Boom!

Pontus: But the problem is, how many ballads do we have on here? Five? I mean, it's a nice ballad but it drags on a bit. However that pre-chorus, the "Better think awhile" part, that is powerful and unified. But you're right, it's a wall of sound, or more like a wall of keyboards.

Martin: Like Tate says, it's noisy. There's a lot going on.

Pontus: Yeah, but in the old days, they would have added something surprising and that is gone, right? It's very straightforward, even though Rutherford plays some good rhythm lines. Of course the playing is good. I'm just finding it sort of straightforward or obvious, and perhaps that's not what I'm looking for when I'm listening to Genesis. I actually felt that it would have been better if they'd changed their name when they were reduced to the trio. Of course they didn't, and in reality, the brand was too big to just throw away. But would we have accepted it more if they said this is a new band? Maybe. It's like when Joy Division became New Order. The concept is that the personnel is changed or actually diminished, but at the same time, we have some new or fresh ideas.

Pete: With "Undertow," you have this kind of pop track radio. It's mainly a vehicle for Phil's vocals—he's really coming into his own as a vocalist—and some lovely piano and synths from Banks. I think that the big crescendos on the choruses are nicely done. It's lush and a sort of earworm song and it works really well. It's the type of stuff that they would start to do more and more often moving forward. But it's funny, it gets so loud, but is Mike even on this song? I don't know. Maybe you hear a little bass but it's basically all these synth washes and keyboards. There's a lot going on but it's not like the full band is cranking it up like it was on "Down and Out."

Martin: Things pick up again for another rumbling rocker awkwardly called "Ballad of Big," very rhythmic, but again, so bright with the cymbals, high-hats, and even torrents of high-midrange keyboards.

Tate: "Ballad of Big" is a fun song. I really love the switch, the shift, between the Afro-Cuban shuffle kind of groove, which I think Phil could have played with Brand X on a similar-type song that they were doing around the time, and then this thumping, straight rock feel. And you're right, Tony makes his presence known on the song. Lyrically, this character Big Jim Cooley is reminiscent of like a George Armstrong Custer at Little Bighorn, where he's this big, confident, larger-than-life personality who is in way over his head. Custer attacked a Native American encampment that his subordinates begged him not to do but he did it because he was this egomaniac. That's Big Jim Cooley too. He's this guy who's confident he's able to win a gunfight with almost anybody and then he ends up being killed by Native Americans, just like George Armstrong Custer. That's what I'm reminded of when I listened to "Ballad of Big."

Rand: It reminds me of Jim Croce's "You Don't Mess Around with Jim." Like, this Big Jim Cooley cowboy guy was badass. But yes, the title of the song is annoying, although the song itself is pretty cool, with this rockin' shuffle feel.

Pontus: Yes, I like that shuffle feel. It's a second attempt at the "Eleventh Earl of Mar" rhythm, right? And you've got that sort of straight 4/4 rhythm in a few sections. It's Phil telling a story about an Indian battle, if I understand right. Apparently he's very much into American history. So that was a great idea. But yet again, despite the shuffle, the general sound and volume and arrangement of it is the same bright and almost overbearing sound as the other songs so far. It's not very remarkable, or maybe it would be on its own. I really miss the lack of variation in the arrangements. Like I said, this album was recorded very quickly. I think this song would have benefited if they had worked a bit longer on it and added a few things to make it stand out more.

Martin: You're right. It's almost like they made the whole album at an uncommonly well-recorded sound check, on stage in a hockey arena.

Pontus: Yeah! It's very sort of, "We're gonna use these sounds. That's all we've got." And yeah, "We're gonna write these songs and let's do this very quickly. We're in a flow; let's go and just do it and just get it out and get on tour." Except, fortunately, they are very high-fidelity sounds.

Pete: "Ballad of Big" is more of a rocker, and quite catchy. You've got some nice, busy drum in here and some almost angry riffing from Rutherford. So this is one of the songs that has more guitar on it. And even though he's not much of a lead guitarist, he adds some nice textures and riffs here and there. I love the melodic middle section, where we have that full Hammond organ thing going on and those rich vocal harmonies. Then they flop back to that more furious beginning structure, which kind of pops in and weaves itself throughout the song.

Then we're back to the symphonic part again, which is nicely done. Interesting though, he's singing about cowboys and things like that. There's this Wild West motif that shows up on a couple songs, which is kind of weird for Genesis, totally different than what we talked about with respect to the earlier albums. They're starting to incorporate different ideas for lyrics that are odd for a prog band. It's not fairies and nymphs and religion.

Martin: Then we swing back to panoramic ballad mode for "Snowbound." But there's a definite progression, because their choruses are really breaking through as strong and accessible and potentially connecting with more and more people, I figure. And man, given the lyrics of that chorus, it's sure hard not to get it wrong and call the song "Snowman!"

Rand: I know, I know. I love the way the Mellotron lifts up during the chorus. Right before Phil sings, "Hey there's a Snowman," the

Mellotron makes this ascending swooping sound. It feels like you're lifting right up into the sky. Great song.

Pontus: I agree that "Snowbound" has a great chorus, but just okay verses; it's a bit samey there as well with the arrangement, all drenched in these cold keyboards. It's a story about children finding a snowman. It's a good enough ballad, but again, it sounds rushed to me.

Tate: We're continuing with this theme of ice and snow. This could have been a single. It's got great acoustic guitar from Mike Rutherford, the sole writer on it. And he must love snowmen because the lyrics talk about what a great snowman it is and praying for the snowman. I don't know; maybe he liked to build snowmen a lot when he was a kid. But it reminds me of "Your Own Special Way" as well. So yes, "Snowbound" could have been a single and I think it would have would have been played a lot.

Martin: It could have become a big Christmas carol maybe, like the John Lennon and Bruce Springsteen songs.

Pete: Yes, maybe so (laughs). It's a lovely little song. I've sometimes come down on Genesis for they're more pop-flavoured stuff, but I always really liked this song. Phil's vocals are absolutely intoxicating. I like the dreamy, slow build to it. The keyboards are really nicely done. "Hey, there's a snowman." I remember being a kid listening to this and just loving it. As someone who grew up in the Northeast, in New York, I always loved winter and loved making snowmen on the holidays. So there was always something about the song that kind of swept me away. It's just so gorgeous, and charming. The melodies are great. There's not much going on here musically, but it doesn't matter. It's all about that vocal that just kind of takes you through the whole song. Phil Collins, when he's on his money game, that's what he can do. He can just charm you with vocal melodies.

Martin: Okay, we're back to spider-legged prog with "Burning Rope," dramatic, expansive, a song that's very much sympathetic to the previous two albums.

Tate: Yeah, "Burning Rope" is definitely a sign that Genesis have not forgotten their prog roots. I think Steve Hackett would have liked the song. Okay, so going back to what I was saying about "Down and Out," where you could trust Mike Rutherford to come up with a great solo on songs of this nature, this is where that assumption is reinforced. Because Mike Rutherford plays a spectacular guitar solo in the middle of the song. He's letting the listener know that we don't need Steve Hackett anymore. I'm the guitar player and Daryl Stuermer is going to play these parts live and he'll be great.

The lyrics portray someone telling another person that they need to take care of themselves, reminding them that life is too short to surround themselves with negativity. And the song's conclusion is wonderful and majestic and shows this hopefulness. Yeah, "Burning Rope" is a highlight. I would suggest this song to people who dismiss the Phil Collins era as being this poppy, commercial, boring thing. I'm like, "No, it's not—listen to 'Burning Rope.' Your mind will be changed."

Rand: The idea of climbing up a burning rope to escape a mob—oh, my God. The way they descend down that melody line chromatically, that's all Mike on that synthesizer guitar. From the very beginning, he's on that thing. It's a majestic piece, and arguably the most progressive song on the album.

Pontus: Great beginning, another fine melody. It reminds me of "One for the Vine." It's the same sound picture but the song is better. The songwriting actually holds together and you remember the song, especially that, "And the man in the moon" part. It's a clearly worked-out song, actually with one of the first really great instrumental sections we get on this album. It's short, only a couple minutes, but it's memorable.

Pete: "Burning Rope" has this dramatic opening dominated by these majestic synth melodies. I love the rolling drums, the piano, the gentle vocal and I love the chorus. It's just so lush. And then you've got that atmospheric middle section, which leads into, I think, one of Michael's best guitar solos on the album. He doesn't do a lot of them, but this one is tasty and melodic. There's nothing virtuosic about it but it really fits the song. Sometimes you don't need to do some kind of wacky solo. It's just a nice little passage.

That middle section adds some nice prog elements to what is actually quite a haunting song. It's quite haunting lyrically too, sort of about how the only real survivors on the planet are the elements themselves, and how any one person's accomplishments in the end are pretty meaningless. The use of nature imagery—the seasons, sun, rain, snow, Mother Nature, the earth—that's becoming a regular conceit for these guys, and will be there moving forward as well.

Martin: Side two opens with "Deep in the Motherlode," and I'm feeling a connection arrangement-wise to the opening sequence of the last song, but also to the grandeur of "Squonk," given the big, thumping beat.

Tate: Absolutely, "Deep in the Motherlode" starts the second side of the album with a vengeance. It's a really cool song that I like to imagine as part of *Invisible Touch* for some reason. I love the fact that Mike Rutherford quoted Horace Greeley with the "Go west, young man" line, because the slow shuffle framework makes sense for envisioning some 18th century American family traversing the dangerous environments of the Oregon Trail or Santa Fe Trail in hope of finding reward at their destination, like with agriculture or the California gold rush.

Rand: Yeah, our setting, once again, is the American Wild West. This is about the gold rush, and telling everybody you gotta get out there and stake your claim and all that. You know it's like the Oklahoma gold rush, with the Okies all going to California. There were these gold mines there around between Sacramento and Reno and it was quite a boom. Once again we have Mike prominent on guitar synthesizer, doing those chords and stuff and being skilled at using this technology. If he had been playing a guitar that was all fuzzed-out, he wouldn't be able to get clean chords like that. He's playing more than one note at a time. So if he had the original fuzz box sound, it would be all muddy and you wouldn't be able to differentiate between the two notes over the synthesizer. It's got both sustain and fuzz but it's clear. I love that song. There are a lot of contrasting musical passages, which is something I like with my Genesis.

Pontus: I have to be honest with you: I find "Deep in the Motherlode" quite boring! It doesn't go anywhere, there's not much of a melody and it's just drenched in synths. The best part is the opening chords. I can't stand that middle section. It just drags— nothing's happening. Even in the '70s, these guys knew how to write a good song but something is missing here.

Pete: It's interesting how they kick off side one and side two, with the more kind of upfront, upbeat, rockin' stuff. You've got the big, driving riffs from Rutherford and the symphonic keyboard swells. Phil's vocals are imbued with all these tones as if he's playing different characters in the song. You've got these hushed whispers set against these more soaring sections—it's really nicely done.

And as you guys have alluded to—and quite odd to hear from Genesis—we're back in the western part of America, heading across the plains and all this sort of thing. They tackle lyrical tropes that represent a jarring, complete contrast to what they've done in the past. Excellent, propulsive drumming from Phil and some nice little guitar patterns from Mike. But yes, each side is kicked off at full volume, and then they get poppier deeper in.

Martin: Next is "Many Too Many," and again, despite this being a ballad, I'm distracted by how bright and even braying the synths and the cymbals can be. There's a lot of this sizzly, full-volume playing, even on the slower numbers.

Tate: Yeah, "Many Too Many" is definitely a ballad, but it builds. I can envision this song as part of *Abacab*. The beginning of it reminds me of "Man on the Corner." Great vocals from Phil on the song and good guitar layers from Mike Rutherford, plus a good solo from him at the end. It's just a quality pop tune. And there's a lot of "Oh mama" in this song, which kinda makes you wonder if there's some connection to "Mama" from a couple albums later (laughs).

Pete: "Many Too Many" is another one you'd put in the pop song category. It's got strong hooks and some prog embellishments here and there. Collins sounds great on this and you've got these dreamy keyboards which kind of adorn the whole arrangement. We even get some nice little lead guitar fills from Rutherford. As expected, it's nothing virtuosic. He's still learning how to play guitar authoritatively, but I think it fits the song. Nice song, not one of my favourites.

Rand: "Many Too Many" is one of Tony's. He says it's his favourite song on the album. And you're right; it's another one of these that starts really quiet and soft and mellow, but it builds up to become this wall of sound. And that's all due to Tony, who brings all that power and just fills all the gaps. Any music that's guitar and bass and drums, and even piano, if you just have those elements alone, there's always going to be gaps, where you pull your hands off the instruments. But these orchestral swells you hear fill all that in, and so "Many Too Many" sounds almost heavy in places, as they build toward these climaxes, essentially.

Martin: Do you know anything about them deciding to change from a group credit to individual credits? That begins with *A Trick of the Tail*.

Rand: Yeah, that's true. When I bought *Selling England by the Pound*, I remember seeing on the back, "All Titles Done By All" and apparently that turned out to be a lawyer's nightmare. I imagine that Tony Stratton Smith probably said, no, you guys need to start getting your individual credits. But that was a lawyer's nightmare, because nobody knows who to send the royalties to and then when Steve Hackett leaves, that changes everything.

Martin: Yeah, the only songwriting crediting on *The Lamb Lies Down on Broadway* is right on the record label, where it says "All titles written, performed and arranged by GENESIS." Peter however gets credit for the story printed in the gatefold. All right, back on track; Pontus, any thoughts on "Many Too Many?"

Pontus: It's another boring ballad! (laughs). Very pop rock. We've truly moved away from progressive rock and we're in this sort of middle-aged, Fleetwood Mac pop rock vein.

Martin: It's almost like when glam gave up the wildness of '72, '73, '74 and became City Boy, Pilot and Sailor, or maybe Mott as opposed to Mott the Hoople. The bands were dressing a little more corporate, in floral, button-up shirts and maybe leisure suits. You know, cleaning up, ditching the makeup. Sweet is another good example, after the heavy metal phase, from *Level Headed* onward.

Pontus: Yeah, you've got classic Slade or T. Rex, "20th Century Boy," and then suddenly you're in a sort of soul thing, right? It gets more professional and all the passion is gone.

Martin: It almost becomes the UK version of yacht rock. And maybe Genesis in this period is becoming this increasingly aristocratic and mannered version of a prog band. It's like when punk became not post-punk, but power pop and American new wave.

Pontus: Yeah, you have to have a good song. Like Patti Smith, if you're going to do a pop song after doing a punk album, you have to have "Because the Night," so people can focus and go, "Oh, that's a great song; I can hum it." You survive through the quality of the songs, and I think that's what's failing here—the songwriting is unremarkable.

Martin: It's also disorienting to get a single LP album from Genesis with 11 songs on it.

Pontus: Yeah; it's 54 minutes long and I find myself asking "Why?" At 43 minutes, it could be a much more cohesive affair. It speaks to the state of mind of the band at the time. Because if you compare it with *Duke*, they're in a happier, more cohesive place, even though it's actually even longer. You have "Misunderstanding," which is just a pop song but it's going somewhere. You can actually hear the sense of purpose in it. If you ask me to play "Many Too Many" in my head, I can't—it just escapes me.

Martin: I find that "Scenes from a Night's Dream" integrates the pop into the prog a little better, meaning that the prog is there as a foundation, the pop is stronger, and it overlays onto the prog well. In other words, this is an effortlessly accessible song, with the prog delivered almost surreptitiously.

Tate: Yes, this is a really cool and bright, synth-driven song with funky drumming from Phil. Again, as you've been bringing up, it's such a trebly album, and Phil contributes to that big time, using the bell of his ride, using open high-hat, lots of crashes and even cowbell. Lyrically, it's a throwback to the Peter Gabriel era. I like the reference to George Washington and the cherry tree, even though that's a myth. Tony turns in an entertaining synth solo and yeah, overall it's just an energetic, enjoyably song.

Rand: Oh, I love "Scenes from a Night's Dream." "Follow You Follow Me" was chosen to be the single by the management or the record company or whatever, Atlantic Records. But if you ask me, "Scenes from a Night's Dream" would have been a great single. It's so poppy and happy-sounding. I can't say enough about that song. And it's not easy to play, You hear "Nemo, get out of bed!" and then there's that chord pattern. At this point, as long as I've been playing keyboards, I still find that difficult, especially to do it at the speed that Tony does it. But there are so many things going on in this song. It's goofy, but it's poppy. It's like pop prog. It's the type of prog song that could have been a hit.

Pontus: Yes, finally we get a bit more energy (laughs). It's almost got a disco vibe, like a Bee Gees number from that era. It sounds like something you write when you don't know what to write and you want to just get something out. Remember when we talked about Queen *The Game*? This is very much structured the same way, where you have the best bits at the beginning of the album and you have a good side one closer so that people are going to turn it over. Then you have the filler, but then they close out with two great songs. So it's very much like they know they don't have that much to offer, but the way the album is sequenced, you get rewarded in the end.

Pete: "Scenes from a Night's Dream" is an interesting little story about a child's nightmares, probably generated from eating too close to bedtime and also reading too many—or getting read too many—weird little fantasy fairy tale books before bedtime and then having all these weird dreams. We hear about dragons and nymphs and giant mushrooms and goblins and princesses and princes and all that kind of stuff. It's a quirky, little, proggy pop tune with some nice transitions and instrumentation.

But it's so brief. I would have liked to have had a longer middle section with some more keyboards or a guitar solo. Banks really makes this song. His tones are so bright and shiny. It's really well recorded. I'm not exactly sure what equipment he was using on this album but it's really glorious-sounding. Plus Phil does a really nice job on here in true Peter Gabriel fashion, kind of applying his voice, using different tones and timbers and textures to portray different characters throughout the song. Obviously he learned from Peter how to do that, but he's developed it well throughout this whole period.

Martin: Next we have "Say It's Alright Joe," which Mike envisioned as a sort of Dean Martin bar-room drunk song. But it's gone way beyond that lyrically, leaving much open to interpretation.

Rand: Yeah, but I think we can agree that it's pretty depressing. I've seen it live. So they actually set this up where Phil Collins is sitting at a bar. And one of the roadies or something is playing the bartender and a spotlight comes down on Phil and he's just depressed. He's in a trench coat and he's got a drink in his hand. He looks really bummed-out and he begins, "Say it's alright, Joe. I need another drink." So Joe is the bartender. And where did they get Joe the bartender from? Jackie Gleason. But anyways, yeah, I don't think it's a great song. I just think it's something they needed to take up space. It's got a lot of sad, morose chords, a lot of minor chords. The whole song is in a minor key.

Tate: In my interpretation, the protagonist is reflecting on the memory of a good friend or family member. Mike Rutherford's bass is really prominent in the mix in this song; that's something you don't really hear a lot throughout Genesis albums in this era. I really like that. The pickup from the dreamy intro really takes you by surprise and there are really cool guitar textures from Mike as well in that. I like the surprising nature of this song.

Pontus: "Say It's Alright Joe" is another filler song for me. When you think they're going to go for it—and this goes for the last song as well—and that there will be a section that will give us something else, they hold back. So the tendency to streamline things is constantly disappointing me. I want something to happen.

Pete: It's easily my least favourite. It's a weird, kind of mid-level, haunting pop song, with these whispered vocals throughout. The chorus is nicely done, as are all the choruses on the album, and there are some cool keyboards. In my mind, Tony can do no wrong on this album. This is more his album, I think, from a musical perspective. Otherwise, the song doesn't interest me that much. But yeah, it's another foray into their weird kind of theatrical pop music that still has one toe in prog. But you can hear them deciding to be a pop band.

Martin: "The Lady Lies" is one of the more complicated and layered 6/8 songs I've ever heard. They manage to hang onto that rhythm despite some pretty exuberant prog playing.

Tate: It's another one of my favourite songs on this album. I know the main feature of the time signature is that it's in some form of three, but to me, I'd frame it as this very bouncy sort of 12/8 shuffle. Great drumming on here from Phil, with this busy use of ghost notes and clanging of the bell of his ride cymbal. Plus his toms sound really good. The song would take on a whole new life in the live setting, where Phil would instruct the audience where to cheer and boo depending on what the characters did. Great synth solo from Tony Banks and solid but energetic support from everyone else underneath that. Phil puts on a clinic throughout the song. It's maybe his best drumming moment on the album, and the sort of roiling groove of it is helped because you can really hear Mike's bass playing in the mix. At the end of the song, it feels like everyone is playing like their lives depended on it.

Rand: "The Lady Lies" is my absolute favourite song on this album because it really rips. Once they start that energetic sort of pomp rock melody, I'm hooked. They sound like Brand X on this song. They do it on *Duke* as well, but it's really one of the last times they ever sort of scoot this fast, at least playing all traditional instruments. And it even has that beginning which sounds like slow stripper music.

Pontus: Absolutely, they actually pick it up, don't they? The drumming is frantic but the melody is strong and can support the almost fusion playing on it. The whole idea of it being a Hansel and Gretel folk tale for grown-ups is a good one. Phil plays well, there's an acceptable amount of variation and there's a lot of energy. But I still miss Steve Hackett. In the end it fizzles out because there's no guitar. It feels like there's supposed to be guitar but there isn't. And of course live, they had a guitarist and the song went in another direction.

Pete: I like how "The Lady Lies" has all these different musical sections to it; it's actually a pretty complex track. And Phil's drumming on the chorus is really nicely done, quite busy, and it sort of sweeps the chorus up in his enthusiasm. There's a pace and intensity and drive to it and it ultimately reaches higher heights than the other songs on the album. And Phil's using different tones on his voice again, from section to section, while Tony keeps things interesting with his various synth textures.

At the lyric end, you've got this poor warrior who's being seduced by what appears to be a fair maiden. But of course, ultimately, she's got some kind of ulterior motive. Anyway, the only thing I miss on this song is guitar, because it's one of the longer tracks on the album, over six minutes, and Mike's not doing a hell of a lot. I say bump it up to eight minutes and include some guitar solo sections. Still, it's one of the more successful songs on the album.

Martin: We close with "Follow You Follow Me," which represents a new level of direct communication with the fans, or more accurately, maybe the first communication with people who suddenly became fans.

Tate: Yeah, good point. "Follow You Follow Me" was the big single from the album, absolutely. It begins with a kind of novel funky guitar intro followed by Phil's funky drumming. Later we get a nice synth solo from Tony. It's a typical love song and it does its job as a radio single. It's another one that I think would have fit pretty well on *Invisible Touch*, given the poppy nature of it. I don't think it quite hits the mark that "Your Own Special Way" does, but it's a good song nonetheless.

Martin: Is it funk? Is it R&B? Is it disco? What is it?

Tate: It's funk. Well, it's funk and R&B. It's not quite disco.

Martin: I suppose it's that arpeggiated guitar that puts it in a funk zone.

Rand: Whatever it is, it was a big hit single for them. Apparently they were going to make a big jam out of that intro and it was going to be longer. But that never came to fruition. The record company says, "No, no, you've got a hit here. Let's condense this for radio." So you have Phil singing "Stay with me/My love, I hope you'll always be." I mean, it's okay; it's not my favourite song. But people who don't really know the prog side of the band and they like the pop side of the band, they all love that tune. Because it doesn't step on any toes.

Pontus: "Follow You Follow Me" is quite light-hearted motif-wise, against the dreariness of so many of the other songs. And it's well composed and executed. The guitar in the beginning reminds me of something else and I've been racking my brains all week about what it is.

Martin: That arpeggiated guitar lick throughout reminds me of various Police songs, I suppose "Every Breath You Take" being one of them.

Pontus: Yes, that's it! And maybe "Don't Stand So Close to Me."

Martin: There's one or two on *Regatta de Blanc* as well. Maybe the intro to The Cult's "She Sell's Sanctuary" too. But you know, really, it sounds like a ballad that would be on a disco album.

Pontus: Or a Michael Jackson album. And it would fit on one of Phil's solo albums too. But Genesis took considerable heat for "Follow You Follow Me," even though it's all in the spirit of progress. But they lost some of their identity as well with this type of material. That world of imaginative landscapes, the mysticism, the dreaminess, the way they used to jump from one thing to the other, that's just gone. It's very sort of, "Now we're gonna do a pop album."

But, *Duke*, as I said, is better because it's more varied. The songwriting is better and it sits better within the Genesis world. There are still weak moments. "Cul-de-Sac" is really filler compared to "Turn It On Again," which is a dance song that you can't dance to because the rhythm is all over the place. But on *And Then There Were Three*, something's lacking. I don't know if Collins just helicoptered in and did his vocals and wrote some of the stuff but didn't write or jam with the group, but the album is lacking expression, expressiveness. And everything is drenched in the same quite fatiguing arrangement.

Martin: Pete, what are your thoughts on "Follow You Follow Me?"

Pete: It's kind of a syrupy, sweet song but not an overly happy song, for whatever reason. I've never been much of a fan of it. I mean, the chorus is ultra-memorable and that's what makes the song. It's interesting how it's sitting at the back end of the album—such a weird place to put it. But it set the stage for all the pop songs to follow, so maybe it's at a sort of launch position. But obviously they would do other stuff like this going forward.

To me, the best thing about the song is that spiralling synth solo from Tony. Phil's doing this sort of complicated shuffle rhythm. I don't know, people love it, and that's the important thing, right? People love a good pop song. And I think they finally realised that they could do a song like this and could actually make a dent on radio. So going forward, they're like, hey, you know, we're pretty good at this. Or we're getting good at this. People love this. So yeah, never one of my favourites. If there wasn't that great keyboard solo, I would have no use for it. I just love that. It reminds me of "Lucky Man" by ELP. That's a song that I never really liked much at all, but then you've got this amazing mono synth solo from Keith Emerson at the end. Similarly with this song, I'm waiting to get to the cool solo and the rest doesn't interest me much.

Martin: All right, any closing remarks or leftover points anybody wanted to get across? How about how *And Then There Were Three* fares against the next one, *Duke*?

Tate: *Duke* is much more in the commercial vein than some of the stuff on this album. You don't get as many significantly proggy things like "The Lady Lies" and "Ballad of Big." By *Duke*, they've pretty much gotten all of that out of their system. There's "Misunderstanding" and "Turn It On Again," which is a pop song, but it's got a catchy shifting time signature, so it's still proggy in that sense. But "Misunderstanding," I mean, that's an obvious radio pop song in the way "Follow You Follow Me" is. "Your Own Special Way" is not a terribly obvious AM radio song because it still has that 6/8 bit toward the end. But it seems to me that on *And Then There Were Three* and *Duke* and especially *Abacab*, they're composing songs specifically for radio. ELP were doing that back in the day with "Lucky Man" and "Still You Turn Me On," but Genesis weren't really doing that, I think, until *And Then There Were Three*.

Martin: Have you noticed that these guys write a lot about snow and ice?

Pontus: Yeah, it's a very wintry album. I wonder why that was. Did it feel like that while making it? Even though, I guess it was the fall, in The Netherlands. Does it feel like that when you don't know where you're going? Maybe they were in a wintry sort of reflective mood. As you say, it's a theme that runs through the record.

Martin: Or if it's not too pronounced, the idea strengthens with various songs in the catalogue back to *Trespass*.

Pontus: Sure, and weather or not, *And Then There Were Three* is a melancholy album. *A Trick of the Tail* is comparatively happy and uplifting and in-your-face. You're in a good place listening to that record. But this is a bleak affair. It's quite cold and dark. There'd be more energy if there was more guitar. But this is very much the Tony show.

Pete: Yes, it's an interesting dynamic between the three of them on this record. I've always gotten the impression that Tony is cranky and very controlling and that Mike is more easy going. I think the most driven of the three is Phil but then again Phil always seemed like a fun guy. I would love to hang out with the three of them to see if my impressions over the years are confirmed, but I somehow doubt they would be. But Tony, in interviews and in stories that I've read, he seems to be the guy who's the real businessman, the cranky businessman in the band, whereas Phil strikes me as the guy you want to hang out at the pub with and have a few pints.

Rand: You asked about *Duke*. I love *Duke*, but I think it suffers from too many ballads, for one thing. And it's too long. I don't think they needed to make it that long. I mean, "Please Don't Ask" and "Alone Tonight," those were all songs that were written for or about or by Phil Collins, because he was going through the second divorce and I just don't think that people need to hear all that stuff.

When it comes to *Duke*, my favourite songs are the weird ones, like "Man of Our Times," which is really intense and heavy. Nobody ever talks about that song. And "Cul-de-Sac" is another good one, with weird chord changes. "Duchess" is really cool and "Behind the Lines," man, what a great intro. But once we're into the verses, it sounds reggae to me. When they slow down and relax into that verse part, I'm going, "That's reggae!" And then "Duke's Travels" and "Duke's End" I like a lot. "Turn It On Again" and "Misunderstanding" I've just heard too many times and I'm burned-out on them. Sly and the Family Stone should have sued this band for stealing "Hot Fun in the Summertime." It's the same exact thing (laughs).

Martin: I tend to think *And Then There Were Three* sits smack in the middle between *Wind & Wuthering* and *Duke* in pretty much every way imaginable.

Rand: I think it's mostly a prog album with a couple of pop songs. Definitely "Follow You Follow Me" is squarely a pop song and "Scenes from a Night's Dream" is like a *Magical Mystery Tour*-type pop song. It would have fit really good on a Beatles album back then. I love that tune. But the rest of it, "Down and Out" and "Undertow" are prog. "Ballad of Big," I think that's just kind of rock. "Snowbound" seems prog and "Burning Rope" is definitely prog, as is "Deep in the Motherlode" and "The Lady Lies." So it's maybe two-thirds prog and one-third pop. When they go into *Duke*, they're starting to realise that the simpler we play, the more money we make. And then Genesis is on this incline of success versus a decline of artistic integrity. I'm not saying that they don't have any integrity on the rest of the Genesis albums, but they left their prog fans hanging in the wind, you know?

And Then There Were Three

Behind The Lines: Genesis on Record 1978-1997

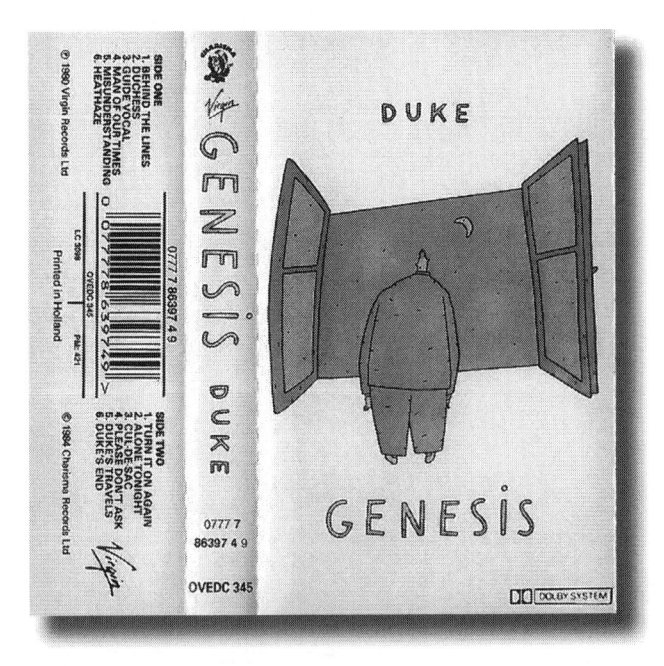

DUKE

March 28, 1980
Charisma CBR 101
Produced by David Hentschel and Genesis; assisted by Dave Bascombe
Engineered by David Hentschel
Recorded at Polar Studios, Stockholm, Sweden
Personnel: Phil Collins – lead vocals, drums, drum machine, percussion, duck; Tony Banks – keyboards, backing vocals, 12-string guitar, duck; Mike Rutherford – guitars, bass guitar, bass pedals, backing vocals
Additional musicians: David Hentschel – backing vocals

Side 1
1. Behind the Lines (Banks, Collins, Rutherford) 5:31
2. Duchess (Banks, Collins, Rutherford) 6:40
3. Guide Vocal (Banks) 1:18
4. Man of Our Times (Rutherford) 5:35
5. Misunderstanding (Collins) 3:11
6. Heathaze (Banks) 5:00

Behind The Lines: Genesis on Record 1978-1997

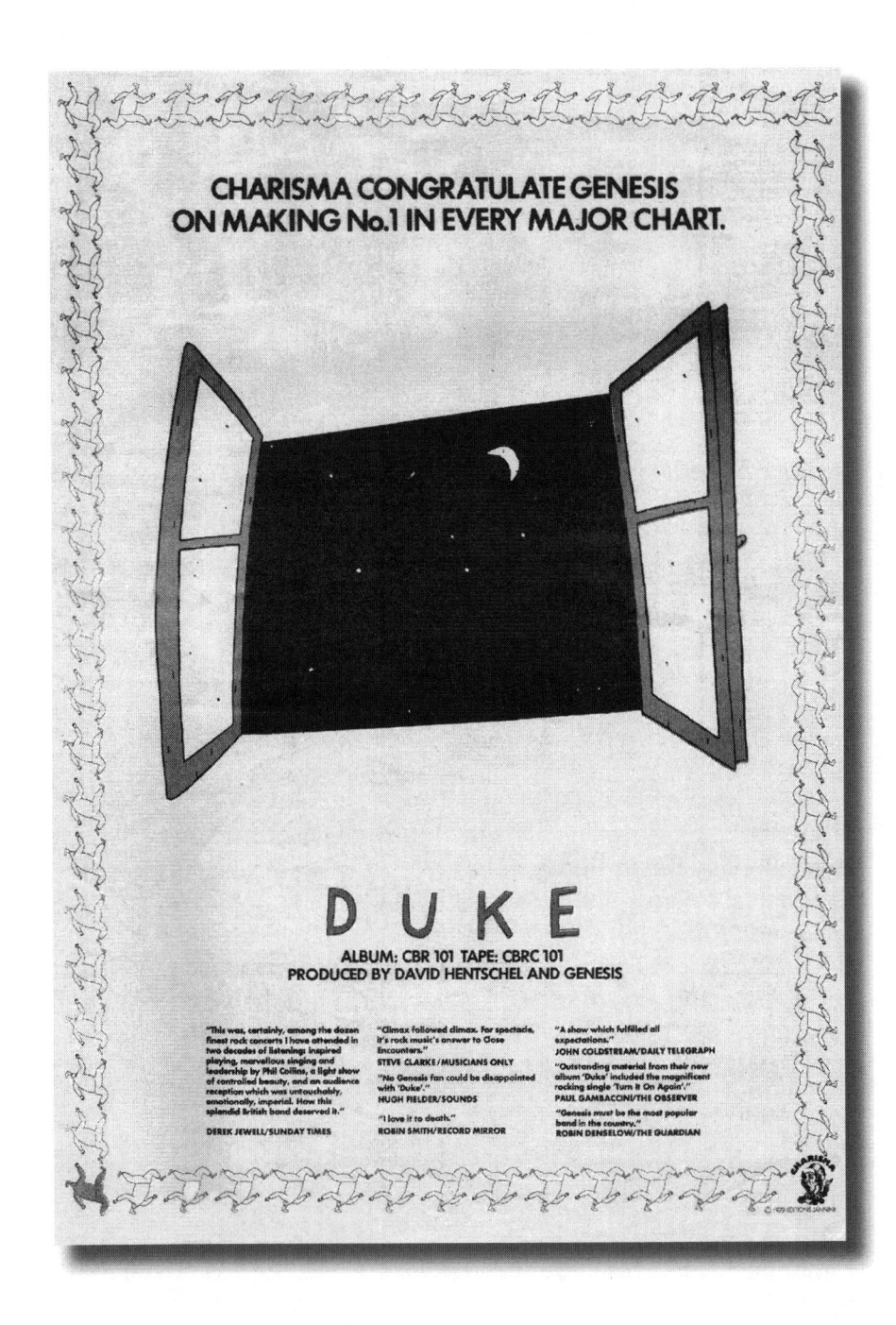

Side 2
1. Turn It On Again (Banks, Collins, Rutherford) 3:50
2. Alone Tonight (Rutherford) 3:54
3. Cul-de-Sac (Banks) 5:02
4. Please Don't Ask (Collins) 4:00
5. Duke's Travels (Banks, Collins, Rutherford) 8:41
6. Duke's End (Banks, Collins, Rutherford) 2:04

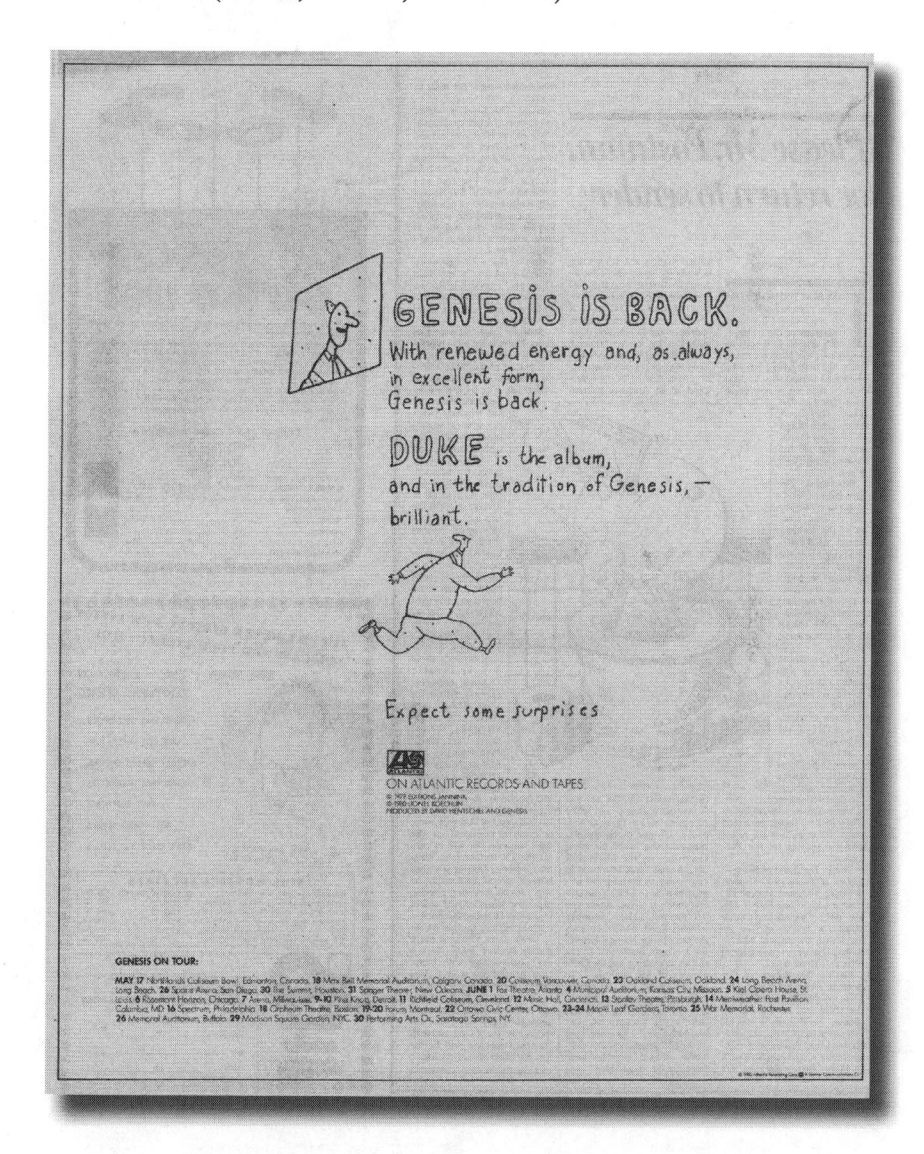

Behind The Lines: Genesis on Record 1978-1997

A *Duke* Timeline

March 3, 1980. "Turn It On Again" is issued in the UK as an advance single from *Duke*. Appearing on the B-side is "Behind the Lines." The A-side reaches No.8 on the UK charts.

March 13 – May 9, 1980. The band conduct an extensive tour of the UK in support of *Duke*.

May 17 – June 30, 1980. The band support *Duke* in North America.

March 24, 1980. Genesis issue *Duke* in the US, followed by a UK release four days later. The album hits the No.1 spot on the UK charts and achieves a No.11 placement on Billboard.

May 1980. The first single from *Duke* issued in the US is "Misunderstanding," backed with "Behind the Lines." It reaches a healthy No.14 on the American charts.

May 9, 1980. "Duchess" is issued as a single from *Duke*, backed with the non-LP "Open Door." The song achieves a No.46 placement on the UK charts.

May 30, 1980. Peter Gabriel issues his groundbreaking third solo album, informally known as "melt." Drumming on four tracks is Phil Collins, with "Intruder" being particularly inspiring to both Peter and Phil from a percussive point of view.

July 21, 1980. *Duke* is certified gold.

August 1980. America sees "Turn It On Again" as a single, backed with the non-LP "Evidence of Autumn." The track reaches No.58 on the Billboard charts and No.55 on Cash Box.

August 29, 1980. "Misunderstanding" is issued in the UK as a single, backed with "Evidence of Autumn." It reaches No.42 on the British charts.

October 13, 1980. John Martyn issues an eighth album, entitled *Grace and Danger*. Drumming on the album is Phil Collins.

Behind The Lines: Genesis on Record 1978-1997

January 9, 1981. Phil issues "In the Air Tonight" as a single. Its innovative gated drum sound sits on a throughline from "Intruder" on the third Peter Gabriel album en route to 1983's "Mama."

February 13, 1981. Phil Collins issues his debut solo album, *Face Value*. Fired by the single "In the Air Tonight," it's a huge success, currently certified at five times platinum. The album also includes a version of Genesis song "Behind the Lines." Co-producing is Hugh Padgham.

Behind The Lines: Genesis on Record 1978-1997

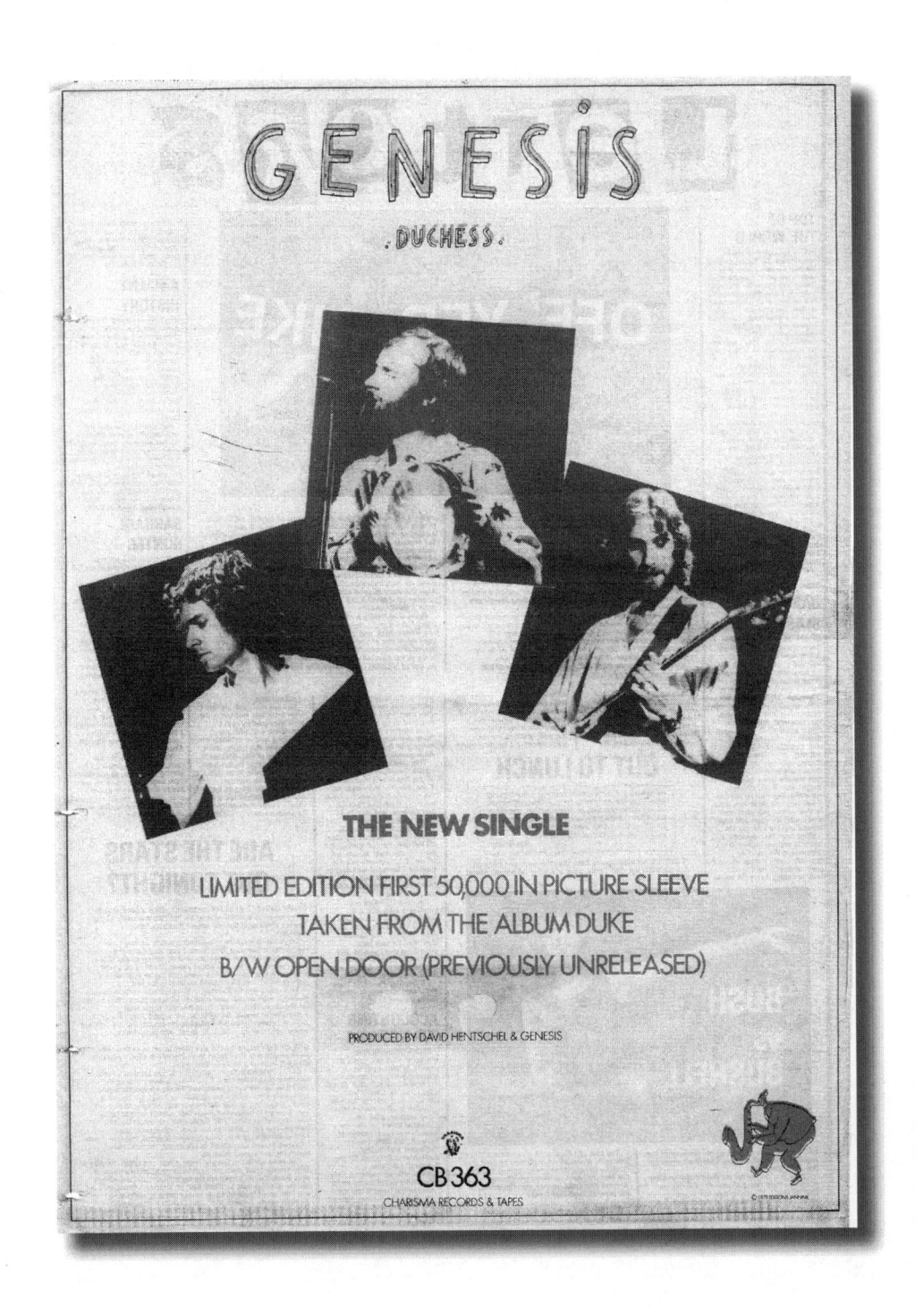

Martin talks to Todd Evans, Douglas Maher, Luis Nasser and Pete Pardo about *Duke*.

Martin Popoff: Let's begin with this: is *Duke* the start of a new era for the band, or are we being fooled by the white cover art?

Todd Evans: Yes, there's the debate about whether *Duke* is them transitioning to pop music. I used to have a recording of an interview with them right around the '83 album and the interviewer brought that up and Tony Banks answered and said, "We've always made pop music; you just never played it." And then Phil Collins makes a joke about it and says, "Oh, we gotta separate these two." But then Tony starts talking about "Counting Out Time" and other songs from the earlier era and they're like, "We were trying to do this all along. We just got better at it as the years went by."

But my situation with this album is this. I remember when *Duke* came out and I saw a poster of it in the record store. I was already into Yes and Rush in a big way by that time, and I thought Genesis is a band that I'm gonna like and I've just got to get started with them. But as it turns out, I didn't actually hear any Genesis until after I bought *Face Value*. That's about when I started, somewhere around 11th grade. But yeah, it's a great album and the guys seem to like it too. "Behind the Lines," "Duchess" and "Guide Vocal" are great. They've come and gone from the set list, but they've been pretty consistently played. "Duchess" was played on the last tour.

Luis Nasser: Well, here's what I will say. I think that *And Then There Were Three* is unfairly maligned, okay? However, *Duke*, from my perspective, is the last truly great Genesis album. This is where the three guys finally got comfortable writing for themselves. The only thing I don't like about *Duke* is that they completely ruin the sequencing of the album. One of the worst things that artists can do is try to please an audience. Because, first of all, you can't read minds, and secondly, you have to start off by pleasing yourself. But you do have to put your best foot forward. You have to be really, really proud of your work. You shouldn't be second guessing it by trying to read the tea leaves of the marketplace. So, from my perspective, this record would have been stronger if they had left the *Duke* suite as one side and they had the other side with strong singles, the standalone songs.

It's an album that people generally like, but the very traditional Genesis fans love to hate, which I don't understand. If people doubt it, all they have to do is go to YouTube and listen to the Lyceum concerts from 1980 where they actually play the *Duke* suite in order live. And then they throw in "Misunderstanding" and all the other things. It's an absolutely killer presentation of these songs. But yeah, I don't understand why people trash this album. *Abacab* also has some incredible music in it, but *Duke* is a very different record. *Duke* is very much a Phil Collins record. He's going through a lot, right? He's going through his divorce and he's working on *Face Value* and then they're doing this thing. So, *Duke* is basically a concept album about a guy who's kind of reflecting back on his life. Which is what you would expect that a guy going through a painful divorce would be doing. I made all these choices and where exactly did they lead me?

Doug Maher: Absolutely. That looms large here. *Duke* demonstrates that a lot of issues around, I guess you could say, paranoia, self-doubt, anger, loss and fear are really deeply rooted in these human beings at such a young age. And I don't know whether that's coming out of living in Britain after World War II or the school system or what. I don't know what their childhoods were like, personally, to be honest with you. Other than specific tales here and there and whatnot. And how many of those are really in-depth?

Martin: Hard to believe they were like 18-year-olds when they made their first album.

Doug: Absolutely, and I was pretty young when I was introduced to *Duke*. I was born in 1974 and I was introduced to *Duke* the same year as *Permanent Waves*. That was my first introduction to Rush because of all the kids that we hung out with in the neighbourhood, they weren't playing *Nursery Cryme* (laughs). They weren't playing the vintage Genesis at that point, because they couldn't relate to it. And then suddenly *Duke* comes out.

But with respect to their young age, that's kind of where I'm going with this. You take this journey with this band, and there aren't a lot of bands you can do this with. A lot of them have wrapped it up by the time you get to the tenth album, and here we are and it's just 1980. I think by the time they get to *We Can't Dance*, they've had a full career. At that point, I think you saw these people almost finished completely as creative musicians. I really think that they were spent.

The loyalists might say it's all about the Peter Gabriel era, but some bands mature, and that applies to Genesis. You don't see too many bands writing this deep and complex and mature this late into their career.

And I think it's really noticeable by Phil Collins and his solo work, that once you got into the '90s with his solo work, it wasn't that good. Once you get into "Everyday" and the Disney stuff and whatnot, the songs weren't that good. It underscores how they were creatively spent. *Calling All Stations* was them just kind of holding on, with. "Shipwrecked" maybe being the exception.

But outside of that, Genesis is a band that I can't compare to any other, and that's pretty difficult to say. What I do know, if I'm being honest, I think that they should hold the mantle as the true godfathers of progressive rock. I know people love to say that about King Crimson and Yes and whatnot. But I think Genesis did something that truly defined not only progressive, but they managed to stay progressive all the way to the end. And if you take a band like Yes, or you take the usual suspects, Rush and what have you, they kept tinges.

But it's nothing like Genesis. To the end, Genesis were like, yeah, here's a ten-minute song and here's another eight-minute song. And they were still able to sell millions of albums and play stadiums and be far more popular. Even though they were huge here in America, I still believe they were and still are far more popular in Europe and around the world.

So I think with something like *Duke* to me, because everything is centred around your age and when you were introduced to a band, that's where the favourites come in. But in the wider world, *Duke* is a jump-off album, where the old-school fans made that decision: am I still in? It was kind of the *Signals* of Genesis, where fans who had been along for the ride, they're like, I'm either sticking with this whole train here that's been going on right to the end or I'm out, because I'm a loyalist to the old stuff. That really happened with Rush with the *Signals* album. I compare the two musically and lyrically, as well as the fan bases and the album/tour/album/tour cycle, both at ten records, both around the same time.

It's important to put that into context. I just don't understand the mocking or the hate or anything else that's projected onto *Duke*. Phil Collins made a career off of *Duke*, in a way, if you think about it. There's absolutely no way that you can look at it any different, writing an album that essentially was about this fictional character,

Albert and whatnot, and Phil going through this whole process with his marriage. That launches Phil's *Face Value* and everything else that you wind up getting for the rest of his solo career.

And so basically, if you're saying that you don't like *Duke*, then you don't like anything from Phil Collins as a solo artist. Because there's no person who is able to really express this kind of pain so well. If you put aside Billy Joel, who seems to tap into another kind of love, Phil Collins has mastered the ability to describe dysfunction, whether it's self-made or circumstantial or by happenstance, something that might not have happened because of what he did, like, say, his wife having an affair on him. Multiple affairs. Phil chose his art, and I think Genesis need to be remembered as the result of that.

I think without Phil going through the turmoil—turmoils, I should say—in his personal life, I don't know if they would have lasted throughout the '80s commercially. They wouldn't have had the commercial success. When you look at where music was going, you saw what Yes did with *90125* and *Big Generator*. These are like fluke records, if you will. It's like, okay, here's a couple hits. This isn't going to be some masterpiece, but you're going to get radio-friendly tunes. Whereas Genesis, Tony Banks writes a lot of dark music, and Rutherford and Banks, I don't think they get enough credit for having… I don't want to say it's for having their feet planted on the ground or they seem to take this dystopian view or loneliness view in just about everything that they write.

When Collins comes in, Collins is more experimental. Collins tends to want to create this bigger picture and humanise it more. Where I would say Banks and Rutherford tend to have this more generalised view that we've got to have some fear in there. We need to have some concern here; we need to have some worry here. Phil is more in touch with the human condition. And I think that's displayed by the success in their own solo careers, too. I don't know about you, but when you listen to Mike + The Mechanics, you have this sense of loneliness, and not just in *The Living Years*.

Martin: Man I don't think there's another band that represents the '80s any better than those guys.

Doug: Yes! It's unbelievably '80s-sounding. Look, no disrespect, I love Paul Carrack. I think Paul Carrack is one of this generation's best singers. What he did out there, I don't think he gets enough credit.

But my problem is that you get an overkill with Genesis. You start to say, all right, is this relatable any longer? Phil talking about what's going on in his life, he managed to pull off... I don't think one album, but I think back-to-back albums with *Abacab*, essentially writing about his separation and his divorce. And not only getting away with it, but doing it unbelievably well and successfully.

And yet Phil Collins, of all people, tends to say that *Abacab* underperformed, didn't live up to any particular expectations. And the fact that *Abacab* had zero representation on the final tour made me irate. How do you not include that? In America especially, where, beyond RIAA certifications, it's about how popular are those songs today? Did they have a lasting impact for decades? I understand playlists are going to change and go in and go out. But *Abacab* and *Duke*, those singles are on today around the clock on classic rock stations, on satellite radio and everything else. And yes, the '83 "Mama" *Genesis* and *Invisible Touch* albums have spawned monster singles as well. They were always able to produce hits because of Phil Collins. And Phil knew that, so why not double dip and have a solo career? That's why people got burned-out on Phil because he was everywhere. To me, Phil Collins became a more talented and popular version of Barry Gibb.

Martin: Pete, and how about yourself? Is there any extra significance to *Duke*?

Pete Pardo: Well, coming out fairly early in 1980, I think it's closing the door on the '70s. Still, there are similarities to *And Then There Were Three*, including that fact that David Hentschel is producing. It definitely sounds like a band with no question marks over whether they can continue as a trio. Now they're like, okay, we got it here. But they are even more so embracing their pop and maybe arena rock sensibilities. There's still plenty of prog, but it's prog for a new decade, like we would see with other prog bands from the '70s, when they started to move into the '80s, usually reconstituted in terms of lineups and even new bands, in the case of Asia. There are new sounds with advancing synth technology, new production values, sharper songwriting, new guitar gear and recording methods. So yeah, there's definitely a shift on this album, and notably toward a certain softness from a production standpoint. Which makes it seem like there's more time between the recordings of these two albums, this with *And Then There Was Three*, even though it's just two years.

Martin: What are your views on the album cover? It's almost an anti-cover, when you think about what this band's canon of covers is so far.

Doug: Yes, starkly different. It's by Lionel Koechlin and it was based off of a children's book, *L'Alphabet de Albert* or *Albert's Alphabet*. I mean, the simplicity that's there, it captures that loneliness but in a beautiful landscape. I know it's French, but you rarely saw artwork like that.

Pete: They're no longer using the logo, and you get this weird dude with the big body and tiny head. It's all very kind of cartoony-looking. And then you look at the track list and you've got two duke songs and a duchess song so you figure something's going on.

Luis: I love that artwork. It's obviously minimalistic and I know some people hate that figure, that main character Albert. Like *Lamb*, it's very white, with this little figure thrown into that whiteness like he's caught in a state of limbo.

Martin: Can you provide any additional insight on how the band is modernizing for the new decade? I imagine a lot of that necessarily has to come from Tony.

Luis: Yes, and he's using more Yamaha stuff. But he's using the cartridge, you know, because they didn't have what I call the Velveeta sound dialled in yet. Those very swirly pads that have like a hundred things in them. You hit a single key and it fills out the sound spectrum. He wasn't doing that. And again, they use the drum machine as a keyboard, almost, which is interesting. It's not "In the Air Tonight." It's still very much Genesis. And they will continue to do that with "Dodo" and some of the stuff from *Abacab* where it will still resonate as old-school Genesis, the heavy-duty prog band.

To this day, I still hold dear that if you listen to *Three Sides Live*, that opener of "Turn It On Again" into "Dodo" into "Abacab" is one of the most amazing rocking-est live pieces of music I've ever heard. Chester Thompson kills, and when they do the double drums, that kills too.

So that's the other aspect. The studio album is not as good as these songs were live, because you're missing Daryl Stuermer and you're missing Chester Thompson. Where I would say that things suffer is in not letting Daryl take the lead guitar role. Mike Rutherford is a great bass player, and he plays lots of really cool arpeggios and 12-strings and all that. His guitar solos are "meh." But you could argue that that speaks well of his ego, that instead he's doing what's best for the song.

Martin: All right, let's get into the songs. *Duke* opens with "Behind the Lines," which is so important that we had to name the book that!

Luis: Absolutely, and it's part of the suite, which is the sweet spot of the album for me, pardon the pun. But they chose to break it up. The fortunate thing about where we are now is that you can reassemble the album the way you want it. "Behind the Lines" is Albert looking back on his life. He had this diary, and he's looking back, with a melancholic kind of "what is" or "what if."

But the music is just brilliant, with complex chord movements that are hard to pick out. You don't really hear them; they're not in-your-face. They're not fat jazz chords, necessarily, but they're not, you know, three-fingered chords either. They utilise a lot of the tricks they learned through the years with Steve Hackett, how to unfold the chord and send some of the notes to this register and send some to another one. It's a beautiful song. And the drums are great. The drum sound on this album is huge, even though the electronic drums are being incorporated. But I like that they don't take over. It's there as a texture.

Pete: I agree, and yeah, "Behind the Lines" is a terrific opener that pulls you right in. You've got those big symphonic keyboards just exploding right off the bat, although the biggest thing for me is that Mike sounds like he's figured out how to play lead guitar at least fairly well. He doesn't sound as shy about it, like he's doubting his skills.

So he's also there pretty quickly, and confidently, on "Between the Lines." I wouldn't call it a Steve Hackett-type guitar solo. He sounds more inspired by the guy who was playing live for them, Daryl Stuermer. And I agree with Luis. I never understood why they never allowed Daryl or Chester Thompson to play on these records. They'd been loyal sidemen for them on the road with Genesis for years and years and never appeared on a studio record. I guess I understand. You gotta pay them more to come to the studio to work. But to me, Rutherford's guitar playing on this album seems influenced by what he was seeing on stage next to him every night with Daryl Stuermer.

At the percussion end, Collins' drumming is acrobatic and powerful. It's interesting how there's no singing until like two-and-a-half minutes into the song. And it's almost amusing how big and bombastic and traditionally Genesis it is at the beginning, and then all of a sudden, the full band comes in and it's kind of relaxed and funky, right? The keys are providing this horn-like effect, but it's catchy and actually quite dramatic. And then you've got a nice guitar solo. I've always loved this track. So yeah, that funk groove, the bright keyboards and the similarly shiny drum sound are all things that function to bring Genesis more into the '80s.

Martin: That whole opening sequence is pretty amusing. It's like a Broadway play, right? I can see everybody shuffling into the theatre while the orchestra in the pit plays that.

Pete: Yeah, and then everybody sits down as the music settles down. It's almost like you've got Genesis and Earth, Wind & Fire coming together here in a weird way, even though it's subtle. I mean, they'd get even get funkier going forward.

Doug: All right, so you had "Duchess," "Misunderstanding," "Duke's End," "Turn It On Again" and "Behind the Lines" all as part of the suite. That was originally supposed to just be one side. And they'd have the remainder of the material on the second side of the LP. Anybody who's really familiar with any information about this record, dating back over 40 years, is kind of familiar with this. If you're reading a book on Genesis or if you're having a conversation about Genesis, you know the story of *Duke* and you know the character, Albert, that is this fictional character, if you will, that is essentially taking this almost exact crisis path taken by Phil Collins.

So I'd like to say that Phil Collins is Albert, in a way, even though I know he was basing it off somebody else. There's no title track, but there's this "duke" theme. What's the connection? How did we get here? The lyrics refers to a book, a whole bunch of times, which reads like a photo album. But more to the point, it sounds like it serves as a symbol between himself and his love interest in it.

"Behind the Lines," I feel like it's this Pete Townshend thing. You remember how you had the Who record called *Face Dances*, and then you had "Face Dances, Pt. 2" on his solo album? "Behind the Lines" appears again on Phil's first solo album, *Face Value*, where it sounds much different—perkier, funkier—than what you're getting with Genesis. So you have this crossover thing and it's weird that that happens. It's like, are you branching out as a solo artist there or are you not? These are little struggles I have between this and *Face Value*. It's like a divorce love letter to his wife, and Phil takes the band along with him. To be honest, he made a career out of doing it as a solo artist. Phil has a fantastic ability to tap into the human condition, notably the misery from failed love, or trying to make love work.

Martin: What is the significance of "Duchess" on this album?

Doug: They're using the Roland CR-78 and it's the first drum machine track in Genesis' history. Phil refers to his ex-wife as the duchess. It's part of the suite, with this back and forth, up and down, rise and fall, if you will, much loved and tragic female performer, this big star from the beginning of her career to her time at the top to her decline and eventually hitting the bottom.

Luis: "Duchess" begins with that kind of ostinato from the drum machine, and then we're into the story of this woman, this famous singer that Albert has some kind of connection with. It speaks about the follies of fame, how fickle fame can be. Ironically, it speaks about something that was going to happen to Genesis themselves, which is if you really want to become mega-successful, you're kind of making a Faustian deal, because the taste of the audience at that level is incredibly fickle. And the pressure for you to come up with another mega-hit is enormous.

Then you see the downfall of this character and how this affects the relationship and all that. It's quite sad, in a way, because without being openly autobiographical, it's really Phil Collins putting his heart on display, and that is something that was not present on older Genesis songs. Peter Gabriel never really talked about himself. That's a very British thing. But Phil Collins just decided to lay it all out, which is a big change at the literary end and style of the band going forward.

It may be difficult for us mere mortals to relate to being a superstar, but it's not difficult to have empathy and relate to a human who is suffering. That's why I like "Duchess" so much. And the music matches the melancholic vibe of the words. It's grandiose but not at all melodramatic or maudlin. We're told that life ends, and you better make the most of it while you can.

Martin: That percussive intro is significant, with a sort of throughput from the Brian Eno albums to here and Peter Gabriel's third album, and onto "In the Air Tonight" and parts of *Abacab* and *Genesis*.

Pete: Yeah, it's haunting and quiet and dreamy, a sort of floating arrangement and then the vocal starts happening. But as it progresses, "Duchess" becomes one of the great singalong songs on the album. It's majestic pop, but it still sounds like Genesis and I love the way it starts and ends in similar fashion, with that long intro and then the fade-out—really, really good. In the middle there's Phil at a proper kit, bombastic for a ballad but perfectly balanced and tasteful and recorded really crisp. But it's Phil's vocals that steal the show on this one, even though there's some historical significance to these kinds of synthesized, programmed drums. Really good track.

Martin: Next is "Guide Vocal," an oddity in the canon, as it's less that two minutes long and yet, kind of a real song.

Doug: According to Phil, the character Albert was a born loser and he falls in love with Duchess who dumps him. "Guide Vocal" is apparently Albert expressing bitterness at this. Albert went on to fall in love with, let's see, the television (laughs), in "Turn It On Again." And then, if you will, maybe a cane or a walking stick in "Duke's Travels." That's my thinking on this. He ends up at a retirement home for losers called Duke's End where he reviews his life. And you're getting those return visits with respect to musical themes, like Dream Theatre does or Rush does, where you go back and revisit the earlier parts of the album. *Hemispheres* does that.

Martin: As does Queen with "More of That Jazz." Luis, thoughts on this one?

Luis: It's an introspective piece of music where the guy is in limbo. It's not clear who he is talking to, other than himself. It's kind of this reckoning. It's a way of coming to peace with who you are, which is essentially coming to any kind of peace. Like you say, it's a short song, but it's well put-together, with a great melody. It's a Tony Banks song, but Phil Collins really sells it, and it doesn't overstay its welcome. Even though I'm not a ballad guy, I think this one works brilliantly.

Pete: "I'm the one who guided you this far/Nobody must know my name." It's just a little vocal and synth bridge piece, quite haunting, but it's important to have here because they revisit it again later in the album. It makes its impact.

Martin: "Man of Our Times" feels like a ballad of sorts, but the drumming from Phil is so grand. Plus, I'm just loving that drum sound. I hear Styx in this one.

Pete: Yeah, that makes sense. I've always had a soft spot for this one. I love the big bass groove and the crashing drums. The keyboards are majestic too and the chorus is absolutely unforgettable, soaring. It's just Phil Collins at the height of his powers. You can just picture him with a microphone up high and just like belting it out with his eyes closed. And I love the production on this song. The drums and the keys sound larger than life. Is it a pop song? Is it a prog song? I don't know. But it's so Genesis and so emotional and I've always loved it. It's another singalong song. When I was a kid growing up and listening to this, I would just sit and sing those words over and over again from the stereo.

Todd: Remarkable song, and easily my favourite Mike Rutherford-penned Genesis song. You mentioned the drums. Throughout most of the song, there's almost not a rock 'n' roll beat in it. There's a syncopated thing that happens with the bass drum and then a couple of whacks on the snare drum and it's like this tangled pattern. Then it goes into the chorus and even there it doesn't sound like a rock song. And then finally, the last time they repeat the chorus at the very end, it goes into this full force, double-time 4/4 Phil Collins rock beat. It's like they made you wait through the whole song to get there.

Doug: I know Rutherford said he was influenced by Gary Numan's "Cars" at the time of writing this song. I find it amusing that there's the lyric "Tonight, tonight, oh he's burning bright," and then *Invisible Touch* has a song called "Tonight, Tonight, Tonight." And yes, hypnotic drumming, on insanely well-recorded drums. It's one of those cinematic songs that is better in your own head than Genesis playing it live. Genesis live versus on record is a big issue for me. I don't think Genesis carried over this material well from the record over to the live venue as well as they should have. I thought they fell short on that, in fact with every album and on every tour. They lacked excitement, inspiration, power and everything else.

"Man of Our Times" feels political, and I suspect this song was an influence on Neil Peart's "New World Man" lyric. Only "Man of Our Times" was written in 1979 when Rush we're coming out singing about battles in the hemispheres of the brain and trees at war. It's such a cool song. Phil crushes his China cymbal and his vocal is literally from the bottom of his stomach. But yes, I would venture to call this the template to "New World Man."

Martin: Here comes "Misunderstanding," another lifeline song or a song that encourages the guys to keep going, after the good experience they had with "Follow You Follow Me."

Todd: Yes, "Misunderstanding" is great. I remember when I first heard the album, I was not that crazy about "Misunderstanding." But it's one of those songs that once you are with it for a while, you realise that not only is it a solid song, but you don't get tired of it.

Luis: "Misunderstanding" was them saying, look, Phil has ideas, Tony has ideas, and we want to break free of the necessity of being Genesis. It's them saying, we can call whatever we write Genesis. Which is a risky move, because most of your fans are not going to go along with that. But what they did, essentially, was trade a bunch of old fans for about ten times more new fans.

And then their concerts became this strange thing where they were mostly catering to the people that were filling out the stadium. And the guys that would fill out a theatre, who were scattered somewhere in the stadium, they would get a medley. That would be the bone thrown to them. All right, we're gonna play a little grab-bag or pastiche of three or four old songs that we know you guys like. And for the rest of the people here, this is going to be their piss break.

But I don't mean to complain—I love *Duke*. I know that a lot of prog guys, musicians that are my friends, like Jacob from White Willow, they love it also. And I think for similar reasons—because the songcraft is second to nothing they ever did. All the chops and all the things we love from the past are there, but they have some simpler material as well. And the suite is Genesis at its best.

Pete: "Misunderstanding" is a radio rock song, right? I still remember the first time I heard it on the radio and thinking that it's a little different for them. It's simple and to-the-point, but that chorus is so great. To me this song is like a heavier—and I use that term loosely—version of Supertramp. It's got the sing-along chorus and the song just kind of bounces along. You get those layers of backing vocals very meticulously put-together. I just wish they'd done more with the little guitar break at the end and perhaps extended it out. Still, it's a great radio tune. Is it arena rock? Maybe so.

Martin: I'm hearing Toto, 10CC, ELO, Elton John and The Beatles there. And you know, like before, I'm hearing polite, conservative late '70s glam, with the piano throbbing away, kind of thing.

Pete: Yeah, the piano definitely adds that element.

Doug: When I think about this song, first, I know "Follow You Follow Me" really put Genesis on the map commercially. But to underestimate what "Misunderstanding" did for them would be a crime. MTV began in the summer of 1981, and they really didn't have anything to use from Genesis that was supplied to them from the label. So this was it. This was really the only introduction that you were getting, if you're a kid at that point, to Genesis.

And you're getting this character who's going around almost like a stalker, if you will. Evidently he's stood up for a date, but I think there's actually something deeper going on. Notably, it's the first Collins-written song recorded by the full band. By the way, another bone I have to pick with the band is their inability to put together great set lists from 1980 forward—37 years it took for them to play this song, which is insane. No.1 in Canada, No.14 in the US. It was an MTV staple, as I said, and a complete staple on classic rock and adult contemporary radio stations to this very day. Yet it was nowhere on set lists.

Fantastic song, catchy as hell. It's a song that never gets old. When it comes on, you're comfortable with it. It's not too long. It's a perfect pop song. If I didn't know the entirety of *Duke* is pretty much about Phil's marriage collapsing, I'd say this betrays a bit of a stalker in him at times in the song. At first, I don't think he knew that it was over. But in the end, he drives by her house and realises there's someone else now. It makes you wonder why Phil went through as many relationships as he did. Did these characters, maybe, if you will, actually exist? Was there a reckless, possessive, obsessed Phil Collins or controlling Phil Collins? We'll never know. We get the portrayal now of the elderly, handicapped Phil Collins who gets milked and abused by his ex-wife and cleaned out in divorces.

Now at the musical end, like we discussed with Robert Plant in the previous book, I'm hearing tinges of '50s doo-wop and R&B lines seeping in here, which would be way more prominent in Phil's solo career, on songs like "You Can't Hurry Love" and then the R&B tributes and the Motown tributes and whatnot.

So yeah, I went to Setlist.fm, and saw that November 15, 2021, at Chicago's United Centre, that was the first time that "Misunderstanding" had been played since 1984 (laughs). It's like, what?! What are we doing here? And you know, that's the kind of stupid shit you see with some of these bands. They always have a reason. "Well, you know, we don't find it terribly exciting." Or, "It doesn't live up to our standards today."

It's so funny because let's go back to Rush and *Signals*. Rush did this to "New World Man." It's their highest charting single, and before they played it on the *Vapor Trails* tour in 2002, it had not been in the setlist since 1985, '86 on the *Power Windows* tour. And it was never played after the *Vapor Trails* tour.

So these bands go through this thing where, all right, we've got a catalogue that's this big and we have so many songs that were radio hits, or even big, certifiable hits. But we're not going to touch that. We're not going to go there. I never understood that logic. "Time Stand Still" was another one; that song vanished for decades. And you're just sitting there going, "Why?" You finally found a song that was relatable to the female audience or to the average person who listened to those lyrics. They had an appreciation for what that song meant.

"Misunderstanding" was the same thing. People were thinking of Genesis as the deep, proggy band, writing about stuff that went way over the head of the average John Q Public. And yet it gets tossed?! It's literally now a song that is played on the radio thousands of times a day across the country, never mind what it is around the world. I just never understood that, bands intentionally killing certain songs throughout their career,

If you took something like "Illegal Alien," that song lived on the radio and MTV. That song was popular as hell. Did Phil Collins all of a sudden wake up and go, "We can't touch that anymore."? I don't think so. You didn't have the same amount of polarization going on back then. Nobody gave a shit if you were singing songs about people breaking into the United States, which is happening all day today, every day. The song was speaking truth, but it was putting humour to it. You have a lot of Genesis fans who curse that song and that album. I'm not one of them.

But what I'm saying is, that's a song that's not going to get booed. It's a recognisable hit. People need to protect their legacies and stand up for themselves. I remember Kip Winger talking about the mental struggles over whether or not they should continue to play "Seventeen." Like, what the fuck are you talking about? Seriously, you've got maybe six recognisable hits. Why is this even a discussion right now? I can't do this revisionist shit. I have a real problem with it. So anyway, "Misunderstanding" was absolutely robbed, as far as I'm concerned, of its potential for success in the live arena and what that would have done for the song's continued legacy, not that it needs much help. "That's All" is another one that they screwed over the years too.

Martin: Good stuff. All right, we close side one with "Heathaze," and it's another ballad, only this time the drums take more of a backseat. It's almost turgid from a percussion standpoint, but still melodically interesting.

Doug: So I borrowed from the dictionary, and heathaze is an effect of very hot sun making it difficult to see objects clearly and I'm like applying this to Phil. Or put it this way, the way you describe it reflects the idea of Phil drumming this song in a heathaze. As far as I'm concerned, it feels more like a Gabriel-style Genesis song than a 1980 *Duke* tune.

It's about a man who was in a haze due to a failed marriage or relationship. He seems to refer to seeing other people enjoying each other's company. It really doesn't matter what they're doing, as long as they're together in their love. Finally, realizing he's in this smoky bar is a way for him to snap back into reality and realise what his life is like. So there are these thoughts of the failed relationship and how he can't get past them. The song seems to represent the continuation of doubt, fear and misunderstanding.

Again, back to Rush, I'm reminded lyrically of "The Weapon," "Analog Kid" and "Digital Man." So much of *Duke* really found another life on *Signals* for me. Don't worry too much about everyone else. Live your own life. Don't give them pity or envy no matter how much you are feeling those emotions.

Todd: "Heathaze" is interesting because of how Genesis' lyrical content evolved over time. When you think about "Heathaze" being a Tony Banks song, Tony Banks' lyrics up until that point, and a little bit after too, they're very... I don't want to insult them because I like them. They're good, but they're elegant and kind of stuffy, in a very British way. And this album is where you start to transition to the Phil Collins way of being more direct about emotions, through ballads or love songs. But "Heathaze,' when you hear it, you think, oh, it sounds more like a song from *And Then There Were Three*. But then you think, well, there hasn't been a song like that yet. So it's good that there's one like that (laughs).

Pete: This might be my favourite Phil vocal on the album. It's a dreamy, mellow pop song, but man, it builds up to a chorus that absolutely slays me. And again there's wind and clouds and earth and all this Mother Nature imagery. That whole passage beginning with "The trees and I are shaken by the same winds," when Phil sings those lines, it sends chills up my spine because he sings it with such conviction. It's so emotional and intense. There's really nothing else needed on this track except for gentle synth and piano. You get some bass lines from Michael which are great, but it's just a lush classic that hits me on an emotional level, and less so for any potential musical flourishes. Because I'm notorious for always looking for the musical bits. I don't need them on this song. It's perfect as it is.

Luis: Well, I'll be the wet blanket then. I like "Heathaze," but let me put it to you like this. If you play "Heathaze" for me, I'm gonna enjoy it, but I'm never gonna wake up and say, "You know what I need to play right now? 'Heathaze.'" That's the honest answer.

Martin: Side two opens with the other big hit from this record, setting Genesis up for life, as it were. But "Turn It On Again" is a rocker, maybe even a new wave rocker.

Todd: Yeah, "Turn It On Again" is great. I love the time signature that it's in. Plus it starts with a trick that they do a couple of times later on in their career. The best example I can think of is "Keep It Dark." When you hear that song for the first time, you get this idea of where the one is, the first beat of the bar, but then when it kicks in, it's sort of switched up or turned inside out. And then you have to get used to where the one really is. Clever little tricks like that are what make some of these songs so enduring. It's part of why you don't get tired of hearing them. There's that little bit of challenge, still, every new time you listen to them.

Doug: "Turn It On Again" was a giant hit in the vein of a typical Genesis or Yes or Rush song from the early '80s. It charted okay, but was far more popular as time went on and it became a staple of classic rock radio. MTV in the early '80s would play the live version of this. The joke has always been its catchiness and power to make you move despite being in 13/8. The power to move in odd time signatures while making it impossible to dance to is the curse of Rush. You can't dance to Rush—can't do it. You can't really dance to prog rock period. But they always said that about Rush, that they write great songs but you can't dance to it. That's why it's not appealing to women. You want that 4/4 in there.

Lyrically, in this chapter, in "Turn It On Again," Duke has basically become infatuated with the host of a TV show he's dreaming of. He's thinking about what it'd be like to tell her how he feels, introduce her to his friends, be intimate and have sex with her etc, almost stalking again, except not in the real world. And this stalking thing, really, I think is an underrated discussion when we're talking about this character and Phil. It's something somebody should do a psych evaluation on, possibly through his later Genesis material and his solo material. Is Phil Collins a creep? We don't know.

Luis: Look, people can criticise "Turn It On Again" until they're blue in the face. I would argue that the Genesis songwriting school or collective are responsible for two of the biggest hits ever with weird time signatures. One is "Turn It On Again," which is in 13/8, and the other is Peter Gabriel's "Solsbury Hill," which is in 7/8. And the beauty of both songs is that you don't realise they're in weird time signatures, ever.

"Turn It On Again" is just so pounding and throbbing and well put-together. I have heard demos. This song apparently was not really a song at all. It was just a very short interlude. And the original version was really slow in tempo and was supposed to be more ponderous and I think they were taking themselves a little too seriously. And it was Phil Collins who said, "No, man, let's beef it up. Let's add some drums. Let's rock out with this one." And they sure do. And look, I'm not gonna sit here and tell you that I love the fact that they would later play it on stage with a Blues Brothers section in it and an Elvis medley and all that, because I don't think it's necessary to do that. But then again, it's not my song. They can do whatever the hell they want with it. But the version on *Duke*, to me, is a masterpiece. It's progressive pop and I absolutely love it.

And the commentary. You know, "All I need is a TV show, that and the radio." It's about how fake all that is. "I can show you some of the people in my life." But the guy's fundamentally miserable. There's an indirect or secondary message I get from this song and other songs on the album about how even if you're famous and successful, you can have these fundamental relationship and emotional issues. And people kind of balk at that, thinking, well, you know, what are you bitching about? You're this rich guy, right? You get to tour the world. People imagine a reality, but they don't see that it's very insular. That when you're that famous, you can't just walk out to the grocery store, or go to the local pub for a beer. You have to live in an environment that's completely controlled, cut-off, you're stuck in hotels, you're stuck in airports, you're stuck in your house and your house becomes a bunker of sorts. And this leads to depression. This leads to problems. And I like that the album, albeit indirectly, addresses that situation, that thing that was gonna happen to Genesis where they were about to really snowball into the monster that became *Invisible Touch*.

Anyway, I love "Turn It On Again." I think that song is very underrated among the Genesis fans who only want to hear "The Fountain of Salmacis" or whatever. Those are great songs, but if you can't appreciate a good tune, that's to your own detriment. And this is a great tune.

Pete: Even though "Turn It On Again" was a hit, to me it's darker in tone than "Misunderstanding." Tony's keys are powerful to the point where they're kind of intimidating or foreboding. Phil sounds perfectly at home here, singing these more conventional rock lyrics about relationships etc., even though he's still artful and oblique about it. And I think Mike's guitar textures are excellent.

Now, I come down on bands for doing this, but I think it works here. The whole back half of the song is them basically repeating the main line of the song over and over and over again. But I'm okay with it because they've got all these other vocals appearing underneath it and around it almost in acapella fashion. I think it's a work of genius. To me, this is the first arena rock Genesis song, but there will be more moving forward, beginning certainly with "Abacab."

Martin: Then we're back to the band proposing another ballad. And I do mean proposing. It's like they're experimenting in this space, trying out variants and seeing which subtle stylistic changes bring the magic.

Todd: Funny you should say that. Because as far as "Alone Tonight" is concerned, there's a great story I heard just recently, where Phil Collins was talking about how just before the album came out, they had a meeting with the record company and the record company executive said, "Okay, so the first single is 'Alone Tonight.' Okay, very good. Everybody have a good day." And Phil was like, "Whoa, wait a minute. If you put out 'Alone Tonight' as the first single right after 'Follow You Follow Me,' it will kill us. We'll be typecast. It will be terrible for us."

So they nixed that idea and "Alone Tonight" actually never came out as a single. But I like "Alone Tonight" a lot. It's very simple and has a lot of space in it. Which is odd for a Genesis ballad, but I'm glad that's the case. And the bridge doesn't even have a guitar solo in it. It's like two bass notes. It's just like very sparse for a Genesis ballad. And at the end of it, there's this really beautiful Tony Banks countermelody that's the best part of it, I think.

Doug: "Alone Tonight" is something that Rutherford wrote, and it shows. Lyrically it's pretty generic, about being alone on the road and in life. I guess you can fit it in with the suite, but it's nowhere near as strong as the others. Collins does a beautiful harmony for it, but it's a harmless track, in my opinion.

Pete: Yeah, they can keep this one. It's pop fluff. I never liked this song. This is the one I always skip on this album. Phil sounds great, of course. But what's weird is that you would think that Phil wrote this song but it's Mike's. It would have made a great Phil Collins solo song and it would have been a great Mike + The Mechanics song. It's that type of thing. Maybe it's a moment of levity on this album. But like I say, I hit the skip button. It's a pop ballad I have no use for. I know people who dig it—I don't.

Martin: I feel like "Cul-de-Sac" has a few things going for it. It's fairly proggy but also manages to groove pretty well. Plus it's got sophisticated chord changes, or chord changes that are interesting and non-obvious melodically.

Pete: Yeah, there are a lot of positives. It's grandiose, with more big synths from Tony, lots of ringing guitars, great vocals and the chorus is ultra-memorable. I love the kind of super-intense part that starts at about the three-and-a-half minute mark, which takes the song out in this majestic, symphonic fashion. But that's something they often do; they've kind of perfected that formula. And they do it actually quite well elsewhere on this album. That always hit home with me about this album; they never really forgot their symphonic prog roots. Even though a lot of this album really isn't prog, they throw in these bursts here and there. Which reminds you that they know how to do this better than anybody else. So yeah, "Cul-de-Sac" employs a lot of the different styles that they were doing on this album and in this period and puts them all in one track.

Martin: You know, Tony is such an enigma. I mean, he and Mike can write similar types of songs. And then Mike can write, like you say, a Phil Collins solo song, right? But Tony is hard to figure out. And lyrically, he's no slouch. And lyrically, Mike's no slouch either.

Pete: No, not at all. Yeah, very rarely do you see dumb songs in this catalogue, where the lyrics are trite or just whatever. There always seems to be a lot of thought behind it.

Todd: I always grapple with what my favourite Tony Banks track is, and I go back and forth between "Cul-de-Sac" and "One for the Vine." But I think it might be "Cul-de-Sac." I particularly love the bridge in "Cul-de-Sac." It changes keys really dramatically and then transitions into this really simple Rutherford solo. It's really beautiful and I appreciate that it's simple. Because at this point, Rutherford is not the greatest guitarist. But that guitar solo is so effective.

Then the key goes back down to where it was and they go through the chorus one more time. Next there's this other transition to the end where it changes keys either three or four times, and very quickly, within the course of a couple of measures. Then it goes into this kind of double time thing with the drums. I mean, the last minute of "Cul-de-Sac" is just absolutely brilliant. People don't talk about "Cul-de-Sac" enough. It's a really great moment and I think it's Tony's best Genesis song.

Doug: "Cul-de-Sac" was never performed live. I view it as a much darker, earlier version of "Land of Confusion," looking at nuclear annihilation, with the king or the superpowers lining up for this losing battle. The lyric that always stand out to me is, "You thought you'd rule the world forever/Long live the king, don't spare the loser." Not bad at all for an all-Banks composition. Phil always finds a way to make a vocal powerful and that's definitely the case again here.

Luis: "Cul-de-Sac" is interesting but I like it less than I like everything that's part of the suite. I actually like "Misunderstanding" quite a bit, but as we discussed for the Rainbow book, sometimes when you're trying to be too many things at once, it falls short. With "Cul-de-Sac," they were still trying to be clever, still trying to be Genesis, but they were also trying to go for singles and ballads and songs that would potentially chart. And that combination doesn't always work.

Martin: With "Please Don't Ask," we're right back to the ballad lab.

Pete: Yeah, it's pretty good, but what would you call it? It's like brooding, moody pop. I think the band's ability to shift gears on this album into more emotional and dramatic ballad-form material is evident on this song. The backing vocals are really well done, there are some nice guitar textures and licks, although they're typically understated. That seems to be Mike's MO; they are never upfront. But that's a Genesis thing anyway, including when Hackett was in the band. Keyboards were always to the forefront.

Martin: But there were so many different types that your mind processes them beyond different keyboards almost into different categories of instruments. It's almost like you can defend there being so much Tony by saying it's an army of little Tonys.

Pete: Right, true; it's like he's a band within the band (laughs). Case in point, there's some nice use of soft synth textures and tones along with lots of piano. Phil's a big deal on "Please Don't Ask" as well, with his lush vocals. It's not one of my favourites, but it's a nice tune. I like the melancholy vibe.

Doug: "Please Don't Ask," in my opinion, finds Collins trying desperately to convince his ex-wife Andrea to give their marriage another chance. The couple divorced in '80. "Again and again I ask myself was I wrong?/Oh, but time's a healer and heaven knows I've been strong." When it gets to, "Oh, but I miss my boy/I hope he's good as gold," I don't know if Phil Collins ever written anything so personal. It's relatable if you've gone through divorce and separation and infidelity and things like that. Maybe there are female artists that write like this, but it's rare coming from a man.

Phil's written a lot of love songs, and there are some that just grab you. And you're like, okay, but is it based on someone else? No, this is him. This is his kids. This is his life. That's his wife that those words are directed to. You almost feel guilty for listening in on all this pain and devastation that he felt. He was really given the option—go on the road or stay home. And we know what he chose. It's impossible to ask a musician to do that, which is why the divorce rate is so high, especially when you're working, you know, the last ten, 12 years to get to this level. The average person can't understand that. So if you're a spouse that's willing to accept a traveling musician, you're almost sainthood at that point.

Martin: Genesis close the album with this prolonged 11 minutes of exit music, sending us out of the theatre onto the street. "Duke's Travels" is sort of that but not exactly, but then "Duke's End" most definitely is. Like the beginning, it's hard not to imagine this coming from the orchestra pit below the lip of the stage.

Todd: Yeah, "Duke's Travels" and "Duke's End" are kind of like just gravy at that point, because they deliver what people want from Genesis, with long instrumental parts and something relatively proggy. By the time you get there, you're like, "Great, this too?! Excellent" (laughs). And this is after "Please Don't Ask," which is more subdued and beautiful, but definitely not what the old-school fans want.

Luis: "Duke's End" follows the formula established by "Los Endos." They're revisiting this strong theme with a heavy backbeat and in fact a double drum track that is just driving the song. And the keyboards are very rhythmical also, but everything is in counterpoint. Again, in true Genesis form, they're hitting you up with some complicated chord movement and complicated meter changes, and yet you can always tap your foot to it. To me, that's a monumental accomplishment.

I mean, Yes can't do that. Yes is a great band, but it's homework. You're gonna have to listen to a lot of strange stuff. With *Duke*,

Genesis were able to do the nearly impossible, making prog rock that was also pop that you might be able to dance to. Or if you sit and listen to it, it will definitely stimulate your mind. To me, if they had the suite as side A, that would have really helped the old-guard Genesis fans accept the album. And side B, if you give a conservative prog band a good ballad, they're gonna say they don't like it because it's not prog. But if you give them a good ballad written by a prog band, then they give themselves permission to like it. And I think that's what happens with songs like "Misunderstanding" and so forth.

Pete: At the end here, I guess we're more directly celebrating this guy with the green suit and the tiny head and the big body. And we have some earlier-occurring musical bits reappearing throughout these last two songs. Plus the band is messaging that, okay, we're still gonna do some of that prog stuff. "Duke's Travels" takes all sorts of twists and turns. You've got Tony's banks of keyboards at the beginning, set to the rumbling, tribal drums. And Tony's the master of what I call the spiralling solo, whether it's performed on organ or synth.

At the five-minute mark, it kicks into high gear. You've got these great bass lines and the nimble drums working underneath and then there's this big, soaring synth exploration that seems to go on forever, and you don't want it to end. It's so well arranged. You also get like a nice little guitar run from Mike. And then towards the end, you've got Phil coming in and bringing back the "Guide Vocal" line, which is absolute genius, how they revisit it here. It's almost like you took it for granted. You forgot it earlier on the album because it's just this brief passage. So it surprises you when they bring it back. This is eight minutes of pure prog bliss. Awesome track.

Doug: Ah yes, "Duke's Travels," with the famous Neil Peart roundhouse fill and the Magic Kingdom Main Street Electrical Parade keyboards in it, also with stellar playing by all three. Muse has made a career of ripping off the many hundreds of sounds in this song. It's an incredible musical journey with a sort of circus-meets-vintage ice cream truck keyboard sound beautifully screaming love and devotion from the main character,
Duke. That pretty much sums it up for me.

And I didn't mean that tongue-in-cheek. If you put "Duke's Travels" up against Muse's catalogue, you're gonna hear a lot that's taken from there. And there are positives to be found in that, given how big Muse is, despite not having endless amounts of hits on the radio. But they've found a core following that will fill arenas in Europe. Tool's managed to accomplish that in the modern age too.

Martin: Interesting perspective. All right, anything else anybody wants to get off their chest about Genesis first record of the new decade?

Todd: I'll add that I'm pretty nuts about this album. I go back and forth with *Wind & Wuthering* for favourite album of the whole catalogue. The only shortcoming with respect to *Duke* is that it makes you feel like it's supposed to be a concept album, but they sort of ditched the idea. You're like, okay, look at that; this must be an album about this guy. And then it's not. On the other hand, I think they made the right decision by taking the suite and splitting it up over the album and putting other songs in. But it does give you the feeling that they switched gears, which is heightened by the fact that they were offered three Phil Collins songs, and they passed on "In the Air Tonight." I would have liked to have heard "In the Air Tonight" with Tony's keyboards. Phil did a great job in his bedroom with his keyboards, but Tony would have made that song really scary and menacing.

Doug: So here's the thing; if you go and you look at "Misunderstanding," "Please Don't Ask," "In the Air Tonight," "If Leaving Me Is Easy," "Take a Look at Me Now," "I Don't Care Anymore," "Do You Know, Do You Care," "I Missed Again," "You Know What I Mean," you really see the extent of the main theme of this *Duke* album. Phil Collins is just an insanely talented, brilliant, tortured man. Even when doing the Stephen Bishop song "Separate Lives" for *White Nights*. He just owns miserable, lonely love. He finds a way to make it his own.

Kudos to Tony Banks and Mike Rutherford for creating gorgeous soundscapes and preventing Genesis from turning into Air Supply. You know, Martin, when you get into a lot of Genesis lyrics, like Robert Plant, depending upon who's writing them, there's a lot of nonsense. And there's a lot of lyrical scat that's there. I think Genesis were a bit deeper in the '70s. Peter Gabriel is a much deeper writer. Even to this day, he makes you pay attention to what you're listening to, and it takes a special lyricist to do that.

I also want to note that "Behind the Lines" was the opener on something like three tours. And then, I believe, on the last tour it was the instrumental version. But with that song, we're set up immediately to feel the pain of Phil Collins and his divorce. You're being introduced to what's going on, and in fact it was the first song that they put together for *Duke*. In that sense, it's a place-marker song for me, and a gateway to the rest of the album and like I say, it was popular as a live track.

Plus I wanted to reiterate the point that I don't think there's a band that Rush ripped off or borrowed from more than Genesis. And I mean that as a fan of that band since 1980. On *Duke*, you are hearing so much in the lyrical context and in the musical context that you get on *Signals*, not to mention some of the drum fills that are reproduced extremely closely from this record to that one.

And if you look at the window of when this album was recorded, when it was made and when it was released, Rush is on the road. Then they're doing *Permanent Waves* and into *Moving Pictures*. They're always playing this little catch-up game with what Genesis had been doing previously, an album before. You're starting to hear some of *And Then There Were Three* leak into *Moving Pictures* and things like that. I wouldn't say it's pure plagiarism, but it might be musical grand larceny, if you will, that Rush is committing there throughout their career.

And I noticed that they'd always talk about Genesis, especially Neil, but they put the emphasis on Yes and The Who and Cream and whatnot, as the main catalysts for them. Bullshit—it's absolutely Genesis. And as they were venturing into their synth era, oh my God, it was so obvious that Geddy was doing all he could to grab whatever Banks was doing and somehow put droplets of that into every song.

Martin: "Between the Wheels" is a good one for that.

Doug: Oh my God, hello?! Yes, perfect example. And with "Duchess," you see that theme carried on in "Losing It" on *Signals*, where you have these characters who've reached their peak and lost it. So repeatedly, I would hear these new Rush albums and be reminded of Genesis. The inspiration Genesis had on them until the very end of their career is absolutely present.

Okay, and the final thing I'd like to say is that I lament the fact that I was only able to see Genesis in concert one time—that was it. And unfortunately, it was on the *We Can't Dance* tour. And my walk-away from that was exactly as it was watching them on

YouTube playing Wembley or on MTV concerts and things like that. It was, sort of, big deal, they just stand there. It's a band that lacks personality. Without Phil Collins, you're fucked. Phil's character and his storytelling can at least bring these songs to life, whereas you're getting absolutely nothing from Rutherford and Banks. And essentially, Chester does his job and whatever. My point is that when I saw them live, any entertainment value came from Phil and his personality and relatability. And in parallel, that's exactly what I get from *Duke*. This record is Phil saying to the world, "I'm running the show here."

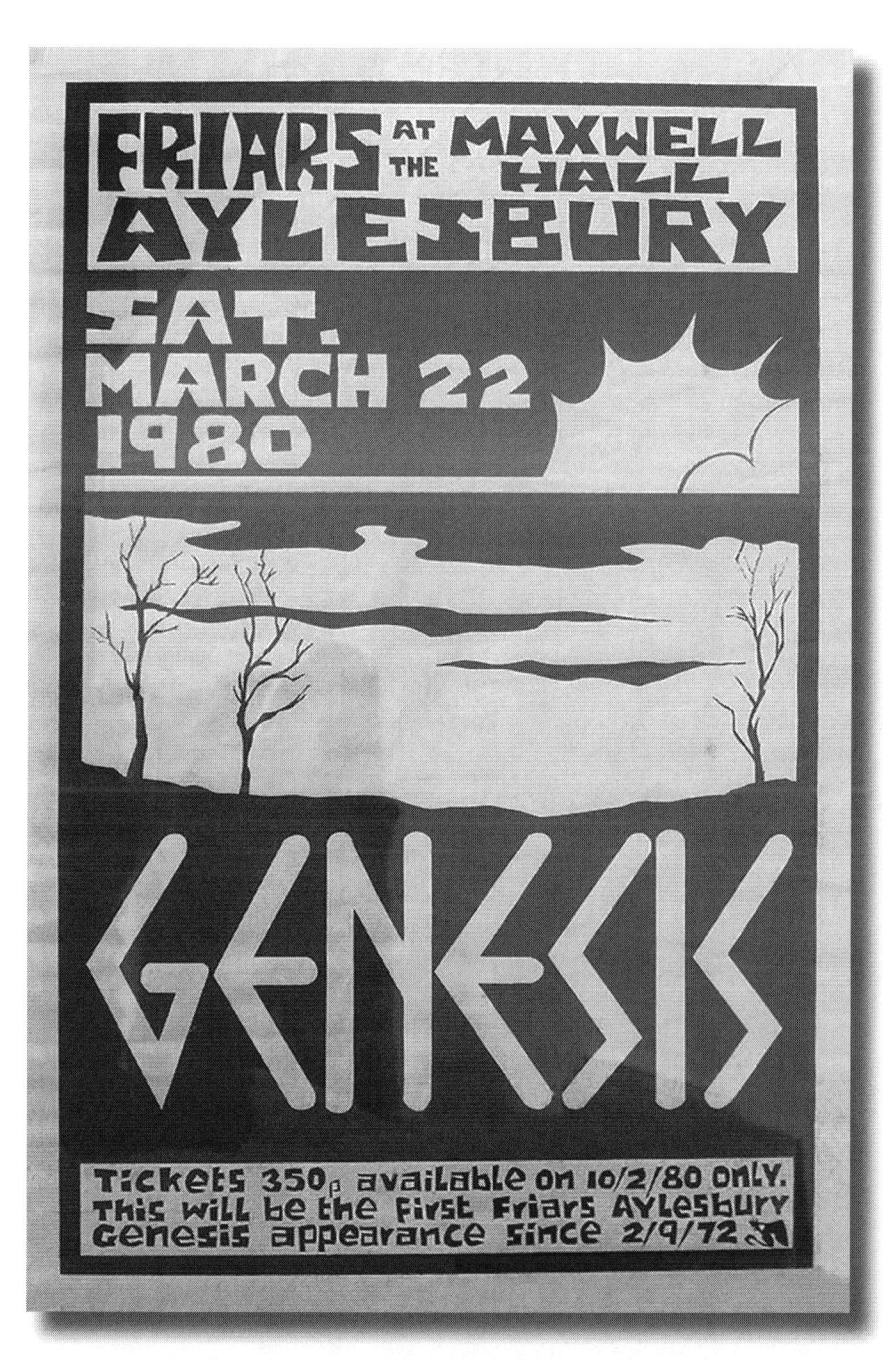

Duke

Behind The Lines: Genesis on Record 1978-1997

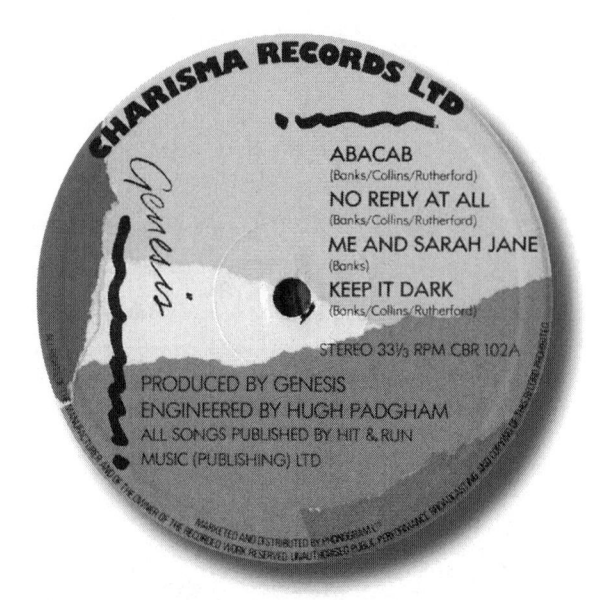

ABACAB

September 18, 1981
Charisma CBR 102
Produced by Genesis
Engineered by Hugh Padgham
Recorded at The Farm, Chiddingfold, Surrey, UK
Personnel: Phil Collins – drums, vocals; Tony Banks – keyboards; Mike Rutherford – basses, guitars

Side 1
1. Abacab (Banks, Collins, Rutherford) 7:02
2. No Reply at All (Banks, Collins, Rutherford) 4:41
3. Me and Sarah Jane (Banks) 6:00
4. Keep It Dark (Banks, Collins, Rutherford) 4:34

Side 2
1. Dodo/Lurker (Banks, Collins, Rutherford) 7:30
2. Who Dunnit? (Banks, Collins, Rutherford) 3:22
3. Man on the Corner (Collins) 4:27
4. Like It or Not (Rutherford) 4:58
5. Another Record (Banks, Collins, Rutherford) 4:30

Behind The Lines: Genesis on Record 1978-1997

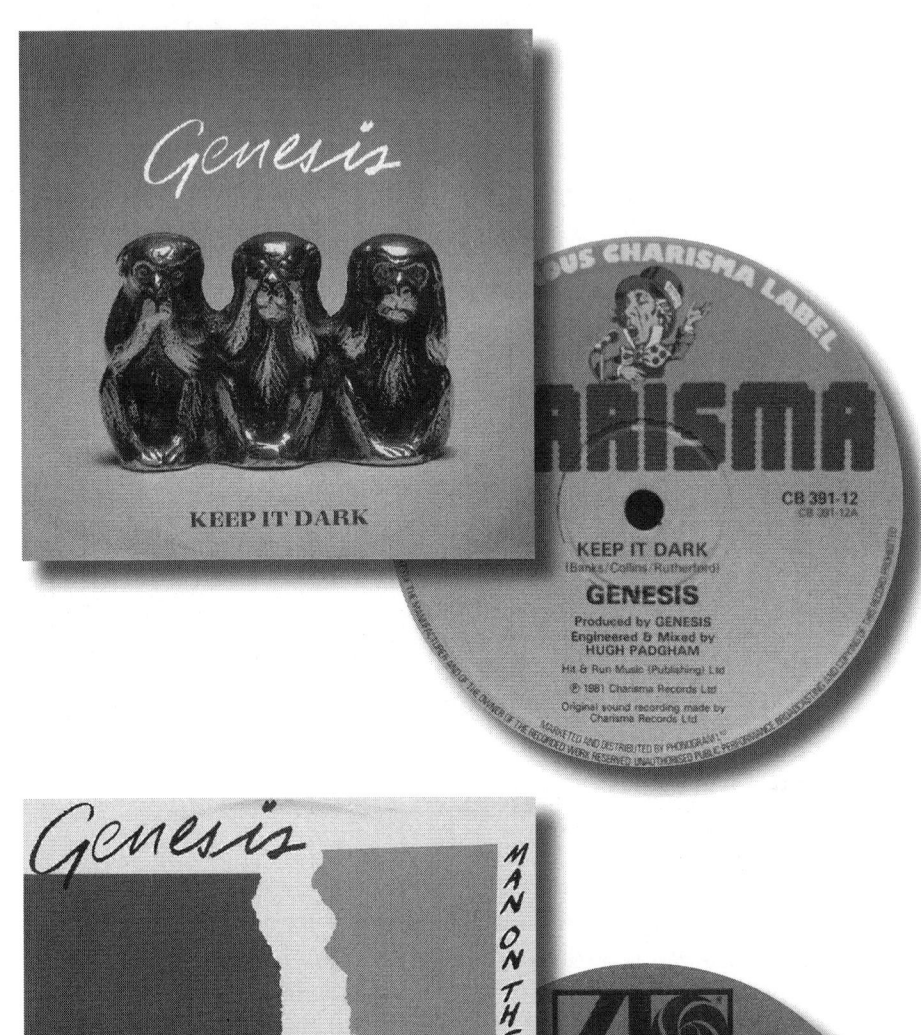

An *Abacab* Timeline

March – June 1981. Genesis work on tracks slated for their upcoming 11th album, writing and recording at The Farm, Chiddingfold, Surrey, UK. They are also self-producing the project.

August 14, 1981. "Abacab" is issued in the UK as an advance single, with "Another Record" on the B-side. It peaks at No.9 on the UK charts.

September 1981. "No Reply at All" is picked as the album's first US single, backed with "Dodo." The song reaches No.29 on the charts.

September 18, 1981. Genesis issue *Abacab*, which peaks at No.1 on the UK charts and No.7 on Billboard.

September 25 – November 2, 1981. The band tour Europe, in support of *Abacab*.

October 23, 1981. "Keep It Dark"/"Naminanu" is collared as the second *Abacab* single to be issued in the UK, where it achieves a No.33 placement.

November 12 – December 11, 1981. Genesis play American and Canadian dates in support of *Abacab*, followed by a couple of big home soil dates to close out the year.

December 1981. The band's American label, Atlantic, issues "Abacab" as the album's second US single, which achieves No.26 on the Billboard charts.

December 11, 1981. *Abacab* is certified gold.

March 5, 1982. "Man on the Coner" is chosen as the last single issued from *Abacab*, backed with the non-LP "Submarine." It reaches No.41 in the UK and No.40 in the US.

May 3, 1982. *Abacab* is certified platinum.

May 10, 1982. Genesis issue the *3x3* EP, consisting of "Paperlate," "You Might Recall" and "Me and Virgil."

Behind The Lines: Genesis on Record 1978-1997

May 27, 1982. Genesis perform on *Top of the Pops*, the results of which are used for the "Paperlate" production video.

June 4, 1982. Genesis issue *Three Sides Live*, which is a mix of live and studio material in the US but is in fact four sides live in the UK. It reaches No.2 in the UK and No.10 in the US. The album is accompanied by a *Three Sides Live* Betamax and VHS video release. "Paperlate," one of the studio tracks on the North American *Three Sides Live*, is issued a s single, achieving a No.32 placement on the Billboard charts. Of note, on the North American *Three Sides Live*, the song is presented as two words, "Paper Late," on both the back cover and the record label

June 25, 1982. Robert Plant issues his debut solo album, entitled *Pictures at Eleven*. Drumming on half the record is Phil Collins.

August 1 – 29, 1982. Genesis play Canada and the United States, followed by European dates to close out the year in early October.

September 7, 1982. Mike Rutherford issues a second solo album, entitled *Acting Very Strange*.

September 10, 1982. Peter Gabriel issues a fourth album, entitled (somewhat) *Security*. It certifies gold.

October 4, 1982. *Three Sides Live* is certified gold.

November 5, 1982. Phil Collins issues a second solo album, entitled *Hello, I Must Be Going!*. Like the first one, it's a big success, currently sitting at triple platinum. Co-producing is Hugh Padgham, and on guitars we have Daryl Stuermer.

Mike Rutherford   Phil Collins   Tony Banks

GENESIS

Daryl Stuermer   Chester Thompson / Mike Rutherford   Phil Collins   Tony Banks

Martin talks to Grant Arthur, Douglas Maher and Bill Schuster about *Abacab*.

Martin Popoff: All right, onto the well-regarded *Abacab* album, and in my opinion, really the start of a new era for the band. What are your impressions, first in a general sense?

Grant Arthur: Well, we've got a new producer on board, in Hugh Padgham, although he only gets an engineering credit. It's a progression from *Duke* but they're streamlining everything. They've taken the prog aspect as far as they could go, which is actually the way they themselves talk about the next one, the shapes album. But with *Abacab*, everything's getting refined. There seems to be a lot of space on this record. I mean, what can they do? The previous two albums are still pretty much the work of the famous progressive rock band, Genesis. To my mind, they are sounding much more like the three-piece that they are. Everything is more open of architecture and there's more interplay between everybody. Basically, it's a perfect blend of pop, prog and art rock. That's what we have here. This is my era, Martin. The shapes cover is my favourite Genesis album. I think that record's absolutely brilliant. A lot of people, like Rand Kelly, will laugh at me, but that's what I feel. I love hooks.

Doug Maher: I'm going to start off by saying *Abacab* is my favourite Genesis record. I refer to 1981 as the year of everything. The record is released in September '81 and it becomes a No.7 album. Phil Collins puts *Abacab* down, but MTV sure liked it; they played the hell out of it, and the song "Abacab" is a radio staple to this day.

So here's your competition: *Paradise Theatre*, Toto, *Difficult to Cure* from Rainbow, you've got *Moving Pictures*, you've got Phil himself with *Face Value*. Earlier on there you got *Killers* from Maiden, *Another Ticket* from Clapton, *Point of Entry* from Judas Priest, *Working Class Dog*, Rick Springfield, *Captured* from Journey and *Coconut Telegraph* from Jimmy Buffett. I'm not even getting into the Juice Newton stuff, Stray Cats, 38 Special, *Wild-Eyed Southern Boys*, you had *Face Dances* from The Who, *Extended Play*, the Pretenders' EP. You had Stones, REO Speedwagon. There's a lot of pop stuff that's there. You've got *Moving Pictures* and then Rush again with *Exit... Stage Left*. Look, you could do a whole book just on what happened in 1981. And with MTV coming along that summer, at that point, you're going oh my God, you know, this is just a monstrous 12-month run. You're about to see the world of music absolutely explode.

And Genesis was part of that, with the videos and the airing of the MTV concert, I don't know, every few weeks of that tour. This blew my mind. I know where it charted on Billboard's 100; that was No.26. But "Abacab" had a dance mix; it was played in clubs and it was on the club charts. Genesis with a dance mix?! What?! What was this band doing three years ago? That's kind of what wound up happening with Robert Plant's "Tall Cool One," as we discussed for your *Pictures at Eleven* Robert Plant panel book, and "Dance on My Own" and "Why." There was like this club mini-disc that was getting marketed around at that time. It was so unusual. It's like, what?! What are they doing here? That was the modernization of Robert Plant into this pop idol, if you will, from a rock idol.

Now we're seeing this same commercial turn with Genesis. It's like, okay, how far are you guys willing to go here? You know, what kind of material are we going to be handed from here on out? If this is a one-off thing and then it's back to full progressive rock, let us know, please. So you're seeing all kinds of chances being taken with the commercialization of this band. And you can see that they fully went "Do it all" because they became the commercial darlings of MTV and of commercial pop radio for the rest of the decade. There's obviously other bands that qualify for that, but when you look at it statistically, Genesis' presence is unbelievable, how they pulled off what they pulled off.

Martin: Good stuff. Bill, are you on board with "Do it all," as Doug puts it?

Bill Schuster: Yes, because *Abacab* is extremely experimental and all the better for it. I misunderstood this record for many years. I always liked the three hits. "Abacab," "No Reply at All" and "Man on the Corner" got played a lot on the radio back in the early '80s. But I slept on some of the album tracks. And that was a mistake on my part. Once I came to the realization that they were deliberately trying to get away from old-school Genesis, and use words more as musical sounds rather than trying to tell a bunch of in-depth, lyrical stories that sometimes interfered with the flow of the music, I was fully on-board.

Basically, they wanted to become something else just to see if they could do it, pretty much, and I think it worked really well. Going in with that mindset, it takes on a new life. Things that were kind of nonsensical, like the lyrics to say "Abacab" and "Who Dunnit?," don't become so important anymore, because now I could see it from the band's perspective. The words to "Abacab" don't necessarily mean anything, but they don't have to. They sound cool and Phil sings them well and they flow perfectly with the music.

Martin: If the record isn't particularly in the same ballpark as *Duke*, the album cover sure is. It's white and it's simple graphically, even more abstract.

Grant: To me, it's like an artistic statement. It's an art rock cover for an art rock album. It's modern art and it reflects what's going on in the music. As for the title, that came from the sections of the title track. Although even though that was the idea, it veers off. As it moves through the song, that's not the order of the parts anymore, plus there's odd time signatures complicating matters further.

Doug: That cover is by Bill Smith, and it started with these different slips of coloured paper. There are a couple of interviews with him floating around where he said that was the biggest payday that he ever had in his career, because he was able to keep the licensing on that, to use for his own purposes. But he pretty much says that Genesis were the most impossible pricks to work with. He started getting these phone calls. He went back and forth and back and forth on something that shouldn't have been that complicated. And that's what he was trying to get across, saying that you're working with this title, *Abacab*, which is essentially nonsensical. It doesn't mean anything. There's no such word.

Yes, I understand that it's verse, chorus, bridge, breakdown and all that. But it's not like that. When you break it down, it would be ACACBACABA or whatever (laugh), if you actually followed how the song went. But whatever; it worked for the bass line of the song, when they were writing it. But Schuster was trying to say, look, we're going for something simple and modern here. And he said they were difficult and obnoxious, especially Rutherford and Banks, who were incredibly hard on him.

Martin: Bill, what else can you tell us about that title?

Bill: Well, as Grant and Doug rightly explained, the song started out with that ordering of the sections—A section, B section—but by the time they were done with the song, it didn't match up. And then they basically said okay, we'll just keep it as it is (laughs). I think that totally fits their whole aesthetic for this thing: "Okay, it's a nonsense word. Yep, that's our title." And the cover is in that same spirit. It came in four different colour schemes, with four different backs as well, with the same abstract blocks or strips. They're just swatches of colour, with no connection to the title. It's very '80s.

Martin: What do you think about the production on this album?

Grant: I love the production. The official credit reads "Produced by Genesis," but we know Hugh Padgham is incredibly important to the process. He knows exactly what to do with the band. I've used this terminology before, but the band really comes together on this album and I think much of that is due to Padgham. Here's where they started with that whole gated drum sound and all manner of experiments with the synths, which sound bold and almost brash at times. And Phil's drums sound magnificent.

Martin: You know what, guys? This is my favourite record of all time for drum sound. It's almost like, there's a cymbal and there's a stick and there's a lightning bolt between them. It's like you're hearing the static electricity of charged air or a lightning strike in the space between the two. Or it's like you can see the soundwaves as the cymbal rocks back and forth. It's like the platonic ideal of a cymbal sound! And I can say just as many weird things about the snare and the toms—so much energy and joy there.

Doug: Yeah. I don't think it can be touched (laughs). I don't think he can be matched. And again, I don't understand this perception that Phil Collins is this schmaltzy balladeer and that's all he knows how to do. Bullshit. He's one of the greatest drummers of all time. And like you say, not only that, his sound is duplicated by nobody except his son. But when Nic solos, he doesn't sound anything like his dad. It has a totally different sound. Yeah, maybe that's just how Nic wants it. But you are 100% right. So many things to say about those cymbals, including the way he plays the bell of the ride.

Martin: Absolutely, and the crashes. And then "Another Record" introduces a whole new extra sound, right?

Doug: That's right; yeah, unbelievable. And those ghost notes that he's hitting. Again, I think Hugh Padgham is a genius at placing microphones around a drum kit.

Martin: He's not famous enough, that guy. It just doesn't make sense.

Doug: No, it doesn't.

Martin: But I feel like a fair bit of that magic is inherent in Phil. It's like it starts on *Wind & Wuthering* and they systematically are taking the analogue characteristics out of it brick by brick, which continues on through the self-titled, which, I think is up over the hill and getting worse at that point.

Doug: I love those records. But yeah, it was more plain ol' electronic Simmons. You still had acoustic drums in different parts, but it was definitely becoming the band that Terry Brown was afraid that Rush was gonna turn into. They were committing that same sin that Rush would commit.

Bill: Yeah, I love the sound of *Abacab*. This would not have worked for *Nursery Cryme*, but it's pristine and perfect for these songs. This is a crisp-sounding album; everything is sharp and tight. It's one of my favourite drum sounds of all time, too. It's arriving in that sweet spot before the harsh and ubiquitous and overbearing sound we'd get in the '80s, from all sorts of bands, including Genesis. This was when the technology was fresh.

Martin: Okay, the album opens as if we're jumping into a swimming pool. There's even a gnarly guitar lick. What are your thoughts on the thrust and parry of the title track?

Grant: "Abacab" is absolutely brilliant, and the first impression I get—after those things you pointed out, of course (laughs)—is that the keyboards are very new wave. The keyboard sounds are new, and what Tony's playing is simple but effective. And I don't think people give Mike Rutherford enough credit, because his guitar playing really stands out. He's like Paul McCartney, the way he plays guitar. When Paul plays guitar, it's almost like those parts can just jump off the record and fly away, just sort of take off. And I hear Mike's parts the same way. But yeah, there's something minimalistic abut this song and the parts of the song and the transitions between them. It sounds like a three-piece rocking out and that's all it needs to be. I could listen to this track over and over and over and never get tired of it. It's like "Turn It On Again" part two, because "Turn It On Again" is where this kind of approach started.

Doug: There's a story I read about these lyrics, plus I heard Phil Collins tell the story. When people look at these lyrics, they're like, what is he talking about? What is this about? We just know that musically it's cool. There's this space that you're being put into. It's just such a great synth-driven song, with this beat that never stops. And yet when you go into the context of the song, it's about Phil's ex-wife banging her interior decorator. So here we are in 1981, and you're still hearing about Phil's ex-wife. He's still reeling, but now we've gone from the loneliness and the emptiness and the sadness of his situation and we're starting to see Phil getting a little angry. He's testy, he's moody, and he's giving you both sides of the story, or the story from more angles, if you will.

Bill: The first thought that crosses my mind when I hear "Abacab" is that instantly, within ten seconds, as you take in that drum sound, you're getting an announcement that the '80s have arrived. The lyrics are quite obscure and mysterious; it's hard to tell what they are about. It's cool that half of the song is pretty much a seemingly unstructured and uncharacteristic jam. And to my understanding, that's exactly what it was—they didn't write that part; they just kept going. And apparently there's a much longer version out there that they edited from to get the album version. I would love to hear that one day, just for fun. Because these guys are tight and they groove well together. Once they get into a groove, they can really stay there. They could have been a funk or an R&B band if they were so inclined.

Martin: Weirdly, "Abacab" manages to be one the heaviest songs they ever did, but also sort of Devo-like futuristic new wave at the same time.

Bill: Yeah, it definitely sounds new wavey. All of a sudden Genesis are right at the front edge of what was going on in the early '80s. They don't sound out of place at all. They sound more like a New Romantics band from the UK than they do like the progressive rock bands they used to be classed with. In that sense, they would navigate the '80s better than all those bands, easily becoming the most successful commercially. I'm not sure they would have done that as well if Steve had stayed in the band, though. As much as I love Steve, maybe it's a good thing he left.

Martin: "No Reply at All" is simply irresistible, as Robert Palmer would say. As a song, an arrangement, just on a creative level, Genesis are really advancing past the more staid and aristocratic band they were on the last three records.

Bill: Oh yeah, this is possibly one of my ten favourite pop songs of all time. As soon as it comes on the radio, as soon as I hear that opening note, I get an instant smile, and I can almost feel it through my whole body. It's just such a feel-good song, and one of Phil's best vocals. It's that sweet spot where he's passionate but not overheated, so to speak. On later records, Phil could get a little overzealous and do this almost scatting thing, especially live, which took away from some of the songs. But here, on this studio track, he's just immaculate.

It's musically busy, but not too busy. It's just always moving, and I think a lot of that comes down to the forgotten man, Mike Rutherford. Mike's bass is all over the place here, kind of bubbling underneath everything. But really, get past those Earth, Wind & Fire horns—the Phenix Horns there—and it's Phil's drums and vocals that are the big things that jump out, even if the beating heart of the song is Mike's bass. That's what carries it along. It's just so bubbly and keeps moving and grooving. And the little bridge where Phil does the, "Maybe deep down inside" bit, oh my God, that's one of his most emotional performances in terms of something I connect with; it just seems very sincere. It might have been a sensitive issue as he's still hurting from the collapse of his marriage at this point.

Grant: I'll also call attention to that bass line; it's one of Mike's best ever. Plus I have to hand it to that guy, because he's really come along since Steve Hackett left. When you listen to *And Then There Were Three*, Mike's not fully come into his own yet as a guitarist, and he's key in that department on this album, although that's not really a factor on "No Reply at All." But the bass playing on this song is killer, very melodic and almost loose as he sort of wanders around and picks his spots. Normally, as a bass player, you want to be tight and in that pocket. But he's almost nonchalant here, which is often how he plays the guitar too. But there are so many competing hooks all over this song. It proves that Genesis can write a pop song and I don't care if the Peter Gabriel cult hate it. These guys are good. And this also has the Earth, Wind & Fire horns, arranged by Thomas Washington. Phil was kind of into that stuff, so he brought it over here.

Doug: "No Reply at All" has a lot going for it, including great bass and this sort of fantastic R&B shuffle structure with all sorts of ghost and grace notes and then up top, this frantic keyboard lick from Tony. The song's about the dissolution of Phil's marriage, unshared love, despair, confusion. It's something we've all been through, in a relationship that has fallen apart or something that you thought that was in a permanent place. He can't get anything from her, as far as being able to get across any sort of communication.

When people hear that song, they think that it's just a typical guy reaching out to a woman. It's not. Again, we're getting the carryover effect. It's almost, in a lot of respects, a sequel. It's not completely, but Phil is lingering now after the fact, trying to understand what his life is now, what he had built to be his marriage, and what he perhaps destroyed on his own volition. But I'm not in a position to make that judgment. I'm not a professional musician, so I can't know what he went through. People make sacrifices all the time and walk away from relationships. They regret it or they walk away from it and say, thank God I did that. I lived that life. I got 15 years of it and I'm good. But as we see, in the '80s, Phil had a lot of work to do.

Martin: I'm super-impressed with "Me and Sarah Jane" as well. I hate to say it, but it puts a lot of the previous generation of Genesis' pop songwriting in the rearview mirror. I'm getting the sense you guys are feeling that as well, that the songwriting is just more toward that Beatle-esque ideal of perfect songcraft. Or whoever else you want might to mention, like Fleetwood Mac or Tom Petty.

Grant: Yeah, I love it. Great chorus, and despite the rock-solid songwriting, it's modern with additional new wave elements. And yet there's also a strong Tony Banks stamp on it. It seems like when you listen to a Tony Banks song, you can tell it's him.

Doug: I love this song, but then again, I love every song on this record. There's a reggae vibe to it, and I love how the programmed beat at the beginning is quite close to that of "Man on the Corner," later on the album. At the lyric end, it's about a homeless man who's created a make-believe girlfriend to be with, since he's alone, and he falls in love with her.

Mike Rutherford, as usual, would say that it's about absolutely nothing, which is what most Banks songs are based on—nothing. That's what Mike Rutherford would say anytime you asked him. I find that really interesting. But the concept of mental illness amongst the homeless... 90% of the time they're homeless—outside of addiction and people running away from maybe an abusive situation because they've got nowhere to go—they find that the majority of it is mental illness that went untreated. That's what got them in a lot of these positions to begin with, that their mental illness wasn't dealt with.

So I think there's something deeper and emotionally appreciative of where Tony was going with this song. Because it's a real issue. And look, this is 1981. This isn't about a situation that's gone away. It's gotten worse. Here in America, Canada, Ireland, England, they all have sheltering issues. Plus people think that giving free drugs out to mentally ill people is saving their lives, that it's preventing them from ODing and they're better off if they could buy and do drugs safely.

The mental health and homeless crisis gets addressed by Genesis over multiple albums, and in Phil's solo career. I address this later on. You hear it again in "Another Day in Paradise" and "Take Me Home." People think "Take Me Home" is just this song about him touring or wanting to get home or longing to be home—fuck that. That song is so deep and so emotional and it's about the mental institution crisis there in England. If you ever do a Phil Collins book, that's something I would love to go deep in on, because what Phil tackles in his lyrics is just so under-appreciated. It's often beneath the surface; he's so good at hiding it. Because he wants a person to listen to a song and think it's about whatever it is that you think it's about. But when you get to those deeper layers, you're like, oh, I see what you're doing here. He's really a masterful songwriter in that respect.

Bill: Nice, yeah, "Me and Sarah Jane" is one of the more traditional-sounding songs, although it would not be out of place on one of the more recent albums. It's a lovely song. I mean, it's Tony—of course it is. It's hard for the man not to come up with a beautiful melody.

As for the lyrics, this character invents a woman to accompany him as he roams the city, essentially. It's an odd, very Tony sort of story, and it somewhat echoes "Anything She Does" on *Invisible Touch*. So I don't know if that's a theme with Tony here or what. But it's a sad story, possibly with a tragic ending on the beach. It's like even though he imagined this woman, he couldn't imagine a happy ending with this woman.

It's probably good to have a piece here with more traditional sounds, perhaps to keep the traditional Genesis fans on board. Because I think "Me and Sarah Jane" and maybe "Dodo/Lurker"—they held the interest of the older fans who maybe didn't know what to make of the rest of the album.

Martin: Next is "Keep It Dark," probably my favourite on the album, up-tempo with that cozy sort of chord movement underneath the main riff. Imagine that—Genesis with a riff!

Doug: Absolutely, "Keep It Dark" is so cool, and a dark horse on the album. I never heard it on the radio at the time and I don't ever remember seeing it on MTV. But VH1 Classic way later on in the early 2000s started playing the song almost routinely, every day, every other day, and I was like, why wasn't this song pushed? It's just quintessential Genesis to me, right up there with "Abacab" itself, with similar futuristic keyboards and driving beat.

And it's a cool story too. It's essentially this guy, or kid, if you will, that gets kidnapped by aliens, and is shown a world that's better than the one we live in. But he's got to keep it a secret; he's got to keep it dark. Can't tell anyone. So there's an interesting opinion that I got from this, that might be more political. There's the whole thing about aliens taking him to this serene, peaceful, beautiful place. But then it shines a light on where he's living, the mass chaos and speech being suppressed and all these other things that are going on there. It puts the listener in this position that you want to go away with them, you want to go to that place, but you can't tell anybody about it. So you get this impression that the aliens don't want the world to know about this place yet, that we're not ready to handle it as a society, as a people.

So yeah, both from a lyrical standpoint and musical standpoint, the song is very underrated, just gorgeous. As soon as that keyboard blasts in on the offbeat, you're going, all right, yeah, I'm here for the ride. This is the Genesis that I love. And Padgham, look, that guy, everything he does is gold. Everything! I mean, our wish list, at least in the people that I associate with, we used to go, fer Christ sake, please tell us the next Rush album is being produced by Hugh Padgham. Oh my God; the fact that that never happened is criminal.

Grant: What I love about "Keep It Dark" is it's so smooth and grooving, yet it's in 6/4. They bring their pop elements into it and they make it work. It's kind of like "Abacab" part two. With the same keyboard sounds and drum fills from Phil, it just seems like a continuation and it adds cohesion to the record, by emphasizing the same sound palette. But it's just great the way they can integrate prog elements with pop. I don't know anybody who can do it better.

Martin: The synth sound reminds me of The Cars or Gary Numan or Devo.

Grant: It's very new wave, and unlike some of the sounds on later records, it doesn't sound dated. When they get into digital keyboards, that's when it starts to date. But these are all analogue synths and they sound wonderful.

Bill: These guys went into this not wanting to have the focus be on the lyrics, but Tony just can't help himself. He has to tell a story. And this is such a cool but sad story. This guy has to make up a story about being robbed and kidnapped, to tell his family, because he can't tell anyone that he was taken away to this alien world that was essentially a paradise. That's a heartbreaking and powerful story. And the music supports it really well. When the narrator is daydreaming about what actually happened, and wishing he could have told the truth, Phil's vocal gets a bit distorted.

And Tony does these simple, otherworldly keyboard sounds, these little strokes or flashes that underscore the sort of alien abduction narrative. So he's serving his story well through sound. I think it's a brilliant piece of musical storytelling to go along with the lyrics there. You feel the sense that the character is returning to that alien paradise in his own mind, living it over again in private, because that's the only way he can.

And it's set to this relentless rhythm track that barely lets up throughout the whole song. But everything else is so cool, it doesn't need the rhythmic variation. The drums just support; there's no fancy stuff from Phil going on or anything. The rhythm track truly is just a rhythm track, and it allows the voice and the keys the space to tell the story. It's very effective.

Martin: Side two opens confusingly with "Dodo" and "Lurker" or "Dodo/Lurker." I suppose the break is at 5:09, beginning with "Meanwhile, lurking by a stone in the mud." But it's sort of up to us, because the back cover of the original vinyl separates them with no timing indicated, the label separates them but gives an aggregate time and finally, there's no lyric sheet. And then I see that's where Wikipedia makes the break too. Funny. I pegged it at 5:09 on Spotify and that's exactly the number Wikipedia uses.

Bill: Yes, and unlike other Genesis suites, there is a clear demarcation because there's no overlap with passages from "Dodo" showing up in "Lurker" or anything like that. What I like about this song is that we get a return of Phil the actor. He gets to use all kinds of different voices here, including these weird guttural vocals and that "Meanwhile, lurking by a stone in the mud" sort of scholarly or news reporter voice. It's funny, but also impressive. He's spreading his wings, but at the same time, returning to a role he had to fill when Peter left. But he's not just Peter's replacement. He uses his Motown influences and whatever weird thing comes to mind and it's effective.

The drums are the lead instrument for much of this song, I think, which again, between Phil's vocals and the drums, it's kind of odd that this is essentially a Tony Banks-written song. It's a showcase for Phil. So, thanks, Tony (laughs). But yeah, the last three, "Me and Sarah Jane," "Keep It Dark" and "Dodo/Lurker," they have some of the most complex and interesting lyrics on the album and they're all Tony songs. So one could argue that Tony is still the best lyricist in the band overall. But it also explains why Tony never wrote the hits. And you can tell he's having fun with his new keyboards, right? It's like he's experimenting with any sound he can find, whether it works or not. And yet it somehow all does, for me. Whatever weird bleeps and blurps he comes up with, I'm cheering him on. It's that kind of album.

Grant: Absolutely; you've got dramatic, majestic keyboards at the intro and also just amusing sort of quirky, new wave keyboards all over the place. I love what Mike does as well, with those arpeggiated little guitar licks. It's magical how it all comes together, and it's also nice that side two opens with full-on progressive rock Genesis.

Doug: A key to this one is Phil's complex, sort of shuffling beat, which is similar to some of the things John Bonham would do. I know the song was originally linked to the B-side track, "Submarine," which was recorded for this record but not included. That became the B-side to "Man on the Corner." Banks was really obsessed with nuclear war in his lyrics, so his words took on a dark tone. He always seemed afraid that nuclear war was imminent. But it's 2024 now, Tony, and nobody's nuked you. But it's a theme in his lyrics and I feel like it carries over to many of his keyboard sounds and melodies too, with a good example of that being the opening of this song. It's almost like his dark thoughts and fears about the future are affecting what he's going to play on his keyboards and synths. "Domino" comes to mind, with the haunting, ghostly keyboards that lead up to the "Blood on the windows" part.

Martin: Was Mike dismissive of just Tony's lyrics or all Genesis lyrics?

Doug: Tony's; just Tony's. No, he respected Phil as a writer. He knew that Phil had stepped up his game. And then, of course, there's the "In the Air Tonight" argument, where Phil was like, "Yeah, I introduced this to the band." And Mike's like, "No, you didn't" and Tony said the same thing: "No, you didn't." And then it took decades for them to sort it out. It might have been 2007 or something, when they were interviewed and it finally came around with Mike saying, "Well, if we were introduced to it, we would have probably fucked it up. We would have Genesis-ised it too much. Where it would have become unnecessarily busy or too long."

But Phil stood his ground. He's like, "No way. I absolutely introduced this. I didn't keep it for myself." "In the Air Tonight" is about his marriage, so that absolutely would have fit in with the theme of *Duke*, which bleeds into *Abacab*. I tend to appreciate the fact that Phil's solo work speaks for itself. Plus Genesis were already getting a bunch of hits. Did it really matter if "In the Air Tonight" was a Genesis song? It really didn't matter, because people were buying both. Plus a lot of people, or at least the average listener, thought Phil Collins songs were Genesis songs and vice versa.

Martin: All right, next we have "Who Dunnit?," which I love, but was altogether a bridge too far for many legacy fans of the band.

Grant: Yes, this actually started out as an improvised track. You could consider it almost a throwaway, but it's still compelling and pretty crazy (laughs).

Doug: You could probably call "Who Dunnit?" the most experimental song on the record, but it's also light-hearted and breaks the tension. I find it absolutely hilarious that it got booed live, when they played it in Europe. That's hysterical to me. If people only saw what was being embraced in America at the time... does anybody remember the song "Fish Heads" by Barnes & Barnes? There were so many weird new wave songs making the rounds, by Devo and the like. Anyway, "Who Dunnit?" is a fantastic song to drive fast to at night. It sounds like somebody drugged the band. Look, I never skip a single track on this record. This is a 10/10 album for me. But yeah, when I've played that song with people in my car, I've gotten funny looks from people of all ages. Whether it's me and my buddies as teenagers, or in our 20s, 30s or 40s, it's like, "Are we really going to sit through this?" "Yeah, we are."

Martin: Love it (laugh). Bill, thoughts on this one?

Bill: Well, it's often considered the most hated song in the entire catalogue by many hardcore fans. But I disagree. The lyrics are goofy, but they're supposed to be; that was kind of the whole point. They were trying to go crazy here and sound abrasive and chaotic and not like old Genesis. It's like they wanted to get as far away from "Follow You Follow Me" as they possibly could.

And it kind of rocks, actually. It's got very modern keyboard sounds, cutting-edge stuff for 1981, really. Phil's singing is an acquired taste on this song and I have acquired that taste, but I can see why people would be annoyed. I'd say the repetition of lyrics is a problem for a lot of people as well. It's sing-songy and simplistic and almost like children's music, I suppose. To me, it's using the vocal more as an instrument and therefore, I'm not concentrating so much on the lyrics. I'm just appreciating the jam.

And it's not that long. Before you know it, it's over and you're onto a totally different kind of song. I think it works well here. As the story goes, Ahmet Ertegun was the one who made them put it on the album. Apparently they were choosing between this and "You Might Recall" and he said, "No, that one has to be on here" (laughs). "Okay, all right." That was not a decision embraced by many fans there, Mr. Ertegun, but cool, whatever you say. I think it fits the album just fine.

Martin: I tend to think that had it been pushed as a single, it would have been a novelty hit along the lines of "Money" by The Flying Lizards or heck, even "I Can't Dance" by Genesis. But even if it was a hit, there are deeper ramifications, I suppose. These are three guys that don't want to be seen as a joke band. All right, what are your opinions of "Man on the Corner?"

Grant: I think it represents a brilliant and intimate vocal performance from Phil, and you get drum machine augmented by real drums; I believe he's using a Roland TR-808. But it's very simple. It's just Tony and Phil. It was a late single from the record and it's absolutely a highlight of side two.

Martin: It's one of these Genesis songs that sounds like it could have been on one of Phil's solo albums.

Grant: Yes, first there was *Face Value*, which came after his divorce, and then *Abacab* was recorded just after that album came out. You read the literature on the band, and some people argue that Genesis ended up sounding like Phil but both of them go hand-in-hand. There were elements both used, like the Earth, Wind & Fire horns, and then the gated drum sound came over from his time working on the third Peter Gabriel solo album.

Martin: Perhaps Phil, Tony and Mike think and write more similarly than we thought, and there's a detectable influence of Tony and Mike on Phil's solo work. Or an influence that seeps in by osmosis.

Grant: I think so. It's a trio now and has been so for a long time, and when they get down to this configuration, they're all on the same page and they influence each other. Because yeah, you listen to *Face Value*, and it sounds like the Genesis of this era. So, sure, I think the present-day Genesis crept into Phil's solo work.

Doug: The homeless man that was mentally ill on "Me and Sarah Jane," I think reappears in "Man on the Corner." It's an unbelievable song that still stands up to this day. Like I said, Phil would revisit this topic on "Another Day in Paradise" and "Take Me Home." "Man on the Corner" became an MTV and radio staple. MTV was doing all they could to get any kind of clips of Genesis, and they got this song from a live concert and it was always on. And it lives on through American classic rock radio. It speaks for itself. I love it. It' a perfect song.

Bill: You've got the hypnotic and ever-present drum machine, soft and quite sparse, which provides a much needed respite after the crazy, chaotic workout that is "Who Dunnit?." So it's well-placed, a nice breather. And as a formerly homeless person, the lyrics hit home for me. It's a pattern for Phil, writing songs about homeless folks. But he's subtle about it here. He doesn't get quite as in-depth as he does later on and I think that's to the betterment of the song. It allows for people to put themselves in the lyrics a bit more easily.

Martin: And it's an early one for them with respect to drum programming, right?

Bill: Yeah, and it's kind of mind-boggling to me that with a drummer of Phil's calibre, that they would choose to employ drum machines. But it works for the album. Phil did enough to impress as a drummer in the '70s. At this point, he didn't have a whole lot left to prove to anyone as far as his technical abilities go. So yeah, it's time to have some fun with the technology, basically.

Martin: "Like It or Not" is in the Genesis tradition of grand or opulent balladry. And when they go to that place, they will often resort to 3/4 waltz time. But it's pretty loud and driving, actually, after the opening salvo, which takes about a minute.

Grant: Yeah, "Like It or Not" is a characteristic ballad from Rutherford, with great melody and almost languid but, as you say, loud instrumentation.

Bill: "Like It or Not" is another somewhat traditional song on the record. I'd say it's pleasant and competent but a bit uninspired. I was thinking that "You Might Recall" should have replaced this one. But I don't know, it's largely forgettable after it's over. I think it's the weakest song on the album.

Doug: It's a love song about hating the situation of not being able to see his love whenever he wants to. There's a lonely doo-wop dance feel to it, with these sort of 1950s keyboards that remind me of carousel music. But there are so many layers to these songs. It's got that '50s influence, but then again, it's so effectively overpowered by Phil's drums. And the keyboards are also extra-loud.

You end up thinking, where is Mike Rutherford in this band?

Mike has the easiest job in history, in my opinion, as far as being a live performer goes. As far as composition and everything goes, I understand there's some heavy lifting there. But I feel like it's Daryl Stuermer who does most of the hard work up on stage. Mike really gets the opportunity to phone it in, compared to everybody else on that stage. Just my opinion on that.

It's interesting that we talked about this for your Robert Plant *Pictures at Eleven* book, but both Robert and Phil have an affinity for that whole '50s thing, the R&B, doo-wop, Motown, the golden oldies or what have you. Phil took ownership of that in the '80s, where he incorporated horns and did covers and things like that. And yet case in point with *Abacab*, you were able to hear these things get sprinkled into very modern, '80s-sounding records and have them connect with rock crowds and rock radio. That in itself is quite impressive.

Martin: We close with "Another Record," which holds one's interest, because it's essentially a pop ballad made tribal and percussive by a strong and moderately busy drum track.

Doug: It's about an aging rock icon who's unaware that his time has passed. I'm dying to know if Phil has revisited this song and reflected at all on the lyrics, given the way the band ended.

Bill: "Another Record," like "Who Dunnit?," is another song on the album that fans did not appreciate. And I must confess that I slept on it for years as well. Phil's beat on this is quote elaborate, but he manages to get a good groove going. You've got to think, is this guy also homeless? Because you've got the line, "Did you ever think of taking him in?"

The intro is a bit amusing, with the atmospheric keyboards and guitar, because it sounds like it's going to be something completely different. It's quite beautiful, but then the serenity of it is broken by this shocking sort of electronic high-hat sound. Then we get synth harmonica, which I shouldn't love but I do (laughs). It's just another one of those weird sounds. It's like Tony said, "Well, this will annoy people. Let's try it." And it did annoy a lot of people, but it's unique in their catalogue. Where else can you hear a synth harmonica? And who would have ever thought that Tony Banks would come up with a sound like that? He's got a lot of creativity in him.

Martin: Good stuff. I just wanted to touch on the extra material related to this album that we got on *Three Sides Live*. Grant, what went down there?

Grant: Right, so the UK had three tracks—"Paperlate," "You Might Recall" and "Me and Virgil"—issued on an EP called *3x3*. We got those three songs, along with "Evidence of Autumn" and "Open Door" on our version of *Three Sides Live*, on the fourth side, while the UK got three more live songs on their *Three Sides Live*, and left off the studio songs. "Paperlate" is brilliant, with those Earth, Wind & Fire horns, but they're all related, with great melodies and riffs. They all have similar tonalities and arrangements.

But think about it, Martin, all those were recorded around the same time. And the thing is, you've got "No Reply at All" that made it onto *Abacab* and they certainly didn't want to throw away "Paperlate." But you wouldn't want "No Reply at All" and "Paperlate" on the same record, because they're basically variations on each other. So they put "Paperlate" on the EP and then the next month, on the live album in the US, and it became a hit, actually. It got a lot of airplay. I think it's a wonderful track. Obviously the recipe worked, but like I say, they already had one of those on the album.

Bill: Besides the confusion of seeing it as "Paperlate" and "Paper Late," it's weird that the UK issue of the live album is called *Three Sides Live* when it's your standard four-sided two-LP live album.

Now, "Evidence of Autumn," I feel is the last gasp for Phil and his '70s-styled vocals. It almost sounds like an outtake from *And Then There Were Three*, rather than the B-side of "Misunderstanding." You've got this pretty opening in the classic Tony style. His playing is lovely throughout, until we get to the cheesy, upbeat section after the lyric, which I'm not a fan of. He gets into this high-pitched, sort of carnival sound, albeit for a very short time, and it totally kills the mood of the song. It's still fun just because it's so weird, but it takes away more than it adds. All told, it's a nice, traditional Genesis ballad, but again, it's one that doesn't necessarily stick with me after it's over.

"Open Door" is kind of similar, although there are no drums. It's another somewhat forgettable Genesis ballad 101. Lyrically, "And when the master calls for me again," I want to know who is this master? And why is this master more important than the love of your life? I don't get this lyric. I want to know who this is that could take someone away. I am moved a bit by the final lyrical section, "Stand in the sun/Shut your eyes and feel the world." But I don't think that the song has really earned that emotional payoff up 'til that time. I don't know. It's kind of hit and miss. It's mostly another Genesis-by-numbers ballad that could have come from any time in the late '70s. I can see why it didn't make a proper album.

I remember "Paperlate" getting played on the radio a lot. It's a strong song. But as Grant explained, the problem with "Paperlate," why they didn't put it on the album was that those Phenix Horns made it too similar to "No Reply at All." They're very different songs when you really get into the nuts and bolts of them, but if they're both strong singles being played on radio as well as competing on the album, I can see why that would be a problem. I know that as a much younger person when these songs were new, I would get them mixed up, at least before I became more of a fan of the band. It's a fun song though. It kicks hard.

Martin: Even though the horns aren't on "You Might Recall," there are keyboard licks that serve the same purpose. Plus the arrangement and general percussive energy of it is in some degree of alignment with both "Paperlate" and "No Reply at All." I think this would have been a perfectly suitable single as well, but I guess the confusion would have been even more amplified.

Grant: Absolutely "You Might Recall" is a pop track, written by the whole band, and again, similar to some of these other songs, even "Another Record."

Bill: It's another one of those where Phil makes the drums sound simultaneously busy and effortless, and somewhat jazzy. His vocal is mostly solid, but I'm sensing some experimentation. It's a bit uncertain in spots. The opening bits remind me of Miami Sound Machine. I'm not a fan of the fade-out on this song. It's kind of foreshadowing *Calling All Stations* and all the fade-outs on that album. It seems rather abrupt. I feel like there was more being added to the song, and then all of a sudden before you know it, oh, all right, it's gone, never mind. It could have used an actual conclusion.

Martin: Any thoughts on "Me and Virgil?"

Grant: Another great track. I like the *3x3* EP quite a bit, but it's the first song, "Paperlate," that's the star of the show. Funny, if you look at the remaster of *Three Sides Live*, they eliminated all that fourth side. I also want to mention "Evidence of Autumn," which is from the *Duke* sessions and was the B-side of "Turn It On Again." It's another ballad and a great track, but should it have been on *Duke*? Maybe and maybe not. That very conservative ballad style was already represented. Also on our *Three Sides Live* was "Open Door," which was the B-side of "Duchess" and yet another ballad. It's art rock mixed with pop, which is basically what *Duke* is.

Bill: "Me and Virgil" is entertaining more so because it's weird, not because it's very good. They tried to emulate The Band but ended up with more of a half-baked ELP joke song. Whereas "Harold the Barrel" worked, "Me and Virgil" I don't think works near as well in that format. The, "Pa, you broke her heart" section sounds like a home cassette demo I made as a teenager, including the hand-beat percussion to go along with my singing. So that's not a good sign. These guys were not teenagers at this point. The instrumentation sounds sort of simple and half-hearted, like they couldn't even convince themselves of the song's merit. So it's an interesting novelty. It's fun to listen to occasionally, just to kind of go, "What in the world are they thinking?!" It's kind of humorous. Plus it's good that they could experiment like that, even when the experiments didn't work. They were risk-takers.

Martin: Nice; thanks for that. And we aren't even done. There are further non-LP tracks that weren't used on the EP or *Three Sides Live*, but showed up on box sets and the like.

Bill: Yes, "Submarine" and "Naminanu." were supposed to be part of a a proposed "Dodo/Lurker"/"Submarine"/"Naminanu" suite, and apparently in that order. It's perhaps a good thing that they just kept "Dodo" and "Lurker." Including the whole thing might have taken away from the flow of the album. "Submarine" is a simple, pleasant, almost ambient piece. It doesn't offer much on its own, away from being part of the planned suite.

"Naminanu" features Phil singing that word, which is very close to "Nanu Nanu," the famous Mork from Ork catch-phrase from Robin Williams on *Mork & Mindy*. So I can't help but hear that whenever I hear Phil. And that show was contemporary to this song. *Mork*

& Mindy ran from 1978 to 1982. So I kind of wonder if Phil was channeling both Grandmaster Flash and the Furious Five as well as Robin Williams back in those days. It's kind of fun, actually, but not really essential. It's not missed by being left off of *Abacab*.

Martin: You know, Bill, I'm taken by how complete, polished, high-fidelity and complicated all of these extra tracks were. These guys were being very creative during this period.

Bill: Yes, they were, and that's not even counting their solo work.

Behind The Lines: Genesis on Record 1978-1997

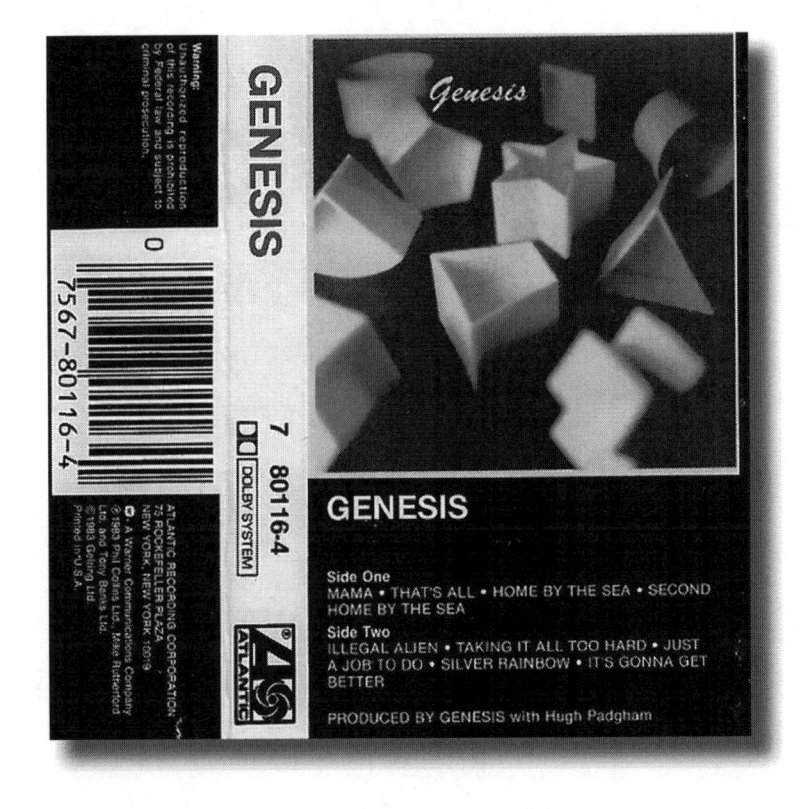

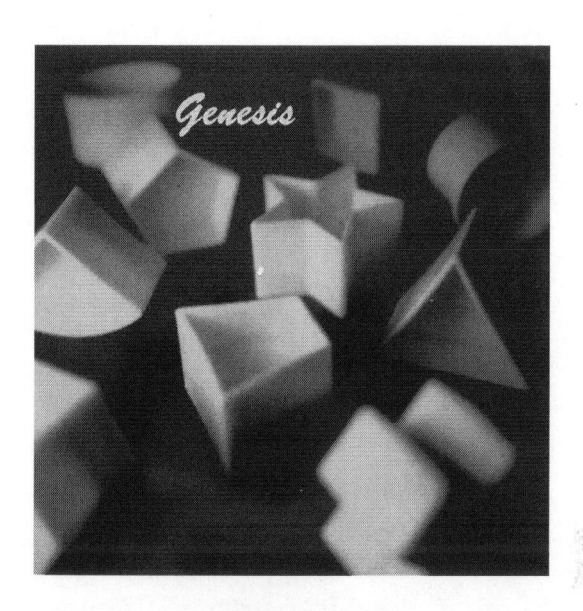

GENESIS

October 3, 1983
Charisma GEN LP1
Produced by Genesis with Hugh Padgham
Engineered by Hugh Padgham
Recorded at The Farm, Chiddingfold, Surrey, UK
Personnel: Phil Collins – drums, percussion, lead vocals; Tony Banks – keyboards, backing vocals; Mike Rutherford – guitars, bass, backing vocals
All songs written by Genesis

Side 1
1. Mama 6:46
2. That's All 4:22
3. Home by the Sea 4:46
4. Second Home by the Sea 6:22

Side 2
1. Illegal Alien 5:12
2. Taking It All Too Hard 3:54
3. Just a Job to Do 4:44
4. Silver Rainbow 4:27
5. It's Gonna Get Better 5:00

THAT'S ALL
HOME BY THE SEA
Genesis

THAT'S ALL
AS SEEN ON "THE LATE LATE BREAKFAST SHOW"
NEW SINGLE BY GENESIS
TATA-1

A *Genesis* Timeline

Spring 1983. Genesis work with producer Hugh Padgham on tracks slated for the follow-up to *Abacab*.

July 15, 1983. Robert Plant issues *The Principle of Moments*, a second solo album. Drumming on six tracks is Phil Collins, who also tours the album with Robert.

July 22, 1983. A British period drama called *The Wicked Lady* sees release. The soundtrack is by Tony Banks. The previous month finds Tony issuing a second solo album, entitled *The Fugitive*. Daryl Stuermer plays all the guitars on the record.

August 22, 1983. "Mama" is issued as an advance single from *Genesis*, backed with LP track "It's Gonna Get Better." It reaches No.4 on the UK charts but only No.73 in the US.

October 3, 1983. Genesis issue a self-titled album, the band's 12th studio album overall. It becomes the third album by the band to achieve a No.1 placement on the British charts, while reaching No.9 in the US. Additionally, the album stays on the UK charts for 51 weeks and the US charts for 49 weeks.

October 31, 1983. "That's All" is issued as a single, backed with "Taking It All Too Hard" in the UK and "Second Home by the Sea" in the US. It reaches No.16 in the UK and No.6 in the US.

November 6, 1983 – February 20, 1984. Genesis tours North America in support of the self-titled album.

December 16, 1983. *Genesis* is certified platinum.

January 23, 1984. An edited version of "Illegal Alien" is issued as a single from *Genesis*, backed with a live version of "Turn It On Again." It reaches No.46 in the UK and No.44 in the US.

February 25 - 29, 1984. The band play multiple dates at the National Exhibition Centre in Birmingham, UK.

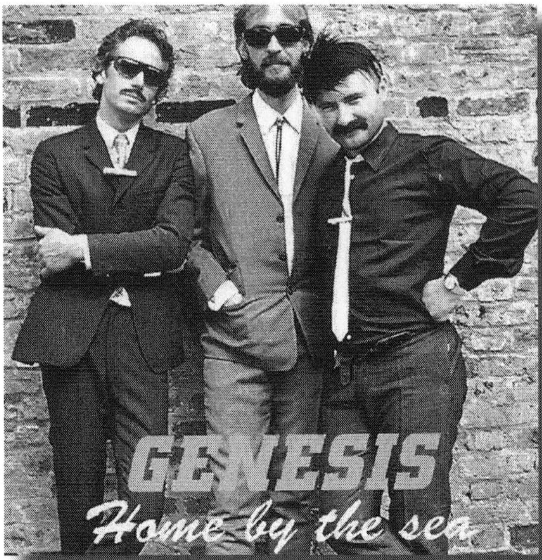
GENESIS
Home by the sea

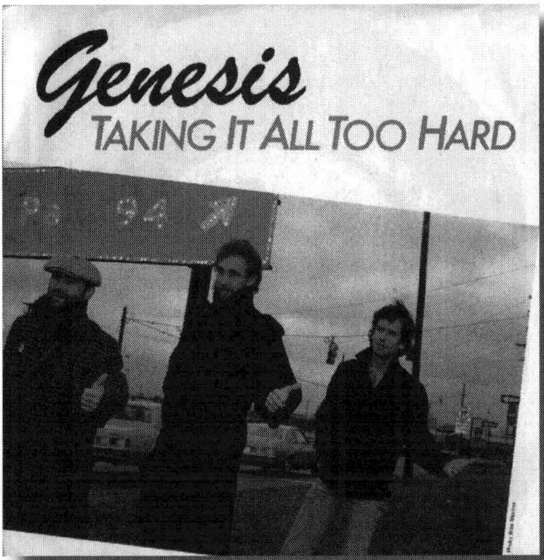
Genesis
TAKING IT ALL TOO HARD

June 1984. "Taking It All Too Hard" is issued in the US and Canada as the final single from *Genesis*, backed with album track "Silver Rainbow." It reaches No.50 on the Billboard chart.

August 4, 1984. Phil Collins marries Jill Tavelman; it is his second marriage. Five years later, the union produces a daughter.

February 18, 1985. Phil Collins issues *No Jacket Required*, a third solo album. The album eventually certifies diamond in the US, with 12 million copies sold in America alone and 25 million worldwide. On guitars is Daryl Stuermer, who also co-writes three tracks with Phil.

Behind The Lines: Genesis on Record 1978-1997

Martin talks to Grant Arthur, Daniel Bosch, Ralph Chapman, Tate Davis, Todd Evans, Jamie Laszlo and Bill Schuster about *Genesis*.

Martin Popoff: I figured the middle album of the seven we are discussing is also pretty central and pivotal from a commercial standpoint, so I've got a bunch of you on the case. I expect a fair bit of disagreement. Let see if that plays out. So yeah, to begin, where does the *Genesis* album sit in the band's history and what function does it serve?

Todd Evans: Well, the thing that was difficult for me was that it was very easy to separate "Mama" from this album, because it came out a month-and-a-half early in both the UK and the United States. The EP I have here says it's the long version of "Mama," which I believe is just the album version. And then it's got a version of "It's Gonna Get Better" on the other side, which is actually extended. But the thing about it is that a lot of people think about this album and they remember "That's All," "Home by the Sea," "Taking It All Too Hard" and "Illegal Alien," and they kind of forget about "Mama."

Now, *Genesis* was the first album that they did where they went into the studio without anything completed. And they worked on it in real time. They started that sort of process with *Abacab*, but with *Abacab* it was different. There they brought in ideas, but they took everything that sounded like Genesis and threw it out. On this album, they didn't come in with anything. They just showed up at The Farm and just started.

Another memory I have is that when this album came out, I used to be obsessive about recording all of those radio shows where they would interview people, the call-in shows like *Rockline* and *On the Record* and all those things. And Tony Banks used to get really defensive whenever anybody said, "Why don't you play prog rock anymore?" He used to say, "You know, we're still writing the same kind of music." And I can remember him one time getting really, really defensive and kind of put-out and saying, "On 'No Reply at All,' I'm playing exactly the same thing as I'm playing on 'The Lamb Lies Down on Broadway.' It's the same cross-handed technique." So very often if somebody said something along those lines, he would say, "Well, what we're actually doing in the songs is actually the same kinds of things that we used to do. We've just figured out how to make them more palatable."

Grant Arthur: And that's what they did. As Tony Banks said, they refined everything. Come on, you can only do the same thing for so long. They just worked along a natural progression and this is where they ended up. These guys are three of the best pop songwriters I've ever heard. I think the sequencing on this record and the recording quality of this record is second to none. There's something about this era that has a certain tonality, just like the '70s stuff had a certain tonality. The way this record sounds, you'll never get this again.

And I don't have any issues with the drum machines on it. It's my favourite Genesis record. I know that's going to make the Peter Gabriel people lose their marbles, but I love it. I've said that *Abacab* represents the perfect blend of prog or art rock and pop; I think that record blends it perfectly. This record's more all over the map. The fact that they open it with "Mama" is a bold statement, given how aggressive it is. It's loud and it's not commercial and yet it did really well on the charts. It just seems so odd that they would lead off with that song.

There were five singles off this record, which is pretty incredible. But there are so many great songs here. Mike Rutherford referred to this as his favourite Genesis album, but he also went on to say that all the classics are on side A and the quirky songs are on side B. When I listen to it, I don't hear that at all. I think it's well-balanced.

Tate Davis: I will say right off the bat, I'm going to be less kind about this album. But yeah, you asked where *Genesis* sits in the band's history. Let me put it this way, which is of course covered in detail in the first book—and thanks, Martin, for having me along for that one too. Genesis, in my view, were coming off a really, really great streak from *Trespass*, pretty much, all the way through *The Lamb Lies Down on Broadway*. Then Peter Gabriel leaves the band and the drummer decides, "All right, I want to try singing 'Squonk.'" The result was *A Trick of the Tail*, which is terrific. And then they put out *Wind & Wuthering*, followed by the double live album, *Seconds Out*, which is amazing. Hackett decides, "You guys didn't turn my guitar high enough in the mix; I'm going to do my own thing." So the three of them—Phil, Tony and Mike—release three more albums and their record sales start to increase quite a bit. They do the *Three Sides Live* album, which serves as a really good snapshot from that era. That brings us to *Genesis*, which of course is successful beyond all expectations, even if, as I say, I have some misgivings about it.

Daniel Bosch: They started with *Duke* and then picked it up on *Abacab* with this idea of writing together more as a three-piece rather than bringing in individual songs. And then they take it to the complete max with this one. There's no individually written songs on this album at all. They've all originated from jams that they did in the studio. They actually started this album with no music at all. They came in with a completely blank slate and then just jammed and jammed and then found the jams that they liked and sort of built them into songs. This is also the album where Phil Collins starts using the Simmons drums, along with his acoustic kit. So you get quite a bit of that on this album, which would carry through to *Invisible Touch*. So that's a big adjustment, the use of not just drum machines, but electronic drums that you play.

Jamie Laszlo: This was my first Genesis album. I bought it when it was released. I remember that the record store had those actual toy pieces on display. Somebody went out and bought the toy and brought it back and they made this display and I bought the album. *Genesis* always reminds me of Iron Maiden's *Piece of Mind*. Because my cousin bought that at the same exact time.

Actually here's the story: I actually bought Loverboy's album, and I remember walking around the mall going, "I should have bought that Genesis record." So I returned Loverboy and got the Genesis and my cousin bought *Piece of Mind* at the same time. We said that when we get home—I didn't know Iron Maiden from shit—he said, "We'll play one track of mine. Then we'll play one track off yours. We'll just go back and forth." Okay, so he played Iron Maiden and I played Genesis, he played Iron Maiden and I played Genesis. He played Iron Maiden again and he goes, "Your turn" and I go, "Keep playing that Maiden. We'll get back to Genesis eventually, but keep playing that Maiden." That's the moment I became an Iron Maiden fan and kind of a metalhead, while listening to this Genesis album going back and forth.

Martin: What else do you remember about what you guys were saying during that session?

Jamie: Oh, with the Genesis? Man, it was like an afterthought. We were both waiting to listen to *Piece of Mind* next while Genesis was playing (laughs). Because I'd heard the first two songs on the radio already, the element of surprise was already lacking as we started this process.

Martin: But you weren't into metal yet. Does that mean you had other albums like *Genesis*?

Jamie: I have my list of cassettes that I bought in order that I've kept track of on paper since 1983. I can tell you exactly what I bought next. But I think once I got into Maiden, then came *Blizzard of Ozz* and *Screaming for Vengeance*. I still bought pop and pop rock but I mean once you get that first taste of metal, you're kind of all-in. And I wasn't buying a lot of albums. I was 13, 14 and I didn't have a lot of money.

Martin: Despite becoming a metalhead, did you and your buddies like the *Genesis* album?

Jamie: Yeah, we were listening to everything. Everybody wanted to be cool. It was December and I was in eighth grade. I was listening to a lot of Duran Duran and Stray Cats before I got this album. And then we got this album and *Piece of Mind* on Christmas break. And I went back to eighth grade and gone are the Duran Duran pins and Stray Cats pins and it was all Maiden. And people were like, "What?! Isn't that a little heavy for you?" I'm like, "Evidently not!" (laughs). But Martin, even though I was buying metal, I was still buying Madonna albums, for crying out loud. I opened up doors without closing doors, is the best way I could put it.

Martin: Did you get home with the Loverboy album? How long did you have it in your possession?

Jamie: No, no, I had buyer's remorse instantly. This was the '83 album, *Keep It Up*, with them on the cover. We walked around for about a half-hour and I said, "I should have bought that Genesis album" and he goes, "Return it." And I went back and returned it. And I'll tell you this: I've never owned a Loverboy album ever (laughs). I'd returned the only Loverboy album I ever bought.

Martin: Why did you want the Genesis album?

Jamie: It was probably the weirdness of "Mama," and just wanting to hear it again, because it's the kind of song that you don't get tired of. The hook isn't too, too big, so it's easy to be like, "Let me hear that again." In my young mind, even though I was naïve, I might have been reasoning also that Loverboy was a flash-in-the-pan kind of band, and I wanted something more substantial, more grown-up.

Martin: What did you think of that album cover?

Jamie: People have problems with it, don't they? I kind of dig it. Here's the thing with me. You put yellow on an album cover and I'm all-in for some reason. That's why I like *Screaming for Vengeance*, and also *Powerslave*, maybe, kinda? I'm just all-in. And of course it reminds me of that toy. A lot of people would have forgotten that toy exists if it wasn't for that album. Because we played with that toy at such a young age. It had the sphere and you had to fit them in, and then you'd twist it and it opened up. That album cover keeps that toy in our memories.

Todd: I like that cover too. And usually when I tell people I like the cover, people roll their eyes and look down at the ground. But the cover was done by Bill Smith, who also did *Abacab*. He'd also designed a bunch of album covers for The Jam, and then he moved on and did Genesis. Apparently, he took the photograph of his kids' toys. Bill Smith Studios also did a bunch of Marillion albums and King Crimson *Thrak*. So for a while there in the '80s and '90s, he was kind of a sought-after guy. I really like the fact that the logo looks generic. I like the simplicity thing they were going for.

Daniel: I'd say the messaging in that cover is that they were continuing to distance themselves from their prog roots. *Duke* and *Abacab* also had minimalist covers, and *Three Sides Live* even more so. This is taking that a step further with those geometric shapes. So they're really trying to get away from the idea that they're a prog band, which is funny, because there are definitely still prog moments on this album.

Martin: What do you think Hugh Padgham brings to the band?

Daniel: Well, he was there for *Abacab* as well. Obviously, he brings those walloping drums that he sort of perfected with Peter Gabriel, and with Phil Collins on *Face Value*. But Hugh Padgham is not an overbearing producer. He's more of an engineer producer, rather than a "take control of the whole project" producer. I find that his productions don't all sound the same, because he tends to go with what the band wants rather than what he wants.

Martin: I tend to have strong views about this one sound-wise, and they aren't exactly positive. From the day I heard it, I've never been able to shake the idea that it sounds like an acoustic album, but instead of vocals and acoustic guitar, it's vocals and every kind of synthesizer imaginable. And I fold drums into that as well, because of the Simmons and the actual programming. Even though the reality is different, since I bought it in 1983 in Victoria, BC, third year university, I framed it as vocals and synths and when I play the songs in my head, that's all I hear. Pretty weird. All right, enough about my problems, what do you guys think of our opening track, "Mama?"

Todd: I discovered Genesis in my early college years, and *Abacab* was the most recent album. So this was my first Genesis album that was a new album that I waited for. And then as the lead single, "Mama" is a crazy, weird, unique song, and when it came out, it kind of blew me away. As the story goes, Hugh Padgham played the Grandmaster Flash and the Furious Five song, "The Message," during the sessions, and there's a laugh in that. And when you listen to that song, the laugh isn't quite as crazy as the one that Phil does. But Phil thought it was funny and just started doing it. And then the other guys were like, you should try to put that in a song.

But it's not just the laugh. It's the way the song is put together. It's got that thing that Genesis had started doing by that point. They did it on "Keep It Dark" and "Turn It On Again," where they start the song with a drum pattern, and then once the rest of the band comes in, where you thought the one of the rhythm pattern is turns out not to be the one. The beat is turned on its head. And that's a great rhythmic trick for a band to do. So it starts out like that.

The lyric is really dark, and then when Tony comes in with his chords, they're also really dark and sinister-sounding. And even what Mike Rutherford is playing supports that mood; Mike is usually the light, kind of poppy guy during this era of Genesis, but what he's playing is kind of weird. So yeah, epic song. When you think about this album, you have to remember that it starts with "Mama."

Bill Schuster: Like Todd, this was my first new Genesis album. I got mine from Columbia House record and tape club along with *90125* and a few others of that era that came out in '83. "Mama" is a great but creepy song. I'm a big fan of "The Message" by Grandmaster Flash and the Furious Five, and I think Melly Mel's vocal on that is great. I spent decades not realizing that Phil had caught that, and I thought that was just hilarious and wonderful when I found out how that happened. Now I can't unhear it because I'm always doing that laugh to my wife just to mess with her. She's put up with worse.

One interesting trivia note about "Mama" is that it's not Phil designing that drum beat. That was apparently created by Mike Rutherford using a distorted sound on a drum machine. He talks about how they became a trio and how in the process, they had to become more of a team and how they helped fill each other's gaps in the songwriting and in the playing, which I think is awesome. I'm a big Steve Hackett guy; Hackett's one of my top five guitar players. But I'm okay that he left and did his own thing, because these guys really came up with something pretty neat on their own that they wouldn't have if he was still there.

Tate: So "Mama," which was the advance single, when I first listened to it, it took a while for it to grab me. What I grew to appreciate is the way it builds. Think "Stairway to Heaven" by Led Zeppelin or "Bohemian Rhapsody" by Queen, or if you want to go lesser known, "Young Is a World" by Budgie. It's one of my favourite vocal performances by Phil, who by the end is shouting. So he's part of that build from a vocal standpoint. Or maybe not shouting, but screaming "Mama!"—awesome. And there's the laugh as well as a really good Mike Rutherford guitar solo. The drums at the beginning remind me a little bit of "In the Air Tonight," mainly from the groove and not necessarily the fills. But "Mama" is a really good song and an unusual way to start the album.

Grant: "Mama" has got that Linndrum machine. They're experimenting with a lot of the latest technology. This came out in '83 and the Linndrum was basically brand new, though I think Prince was using it back in '81 or '82. It's got such a distinct tonality and it's all over the record. The Linndrum kind of defines the record, although it's competing for that status with the Simmons drums, I suppose. But they know how to use it because all these guys are really top-notch. "Mama" doesn't seem like an obvious single but as an opening track, it grabs your attention right away.

Daniel: "Mama" is an unusual-sounding track, even for 1983. It's got the off-kilter drum machine to start with, which, as Bill noted, was actually programmed by Mike Rutherford rather than Phil Collins. Perhaps it benefits from the fact that Mike is not a drummer. You get these wonderful, eerie sort of synth sounds from Tony Banks and a vocal from Phil that starts off really quiet and whispery and a bit menacing. As the song progresses and sort of gathers, it gets more desperate and wild until basically towards the end of the song, he's just screaming out the lyrics. Lyrically, it's a song about getting together with a lady of the night who's a bit older than he is, which is not typical Genesis subject matter. But it's just an incredible and brave choice as a single. The album version's a bit longer; they trimmed it down for the single. Actually, it was issued in four different lengths. "Mama" would become a concert favourite; they would play it on every tour after that.

Ralph Chapman: I'll just add that Mike's Linndrum rhythm was fed through some additional effects to create this kind of sweaty, weird sound, which invoked or created the mood.

Jamie: *Genesis* represented a big step further into the world of pop music, but "Mama" was decidedly not that. And for a lead-off track, side one, track one, it's doubly weird. But here's the thing; this song was released to radio right when I was getting into rock music. I didn't know a ton about music. I was only listening to the radio and I only knew the songs I heard on the radio. And I would only know who sang what song if the DJ told me. So I was still learning who all the legends were.

And I only knew of a crazy guy out there named Ozzy Osbourne. I knew nothing really about him. I didn't know what he sang. I didn't know what his voice sounded like. I just knew there was a crazy guy, that he existed. And I remember I was cutting my lawn one day with my headphones on and this song came on. And it sounded so weird and scary. And I remember thinking, this must be that Ozzy Osbourne guy. Because it sounded weird and scary. I soon learned that there was a big difference between Genesis and Ozzy Osbourne, weeks, maybe months later.

"Mama" still sounds weird and scary to this day. It's funny how a little, friendly-looking Phil Collins was able to muster up those chilling vocal sounds. And that laugh also sounds disturbing to this day. If you think about it, it comes close to those choking-like grunts some death metal bands throw into their songs at the end of the line. Is there a word for that? I'm not sure if there's a word for that vocal, that death metal choke sound. There might be. As for the music, it's obviously very electronic. But does it sound dated? Maybe I'm just grandfathered into some of this stuff, but it doesn't sound dated to me. That's a great question for a 16-year-old, right? But it's hard for me to answer that.

Martin: Okay, moving on to "That's All," the mood has shifted and lifted, although there's still a palpable sense of melancholy. Which makes sense, given the break-up lyric.

Daniel: "That's All" is a complete change of pace from "Mama." It's this basic sort of mid-tempo piano ballad, very beautiful. It's got a great vocal from Phil. The drums don't have that wallop, because they wouldn't sound right on this song. It's quiet drums. But it's very much about the vocal and Tony's piano. Like I said about *From Genesis to Revelation* in the part one Genesis book, *Entangled*, I find there's a definite downgrade in quality from side one to side two. I also remember the video clip, where they're sort of dressed up as hobos, playing the song in an old, dusty factory. I remember watching that as a kid. Like these guys, I came in with *Abacab* and at this point was now waiting for the new singles and the new album.

Todd: "That's All" is something that I started to enjoy a lot more when I got older. It's just a great melody and the Tony Banks piano on it is just really excellent. It's funny, but "That's All" sounds like R&B and it sounds like country but it's neither. But they used to introduce it as their country song. I guess it swings, but really, it's pop. There's a Phil Collins big band album, *A Hot Night in Paris*, and they do a version of "That's All." After you hear that, then you'll think that "That's All" is jazzy and that it swings.

Bill: It surprised me to find out that "That's All" was their biggest hit in the US up to that point. They'd had stuff like "No Reply at All," "Misunderstanding" and "Follow You Follow Me" that, for a long time, I thought were bigger hits than they actually were. Frankly, a lot of those songs I like better than "That's All," but that's a subjective thing. I do like the way Tony takes the lead on it after his more mood-setting keyboards on "Mama." It shows his variety quite nicely.

Tate: "That's All" is a terrific single with a great funky feel to it. I cannot get over how great Phil sounds on this album from a vocal perspective; he's really singing his ass off. Plus we get a great piano hook from Tony and solid solo from Mike on guitar. My favourite part of the song is the end where it goes into the double time feel.

Grant: I agree—brilliant single, and you can hear an overt Beatles influence. This album has some of their best pop songs ever. This one absolutely stands the test of time. As alluded to, this album was written and recorded entirely in the studio based off of them jamming. And from what I read, Genesis themselves thought that they made their best material when they all collaborated equally.

Jamie: It's one of those perfect pop songs. Some people hear the word pop and instantly get turned off, but I do not. There's nothing like a perfect pop song. It's like a perfect ravioli, just firm enough on the outside to keep a good shape and foundation, even though it can be very cheesy in the middle. As Grant referenced, I read that the song was intended to have a melody in the style of The Beatles, and that Phil was attempting to sound a bit like Ringo on the drum part. I don't know if he succeeded at copying Ringo.

I just know that high-hat sound gets me every single time. It's so simple, but so effective right from the start. I'm instantly drawn into that song. It's just so damn bouncy. It makes you feel good, even though Phil sounds angry. It's a push/pull thing with the happy bounce of the song working against Phil's exasperation. Somehow it just works beautifully. If you're trying to write a good song out there, this is the type of song you should be striving for. It's a great blueprint. And after you have the song, then you can add the heaviness, moodiness or shredding guitars if you really want to. Thank goodness they didn't do any of that here. But you have the song first. That's the hardest part.

Martin: Next we have a modest prog suite, as it were, with "Home by the Sea" and "Second Home by the Sea." It mirrors the pairings done on both of the last two albums, a linking through titling of fairly independent songs.

Todd: Yes, that's a really great pairing of tracks. The first part of the song is the song and the second part is an instrumental, a proggier thing with the Simmons drums. And they did that again on the next album. They did "In the Glow of the Night" and "The Last Domino." So they really like that concept. But on the song proper, the way the parts fit together are really nice. Again, I'm a Tony Banks fanboy, so I'm gonna say this a lot, but what Tony's playing is really great and quite innovative.

And the second half, "Second Home by the Sea," is pretty intense, with one of Mike Rutherford's best guitar solos. One of the things I don't really like about "Home by the Sea" and also "Mama," is that over the years, Phil spent a lot of time talking about what those songs were about. You hear the story over and over again, but "Home by the Sea" is about this guy that breaks into a house, climbs in the window, and the ghosts are there and the ghosts are telling him you're gonna sit down and you're gonna listen to our story. And then "Mama" is supposed to be about a brothel. You hear him explain them so often, that I think those songs work better when you don't think about what they're about and you just get into the atmosphere of them. Plus Tony Banks once said that he thought the meat of the album was side one and that side two contained the character pieces. I always thought that was interesting.

Bill: I feel like the band are tight and really in sync with each other on "Home by the Sea." I tried to single out one instrument and my ears kept wondering what one of the other guys was doing, and realizing how well they're playing as a unit. Especially on headphones, you really hear the sort of cohesive crafting. Genesis get looked at as a pop band and as a prog band, but I think people tend to overlook how much they can get into a groove. It wasn't just Phil that had a little bit of funk and R&B in him. Even though Tony and Mike might be the whitest guys in the world, they've got a little bit of funk in them too. It's funny, but "Second Home by the Sea" is kind of a mix of extremely futuristic '80s sounds and '70s prog. It's like the best of both worlds. They're playing a '70s songs structure with '80s sounds, basically.

Todd: I've heard Tony say in interviews that his intention was to be an R&B keyboardist, and things just came out like they came out.

Tate: "Home by the Sea" is a solid, mid-tempo song with another great vocal from Phil and these vital, energetic synth sounds and performances from Tony Banks. Then there's a mysterious outro that flows into the largely instrumental "Second Home by the Sea," which I'm not quite as big on. I didn't think it needed to be as long as it is. The main song is a bit too synth-poppy for me, but again, Phil saves the day with his vocals at the end, with that last verse. It might have worked better if "Second Home by the Sea" was kept to a two-, two-and-a-half minute addendum to the former song.

Grant: Written by Tony, "Home by the Sea" is a minor key track with a strong rhythm to it, with the drums in the pocket with the bass pedals. You can always tell a Tony Bank song because there's a lot of keyboard clutter, which in this case adds to the atmosphere, where it actually sounds like it's been recorded down on the ocean shore. This was another song that was developed from the Linndrum where they jammed to it. But eventually, of course, by the time you get to the end of it, the Linndrum is gone because Phil puts his drums into it. It's not completely pop. They haven't given up the prog or the art rock.

Daniel: I think of "Home by the Sea" and "Second Home by the Sea" as one piece, because they flow together nicely and they would always play them together live like one big suite. But this was the third single, so you've got three singles in a row starting off the album. As Todd says, the lyric is a ghost story about people in a haunted house, which is really cool. Musically you still get hints of the prog Genesis.

Jamie: That haunted house lyric means it's instantly got an edge to it. It specifically involves a burglar who went inside a house and he's held by ghosts for the rest of his life, or forever, I guess. So it's a very cool concept. It's pop, it's prog, it reminds me of songs that Asia recorded where they had a blend of elements of both to create an accessible sound. It could almost be labelled as dance prog.

Grant: "Second Home by the Sea," was really just a song that was conceived over jams. But it's fresh and it sounds like they are actually enjoying them themselves in the studio, getting into the creative process.

Daniel: Phil's playing the Simmons drums, but it's basically just a big, long keyboard solo for Tony. I always loved those extended keyboard solos Tony would play on things like *The Lamb Lies Down on Broadway* and "The Cinema Show" from *Selling England by the Pound*. He'd have these four- or five-minute keyboard solos, and I always was a sucker for those, so I love this suite. Wonderful way to close out side one.

Martin: What is Tony's persona as a keyboardist, his particular character?

Daniel: Tony doesn't necessarily have the chops of a Keith Emerson or Rick Wakeman, but he's got a feel and personality that appeals to me. As a lyricist, he tends to be a storyteller. He's not the one to do personal lyrics. He likes to tell stories, and sometimes they work and sometimes they don't.

Jamie: I know I called part one dance prog but I'll call part two smooth prog (laughs). You've heard of smooth jazz? Well, this is smooth prog. Yeah, the drum machine along with Tony Banks' low, humming, lush keyboards is what gives this that smooth feeling. There are also touches of new wave within the track. And then we get a piece of the same lyrics as part one, but this time Phil sounds less peppy, as if he's being held by the ghosts and having to hear their stories and he's realizing his fate. He's thinking, it was kind of cool at first, but now reality setting in. He's realizing that this is how the rest of his life will be and it's starting to not sound very cool at all. It's a nice way to close out side one. Side one is one of those perfect sides in rock history. It's a nice way to close it out before we turn over the record and hear the disaster that starts off side two (laughs).

Martin: Right, so now we get to "Illegal Alien," which, I must say, has a lot going for it, despite now, years later being controversial. It's got sophisticated chord changes in the verses and it's catchy as hell. I must say, over the decades, my mind would periodically slip and I'd think it was from *Invisible Touch* and not *Genesis*. And I think that's because it's really quite out-of-place here.

Todd: I agree, functionally, "Illegal Alien" is a really good song. I don't want to give them too hard of a time about it, because I don't believe it was meant to be disrespectful. But at the same time, when you listen to through a modern lens, there are quite a few cringe-worthy lines in the song. But I don't think there was any ill intention there, and Tony has said as much in interviews, that there wasn't any disrespectful or racist intention. It's just unfortunate, and not helped by the strange video, or Phil singing it in one of his character voices.

One of the things that they do in the video—and I don't know what this is based on—but the characters in the video are wearing like clothes pins on their clothes. And one of the souvenir items that year, during that tour, was a clothes pin, which had the Genesis logo on one side and it said "Illegal Alien" on the other side. I thought that was so bizarre. I didn't buy one but I found one in a puddle of soda and I've kept it all these years. I was looking for it but I couldn't find it.

Sound- and arrangement-wise, "Illegal Alien" is pretty good. I have no problem with it. It becomes a punching bag for this album and I don't think that's fair. But at the same time, I understand why that happens. And it's interesting. People tend to blame Phil Collins for "Illegal Alien," but that song is predominantly Mike's. And here's the thing. I don't think it has anything to do with being woke. It's just, that wasn't a time when there were people who were trying to turn immigrants into villains—that just wasn't there. At that time, you thought that's the way people talked and the way people looked and it was innocent. So today, I think it's okay to be annoyed or slightly put off by the content and it's also okay cut them some slack for it.

Bill: Oh boy, I usually don't have guilty pleasures, but "Illegal Alien" is the very definition of a guilty pleasure, at least for me, because I've always loved this song. Musically it's brilliant, and like you say, it's catchy as hell. There are all kinds of cool things they're doing in here. And yeah, at the time I didn't perceive anything as cringe-worthy in it. I was 15, 16 when this came out. I agree with Todd that there was no malice on their part. I just think they went about it a bit ham-fistedly. In my notes, I wrote, "Phil comes across as a bull trying to draw attention to the plight of china shops, while knocking dishes all about." That's how I see it.

But yeah, I still I love the song. I'll put it this way. I'll play it at home all day every day, but if I were a DJ on the radio in 2023, I wouldn't play it. Which, believe me, it was played a lot. When this album came out, I was living in Illinois, close to an Indiana radio station. And then I moved to Colorado, close to Denver. And rock stations in both markets played every single song on this album other than "Silver Rainbow," and they played them all a lot. Whether they were mainstream pop hits or not, this album got a ridiculous amount of rock radio play.

Grant: It was a different time. No one thought about these issues and the proof is that Genesis never got any flack for it. You couldn't put that out now, because the woke would lose their marbles, although, really, I don't think it has anything to do with being woke. I like that Genesis can do a song like this and not take themselves so seriously. It's catchy, it's got pop hooks galore and sure, it might set

Yes, there were then three—matching jackets required. *(Charisma Records publicity photo)*

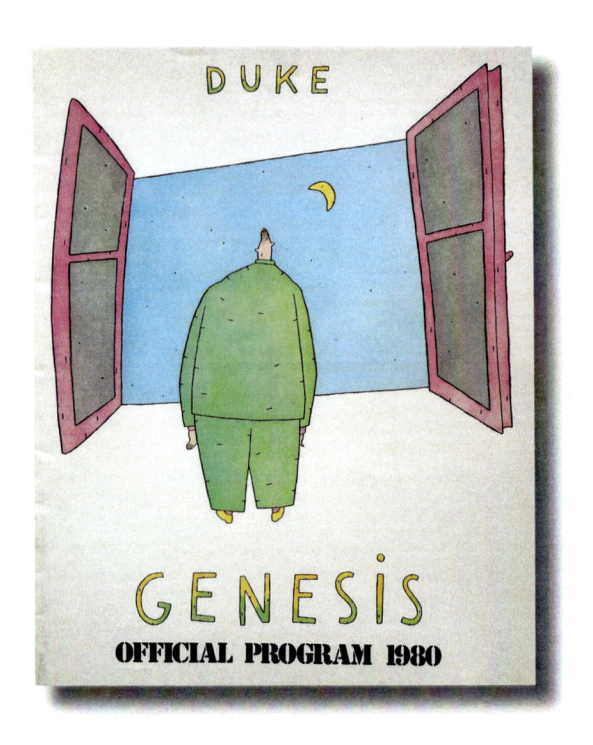

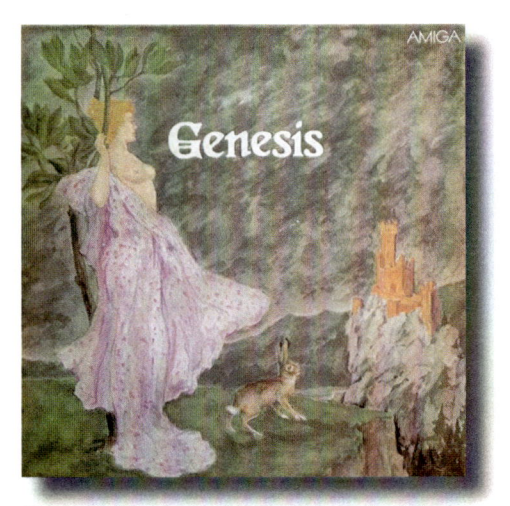

Obscure 1981 array of material from *And Then There Were Three* and *Duke*.

When three equals five. *(Atlantic Records publicity photo)*

Hamburg 1982. *(Ted Sayers)*

Genesis developed their own lighting system to great effect. *(Mike Ainscoe)*

Although on record Genesis remained a three-piece through the '80s, Daryl Steurmer complemented the lineup on stage. *(Mike Ainscoe)*

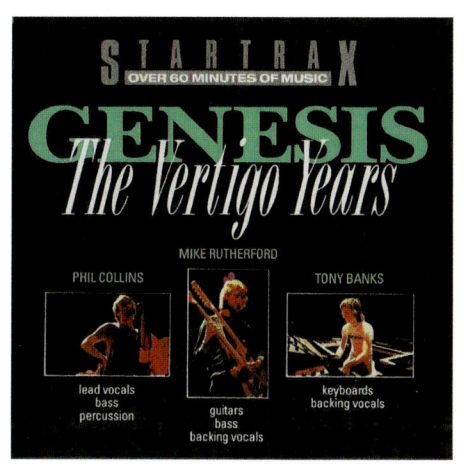

Australian-only compilation of '80s Genesis.

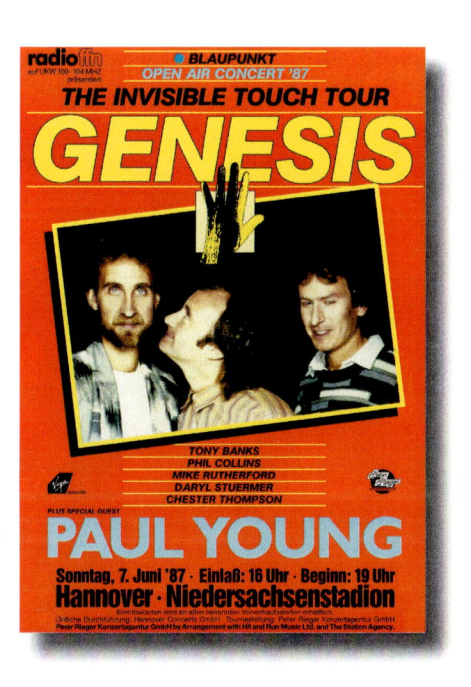

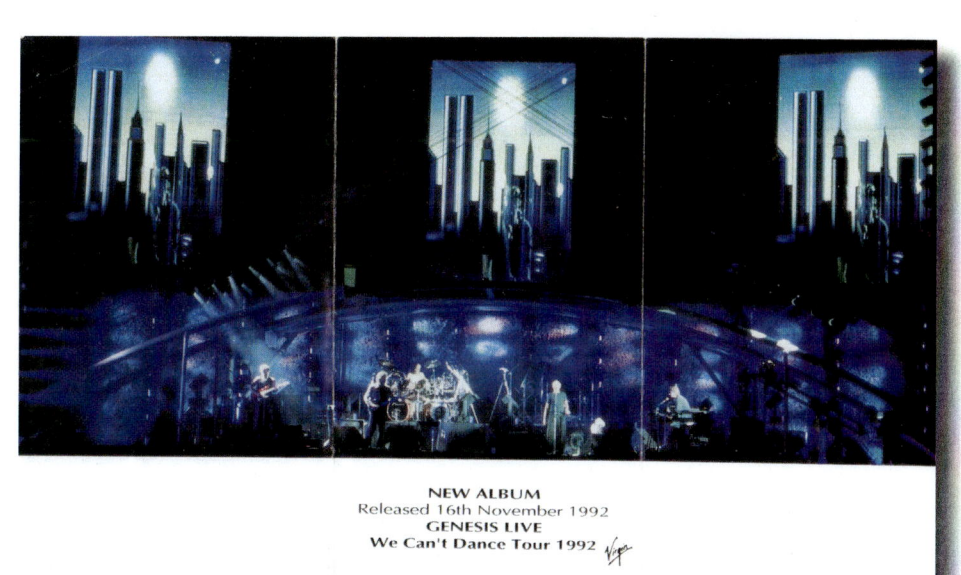

NEW ALBUM
Released 16th November 1992
GENESIS LIVE
We Can't Dance Tour 1992

The short-lived lineup with Ray Wilson. *(Virgin Records publicity photo)*

off those Peter Gabriel people, but hey, it's a clinic in finely-honed songwriting. It sounds like a band enjoying each other's company and having a good time. Hey, it's on the record. Some people like it; some people don't like it. I love it.

Tate: "It's no fun being an illegal alien" sounds pretty silly, but I enjoy it, despite the notoriety that might arise had they tried to put that out today. It's a fun song and probably close to my favourite of all their really poppy songs.

Daniel: Good lord, this song is borderline offensive; it really is. It's a song about Mexican migrants trying to get into the United States, and Phil does this cod Mexican accent, which is really awful. The film clip makes it even worse. They've got these big moustaches on and it really does trivialise what is, to me, a very serious topic about refugees. Musically, it's up and jolly, and I think the song is meant to be taken as a joke. I don't think it's meant to be taken seriously at all. To me—and mileage may vary—it's a joke in poor taste.

Jamie: Oh my God, "Illegal Alien" tries to ruin the album the same way "Who Dunnit?" almost ruined *Abacab*. A lot of people see this as being a racist song. *Blender* listed it as the 13th worst song of all time (laughs). I'm not a fan. Maybe they were trying to sympathise with Mexicans. I'm not 100% sure what the intentions were. But the accent Phil uses is pretty cringe-worthy and has not aged well. And the video, where Phil is dressed up to look like a stereotypical male Mexican doesn't help matters. But here's the worst part: the song comes off as being a jokey novelty song. And if those types of songs are going to exist on an album, they have to be short. You can't go much over three minutes. And this song is over five minutes long. It goes on and on. And you can call the chorus catchy, but that doesn't make it good. After all, the flu is catchy and nobody wants the flu. This could have been my favourite Genesis album if it wasn't for this song. So not only does it try to ruin the album, in a way it kind of does.

Martin: "Taking It All Too Hard" is next, and I guess you could call it a pop ballad, up-tempo, bright to the point of crisp, which applies to the whole album, I suppose.

Bill: It's a nice breather after the exuberance of "Illegal Alien," well-placed there, kind of a come down. I like the song. It's simple and pretty, the kind of thing that Genesis does well when they want to.

Tate: My criticism with this album is that there are some songs that sound too much like Phil Collins' solo stuff and this is one of them. You're starting to get the old-school fans feeling sour because Phil's having a pile of success with the solo stuff and Genesis is also having success and it overlaps and not in a good way. So yeah, "Taking It All Too Hard" is a nice song but kind of bland.

Grant: It's a Rutherford lyric, and there you go—Rutherford with the ballads again. It's a typical Phil ballad, but with Mike Rutherford lyrics. Phil sings these ballads with so much emotion and beauty. You wouldn't have a song like this on the Ray Wilson album. "Taking It All Too Hard" should have been on side one where all the hits are, although that would have really front-loaded it pretty egregiously.

Daniel: I don't think it stands up to any of the songs on side one. What's interesting is that despite this album being generated from jams, when you see remasters and reissues of this album, unlike everything else, there are no bonus tracks or outtakes or B-sides. That suggests to me that they used pretty much everything they had on the album, like that this was all they had. Songs like "Taking It All Too Hard" lead towards songs on some of the later albums that I really don't like, some of those mushy ballads like "In Too Deep" or "Hold on My Heart." It's pointing the way to that part of Genesis that really doesn't appeal to me.

Ralph: Because of the immediacy of the lyric, "Taking It All Too Hard" is one of very few explicit love songs that doesn't cloy. It's so immediate emotionally. I don't want to use the word poetic. It's just Mike Rutherford, once more, having that innate talent to craft something that transcends its apparent genre, that of love song. It's hard to write a great love song; it's a lost art. And whether I was 17 when I first heard it or now, it's a touching song. And Phil is able to convey that effortlessly.

It's also got a wonderful rhythm track, with Phil showing his best Ringo colours, where he's laying back. It's also a song that starts with the chorus, right? I just love that kind of structure, chorus first and then landing on the verse. I don't know why I have such a heavy bias towards how Genesis constructed love songs. Mike Nesmith is another songwriter who seemed to be able to get that pain across in a pop song. It's very difficult to explain what you're feeling, and then doing it so clearly and succinctly, but not making it obvious. There's nothing obvious about that lyric in "Taking It All Too Hard," but just from the title alone, it's comforting. It was a comforting song when I was a teenager and it's a comforting song now.

Todd: "Taking It All Too Hard" is a pretty solid ballad, but I think they got better at this with the next album and the albums after that. But it's got a nice feel to it.

Jamie: They're continuing with the soft pop aspect of their songwriting that started with "Man on the Corner." Some might go as far back as "Follow You Follow Me," but that song still sounds like proggy, layered '70s Genesis to me. People often confuse certain Genesis songs for Phil Collins solo songs, and I can see a lot of people confusing "Man on the Corner" and this song much more than "Follow You Follow Me." I don't mind this song. I will say that every song leading up to this one has a certain edge, even if the edge of "Illegal Alien" is weird and uncalled for. But whether it's lyrical content or Phil's delivery, there's always something brimming below the surface of the songs on this album. So "Taking It All Too Hard" feels out of place, since it lacks any sort of edge. But that's a small gripe. Luckily the next song takes care of all of that.

Martin: "Just a Job to Do" is a percolating pile of fun. There's a profusion of parts, and just as many brief musical hooks. What do you guys think of this one?

Todd: Yes, I agree, and it's an R&B-influenced song, like "No Reply at All," except they used Tony's keys instead of the Earth, Wind & Fire horns. Which, I'm not sure whether that was a scheduling or logistical issue or whether they just decided that they were going to try re-create that vibe on their own. But you can tell when you listen to that track that it's the same kind of thing. The rock station in Atlanta used to play "Just a Job to Do" all the time.

Bill: "Just a Job to Do" is a bit of a Mike showcase. It's a nice rocker about a hitman. I'm kind of wondering if since this album came out in late 1983, if they knew about "Twilight Zone" by Golden Earring, which is late '82, and thought, hey, we can have a hit song about a hitman too—why not? It's the trend now.

Tate: "Just a Job to Do" is one of my favourite Genesis songs. It's funky and it's almost hard rock—awesome. "I've got a line on you!"—great Phil Collins vocal on that and I love the keyboard performance from Tony.

Grant: I agree that it's kind of heavy and hard-edged, even nasty, given the way Phil sings it. Great drumming, very lively. Now this is one where I feel like Phil as a solo artist picked up a few things from what he was doing with Genesis, rather than the other way around. There was a song on *No Jacket Required* called "Don't Lose My Number." If you will play that song, and you play "Just a Job to Do," it's pretty similar. And that's 1985.

Another thing about "Just a Job to Do" is how Genesis make the complicated sound smooth and simple. Put headphones on and listen to this song—there's a lot going on sort of down through the layers. I guess one could say it's because of their history in prog. But yeah, there's the sort of Andy Summers-like guitar from Mike but also synth from Tony that is playing what you normally would expect a guitar to do.

Daniel: "Just a Job to Do" is about a criminal, so we're kind of getting back into "Robbery, Assault and Battery" from *A Trick of the Tail*, lyric-wise. But it's an up-tempo song and fun while it lasts. Still, it doesn't have the staying power of the tracks on side one. I don't dislike it the way I dislike "Taking It All Too Hard." It's great while it's on, but it's not one that tend to stick in the memory bank, an earworm, so to speaks. It's not one you're going to find yourself humming out of the blue.

Ralph: With "Just a Job to Do," again, I'm talking about original mixes because the remix I think altered the atmosphere of it. Whether they used a plugin or not, I'm not sure what they did technically. But that's an aside. I always encourage people to listen to the original mixes, and then listen to the remixes. But "Just a Job to Do" for me, the bass playing on that is superlative. It's just a driving number. Structurally, it reminds me somewhat of "Deep in the Motherlode." Maybe it's the break, that "Keep running, keep running, city to city/Even if you're innocent/You can cause too much embarrassment" section.

I love how the rhythm guitar locks in with the bass and drums. You didn't necessarily hear Genesis do songs like that. Again, one of the great things about Genesis and why I always compare them to The Beatles is that they could take on new things or approaches to songs and do them incredibly well. They were well versed musicians who were startlingly broad in their influences and their capabilities. So it's just a really great, driving tune. And when I test headphones—I love headphones—that's one of the songs I use, because of the way it's mixed and produced and played. It's just a great piece of record-making for the headphone experience.

It's 1983, so it's the second album into the Hugh Padgham experiment, and so what strikes me interesting is that it was their first album where they brought nothing in. They all wrote it together at The Farm, their studio, Fisher Lane Farm. But something like "Just a Job to Do," I would love to have heard the jams that came out of that. I would love to know how they structured and pulled that together musically and how they got to that vocal melody. I know that they did the lyrics later. It's criminal that on the second box set, they gave you a bit of the "Mama" demo. I thought, of all the things to give you, give me something that really shows what a tight band they were, and how at the end of the day, they were still rocking it. But that's the innate talent of Genesis, that they could do a song like that. And they do it again on the next album with "Anything She Does," where it's just compact rock.

Jamie: "Just a Job to Do" is one of my favourite Genesis songs ever. It feels like a hard rock song without having any screaming guitar. It's got a certain heaviness to it. It's hard to put your finger on where it's coming from, but it moves and has the rhythm of a rock song. And Phil's vocals and lyrics are both very aggressive. Tony Banks' keyboards are not as lush as they are on "Second Home by the Sea." And that "Bang, bang, bang" followed by that drum part, I feel like that little moment would put a smile on the face of a lot of metalheads. Also, compared to the other songs, the bass is being played a little quicker and the drums sound a bit more real. Like I say, when you put that all together, it comes off as the quote unquote hard rock song on the album.

Martin: How would you describe Phil's voice? Just generally.

Jamie: British, definitely British. Sometimes you hear a voice and you don't know where that guy's from. I hear Phil Collins' voice and

I go, "That's a British guy." It sounds like a friendly little guy, and he can be sappy and he can be quirky, but he can be aggressive too—and weird. He's got it all, all on his little smiling face of a package that you just want to take him home with you and put him on your lawn (laughs). It's like stay there on my lawn as my little gnome guy.

Martin: Love it (laughs). Do you ever reflect on how odd it is that the band's first singer, Peter Gabriel, has this quite unique voice, and then—surprise—your drummer is somewhat in the same category and he can also sing?

Jamie: They got lucky that he was able to pull off the Peter Gabriel tracks. Yeah, that they had someone in the band who could do that. And when he does the Peter Gabriel tracks live, he can sound very much like Peter Gabriel. And you're right; it's more so because he has that same kind of twangy voice and the same range. He's not trying to do it. When I say being able to do it, he's just doing it. Yeah, they got lucky. Pretty bizarre.

Martin: Remember I talked about how I can't unsee *Genesis* as an acoustic album? "Silver Rainbow" is a key track for that idea. I listen to this and all I hear is vocals and a million synths. And yes, I hear the headache-inducing drums but they are so processed, they may as well be programmed. How does this one sit with you guys?

Todd: I thought it was interesting that Tony Banks once said that the working title of that song was "Adam" because they thought it sounded like something that Adam Ant would do. And they also thought the lyric was kind of childish and playful, so they made the music feel that way. Although I think Tony's keyboards are quite spooky.

Bill: "Silver Rainbow" is the one that the hardcore prog snobs accept. If they're prone to hate the rest of the album, they'll grudgingly say, "Oh, yeah, 'Silver Rainbow' is okay." I can't make heads or tails of the lyric. Good or bad, it makes an impression. Sometimes it's good not to know what the songs are about. I've often joked that your first Blue Öyster Cult book ruined a lot of the mystery for me about BÖC's crazy mythology. And that's also kind of true when you have these Genesis songs explained for you.

Tate: I don't know; "Silver Rainbow" doesn't resonate with me. For some reason, it sounds too much like Phil's solo stuff for my liking. And I actually feel that way about the last song, too, "It's Gonna Get Better," although that one's got a bit of a cool funk vibe to it.

Grant: "Silver Rainbow" is a Tony Banks song, and we're flipping back to an emphasis on art rock as your base with the pop elements added on top, as opposed to a pop song with art rock embellishments. Any bass in it seems to be synth bass, but mostly what you hear is those tribal toms. Some say the song is about sex, but I'm getting the vibe that these lyrics kind of come out of that rambling jam ethic that gave us the music. There was a lot of improvisation on this album, and I feel like it carried over to the words here.

Daniel: I like "Silver Rainbow." It's got the Simmons drums, which work well, and it's got some odd keyboard textures and sounds. Tony Banks isn't just playing lyrical keyboard lines. He was big into sound effect kind of keyboards, and you get that quite a bit on "Silver Rainbow." It's like '80s psychedelia, with a swirliness to it that I like. It's my favourite song on side two.

Jamie: What I like about "Silver Rainbow" is that Phil sings it as a ballad, but the band isn't playing a ballad. In my mind, I always remember it as a ballad, but then when I hear it again, I go, "Is it really?" I don't think so. It's this cool, mystical song that sits somewhere in the middle. There's something very fairy tale-like about it. And here's the thing; Tony wrote two songs for the album. One is about ghosts and the other one is about a land that lies beyond the silver rainbow. So thanks to him, we get into a world of fantasy, twice.

Martin: So we close with "It's Gonna Get Better." I love that opening sort of backwards music sequence. It reminds me that there are better albums to listen to over in Peter Gabriel land. Actually, I don't mean to be harsh; I love this song. The chords are just really cool, and it's in a weird sort of 4/4 time that for some reason has me counting 8/8!

Grant: This is a Rutherford track and it's got a lot of experimentation. The keyboard on it reminds me of Robert Fripp's Frippertronics, his guitar looping thing. Tony evidently sampled something off of some classical cello album to get that sound and it sets a dark mood. But then the mood lightens as it picks up or as it moves along, although it's still very emotional. Wonderful track, with a great suite of vocals from Phil throughout all the different passages.

Todd: The thing I always think of when I think about "It's Gonna Get Better" is this interview they did on *Rockline*, where people could call up and ask questions. And somebody said, "Mike, what are you playing in 'It's Gonna Get Better?'" And they were referring to the synth pedals, you know, the bass pedals. And because, obviously, they're not playing electric bass, Mike Rutherford says, "A Stratocaster, a nice blue one." And Tony interrupts him and says, "I think he means the bass." It's an innovative track; they'd never quite used synth bass in that way. Plus Tony comes in with some eerie and pretty fresh keyboard sounds. If you can't tell, I really like this album.

Bill: I really like the way "It's Gonna Get Better" ends the album on a hopeful note. The lyrics provide a positive message. They're universal. Anybody can latch onto them without needing to be part of any specific group or whatnot. Which is quite nice—they have a universal anthem there. Plus I'd say it's the peak of that drum sound. It sounds dated now, but being dated is often a good thing. In this case it takes me right back to '83, '84. That sound and that period is so special to me, and that kind of drum production acts like some kind of audio time machine. What more can I ask out of a 40-year-old album? And I love Mike's sound on it. Until Todd brought it up, I had no idea that was synth pedals.

Todd: I don't know for sure whether they're pedals, but it's definitely some kind of a synth thing. They may have been programmed.

Bill: It sounds great either way. I like what he did with it. It's an interesting lead instrument, basically. It's subtle, which I like; it's not really in-your-face. You can really get into a groove with it.

Daniel: "It's Gonna Get Better" is an odd choice for a closing track, because it's not particularly dynamic. It doesn't go out on a particularly energetic tone to finish the album out. It's just kind of there. I appreciate the idea or sentiment of the lyric, you know, that things are not going great now but it's gonna get better. I think we all need to hear that sometimes when we're going through tough times. But it's not especially memorable musically.

Ralph: The idea of writing a song that starts, "Reach out, hands in the air" is very Stevie Wonder to me. It's very much early '70s soul music, maybe like something off of *Innervisions* or the one right after that, *Fulfillingness' First Finale*. It reminds me that these guys were still very much rooted in the '60s. Remember that Phil did a whole album of Motown covers. These guys were heavily steeped in soul music.

I thought it was a great way to end the record. The best way to hear "It's Gonna Get Better' is actually when they released the single, the 12-inch single. They gave you a whole extra minute-and-a-half with an extra verse and with different drum parts. I think it's a much better version. It's a more realised version of a set of ideas.

So it's wearing that soul music on their sleeves and it's a great groove. I agree with you that the chords are interesting, and you also pointed out that almost backwards, bizarre keyboard sound that kind of lays into this relentless groove. Phil always played that better than Chester, I thought. But Phil was always really, really good at playing soul music on the drums. Plus that's one of his best lyrics as far as I'm concerned. It's simple and there are no bromides or cheap sentiment. It's just pictures, images, lyrics. "There's a sister and she's standing next to her man"—it's just sparse, economical, evocative storytelling.

And the climax of that song, and how he holds that note... you hear something like that on "Inside and Out" as well. He could just hold a note so beautifully. You could just float on it. I think Phil's incredibly under recognised as a vocalist, because everybody talks about everything else. They don't talk about his raw talent as a singer. You know, I'm trying to put this Phil Collins book together, and as you know, I've done some interviews, and I gravitate towards producers, who just seemed to understand that buried beneath all the shit that's ever been written about Phil Collins, at the end of the day, he's just like McCartney and people like that who've got such massive reputations. His actual raw talent is seldom explored, dissected and celebrated, and "It's Gonna Get Better" is one of the great Phil Collins post-Steve Hackett Genesis moments.

Jamie: I think it's the most '70s-sounding song on the album, not only the way it's produced, but in the way the song is constructed. It sounds like a leftover from the songwriting sessions for *And Then There Were Three*. It feels almost like there was a toss-up between this song and "Follow You Follow Me" for that album, and they decided to hold off on this one until 1983. None of that is probably true, but that's how it sounds. And I'm not saying it's a bad song, although I guess I'm saying that it sounds a bit dated, even for 1983.

Martin: Good stuff. All right, is there anything anybody forgot to say? Does anybody want to attempt to summarise how the band sounded here at the end of 1983?

Tate: Well, overall, for me, the great stuff on here is great and the not so good stuff is decent. I'd give it like an eight-and-a-half out of ten on the strength of "Just a Job to Do" alone. For me, it's situational. The proggy parts on songs like "Just a Job to Do" and "Home by the Sea" work for me. But I must be missing something with "Silver Rainbow" and "It's Gonna Get Better," and then "Taking It All Too Hard," I might be missing something there too. I didn't even like "Mama" when I first heard it and now I really enjoy it. There are still parts of this album that have proggy moments that I really enjoy, and then there are other proggy moments that just kind of go by the wayside for me. It's subjective, because I don't think I could defend it objectively.

My favourite era of Genesis is that span of the first three where Phil takes over on vocals. Those are terrific. And I'll even go a step further. I'm controversial in calling *Trespass* my favourite Genesis album, but I think Phil Collins sounds better on the Gabriel-era stuff on *Seconds Out* than Peter did. It's almost uncanny how great of a job he did. I mean, the *Seconds Out* version of "The Lamb Lies Down on Broadway," Phil sings it so much better than Peter did on the studio album, and that was supposedly the apex of Peter's time with the band.

Anyway, overall, *Genesis* is definitely not as bad of an album as the pro-Gabriel crowd would have you believe. But in my opinion, it's the last really strong Genesis album, because I'm not a fan of *Invisible Touch*. I'm not that big of a fan of *We Can't Dance* either and *Calling All Stations* I think is a pretty big misfire, after Phil left. For me, this is the last really good Genesis album.

Martin: Why do you think *Genesis* was so successful?

Daniel: I think it was so successful because "Mama" was such a huge hit, and "That's All" was very big in the US as well. In the early '80s, big singles tended to drive big sales for albums. This was also coming off of Phil having a couple of really big solo albums. Phil's solo career and Genesis' career were feeding off each other. Phil would do an album, it would be big, and then the next Genesis album would come out and it would be big. That would lead to the next Phil album and so on. The two would propel each other up the charts, as it were.

Martin: Another reason might be that it was just so cutting-edge in terms of its production. It's like the perfect stereo test record for 1983, right?

Daniel: Yeah, it is, except for "That's All," which is a real throwback-sounding track. But sure, overall there's a real sense of state-of-the-art technology being used, with the Simmons drums and Tony's E-mu Emulator keyboard and things like that. One last thing; it's quite a wordy album. Genesis were never afraid of giving us reams and reams of lyrics.

Todd: A lot of Genesis fans only like the early version of the band, up until Steve Hackett leaves, or earlier, when Peter leaves. But there's really innovative music going on after that. I was somebody that liked *Abacab*, but when this album came out, I liked it a lot more than *Abacab*. I thought that the melodic quality was better and that the songs were better and more interesting. If I could think of something bad to say about it, it doesn't have much cohesiveness. Still, it's a good period of the band, one that should be reassessed. Because it's pretty innovative stuff and even, at times, super-weird. Who knows why it was so popular? I mean, it's a pretty strange album. It certainly starts out with a pretty crazy song.

Also, I wanted to comment on something that Bill said. It really is true with this album that there are songs where you're not really thinking about who's playing what. There were parts of "That's All" that I used to think were Mike that are actually Tony. And that's one of the things that's really cool about this band, is that they figured out how to do that. In a prog band, we're led to believe everyone has a role. But in this band, especially on this album, it's kind of all over the place and I think that's really cool.

And I'd go so far as to say that the drums on their own support this narrative, because it's hard to tell what's programmed, what's Linndrum, what's Simmons and what are acoustic drums maybe processed to sound modern. "That's All" is a great example of that. It sounds like he's playing everything and yet nothing sounds like real drums. It also sounds like some of it could be programmed. I can't tell what are real drums and what's some kind of hybrid.

You know, when these albums were coming out, I liked things like "Home by the Sea" and "Second Home by the Sea" and "Domino" because they were proggy. But I thought they were missing some drama that the earlier songs had, and I didn't think these songs had it. But as I get older, I actually like the proggier songs from Genesis' later era even better, because I think they're weirder (laughs). I think they just work better.

There's also this. Tony has said this a bunch of times, that there's singing Phil and there's screaming Phil and Tony prefers screaming Phil. That's really interesting, because I never thought of him as screaming. But when you listen to many of the parts from this album onward, that's actually what it is. And then I guess starting in 2007 when they did that tour, he went back to being singing Phil, because he couldn't scream anymore.

Martin: Do you think the *Genesis* album is this band's *90125*?

Todd: Well, I feel like *Abacab* made more of an impression on people who didn't previously listen to Genesis, which kind of makes that their *90125*. And you know, I gotta say that when *Invisible Touch* came out, I thought it was stronger than *Genesis*. I'm not sure if I still feel that way now, but I thought it sounded better.

Grant: Well, let me put it like this. These guys started out playing prog but now they've gained the freedom to play whatever they want. The beautiful thing is we've narrowed this band down to three core people. I'm not saying that Peter Gabriel wasn't an important part of the core band—he's great for what he does. But Mike Rutherford, Tony Banks and Phil Collins can write pop songs, and in my estimation, some of the best pop songs across all the 1980s were done by Genesis. I'm telling you, when they were down to that trio, there was something about it. People could argue with that or disagree, but I think as a pop music writing machine, they were all over it. Those three guys together did something magical. I'll leave it there.

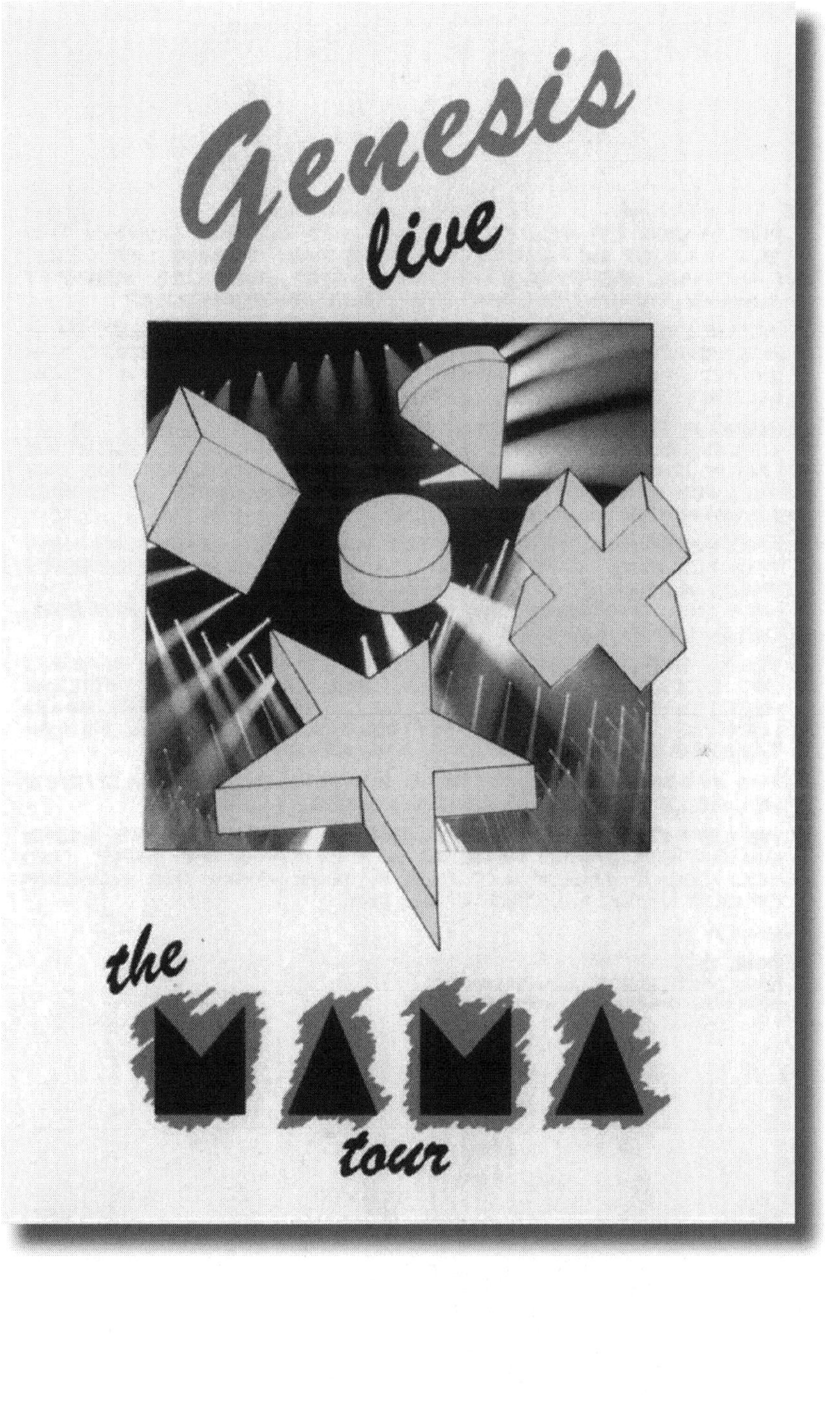
Genesis
live
the
MAMA
tour

Behind The Lines: Genesis on Record 1978-1997

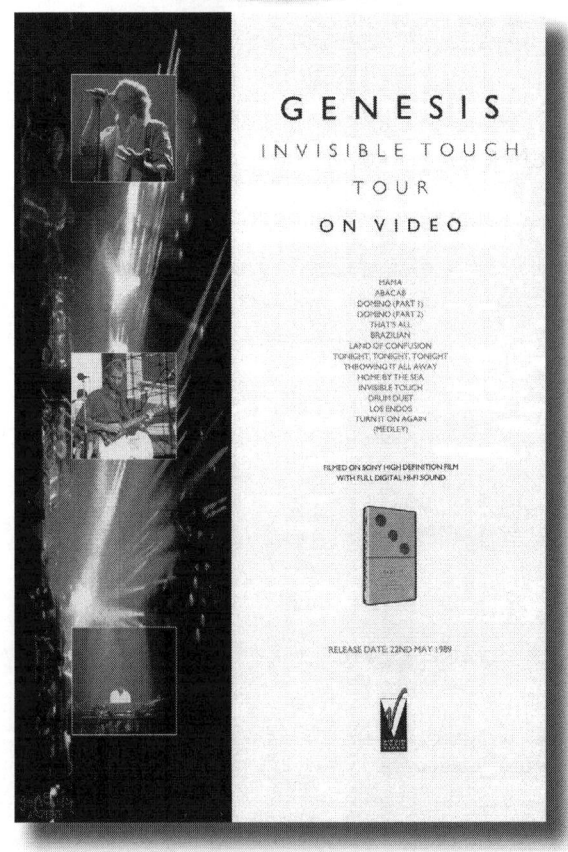

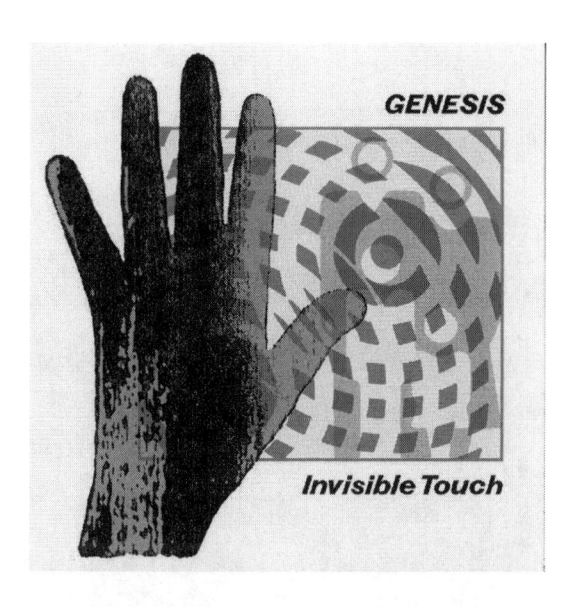

INVISIBLE TOUCH

June 9, 1986
Charisma GEN LP2
Produced by Genesis and Hugh Padgham
Engineered by Hugh Padgham; assisted by Paul Gomersall
Recorded at The Farm, Chiddingfold, Surrey, UK
Personnel: Phil Collins – drums, vocals, percussion; Tony Banks – keyboards, synth bass; Mike Rutherford – guitars, bass
All songs written by Genesis

Side 1
1. Invisible Touch 3:26
2. Tonight, Tonight, Tonight 8:49
3. Land of Confusion 4:45
4. In Too Deep 4:59

Side 2
1. Anything She Does 4:06
2. Domino (Part One – In the Glow of the Night, Part Two – The Last Domino) 10:42
3. Throwing It All Away 4:41
4. The Brazilian 4:49

Behind The Lines: Genesis on Record 1978-1997

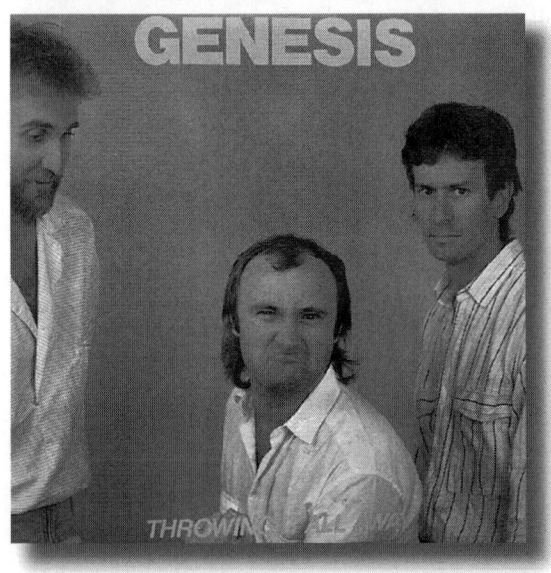

An *Invisible Touch* Timeline

October 1985 – February 1986. Genesis work on tracks to appear on the follow-up to their hit self-titled album from 1983. Producing is Hugh Padgham, with the team working at The Farm, the band's own studio, recently upgraded, in Chiddingfold, Surrey.

October 21, 1985. Mike + The Mechanics, featuring Mike Rutherford, issue their self-titled debut album. Also this month, there's a video release called *Genesis Live: The Mama Tour*.

May 19, 1986. Genesis issue "Invisible Touch" as an advance single from the forthcoming new album of the same name, backed with "The Last Domino." It becomes the band's only No.1 single in the US. The single also reaches No.4 in Canada and No.15 in the UK, where it's certified as a gold single with 400,000 copies sold. On the same day, Peter Gabriel issues a fifth solo album, entitled *So*. It's a big hit, eventually certifying at five times platinum.

June 6, 1986. Genesis issue *Invisible Touch*. The album currently sits at six times platinum in the US, reaching double platinum before the end of the year. It's the band's fourth album in a row to hit the top slot on the UK chart, and it gets to No.3 in the US.

August 25, 1986. "In Too Deep" is issued as a single in the UK, backed with the non-LP "Do the Neurotic." The A-side reaches No.19 on the charts. For the second single, America gets "Throwing It All Away" with the same B-side, with the A-side reaching No.4 on the charts.

September 18 – October 24, 1986. The band tour for the first time in almost three years, supporting *Invisible Touch* in the US.

November 17, 1986. "Land of Confusion" is issued as a single, backed with the non-LP "Feeding the Fire." It gets to No.14 in the UK and No.4 in the US. A famed video is produced for the track, featuring the *Spitting Image* puppets. It receives a Grammy award in 1988 in the short-lived Best Concept Music Video category.

November 23 – December 20, 1986. The band tour New Zealand and Australia.

January 15 – March 1, 1987. The band return for a second US tour leg.

March 9, 1987. Genesis issue "Tonight, Tonight, Tonight," backed with "In the Glow of the Night (Part One)" as a single. It reaches No.3 in the US and No.18 in the UK.

March 13 – 19, 1987. The band tour Japan.

April 1987. "In Too Deep" sees release as the album's fifth single in the US, backed with "I'd Rather Be You," reaching No.3 on Billboard. Additionally, up into 2000, the song would feature in the hit horror movie *American Psycho*.

April 14, 1987. *Invisible Touch* is certified three times platinum.

May 10 – July 4, 1987. The band tour Europe, broken up by a few US dates.

February 11, 1988. *And Then There Were Three* and *Duke* are certified platinum. *Abacab* is certified double platinum.

October 24, 1988. Mike + The Mechanics issue a sophomore record, called *The Living Years*, which goes gold in the UK.

May 22, 1989. Virgin Music Video issues *Genesis: Live at Wembley Stadium*, documenting shows from July 2 and 3, 1987.

August 14, 1989. Tony Banks issues a self-titled album under that band name Bankstatement.

November 20, 1989. Phil Collins issues *...But Seriously*, which certifies at four times platinum.

April 20, 1990. *Selling England by the Pound*, *The Lamb Lies Down on Broadway*, *A Trick of the Tail* and *Wind & Wuthering* are certified gold.

July 30, 1990. The band play Knebworth Park, Stevenage, UK.

April 2, 1991. Mike + The Mechanics issue a third album, called *Word of Mouth*.

Invisible Touch

June 3, 1991. Tony Banks issues a solo album called *Still*. Once again, Daryl Stuermer plays all the guitars on the album.

October 1991. The *Three Sides Live* video from 1982 is issued on laserdisc.

Behind The Lines: Genesis on Record 1978-1997

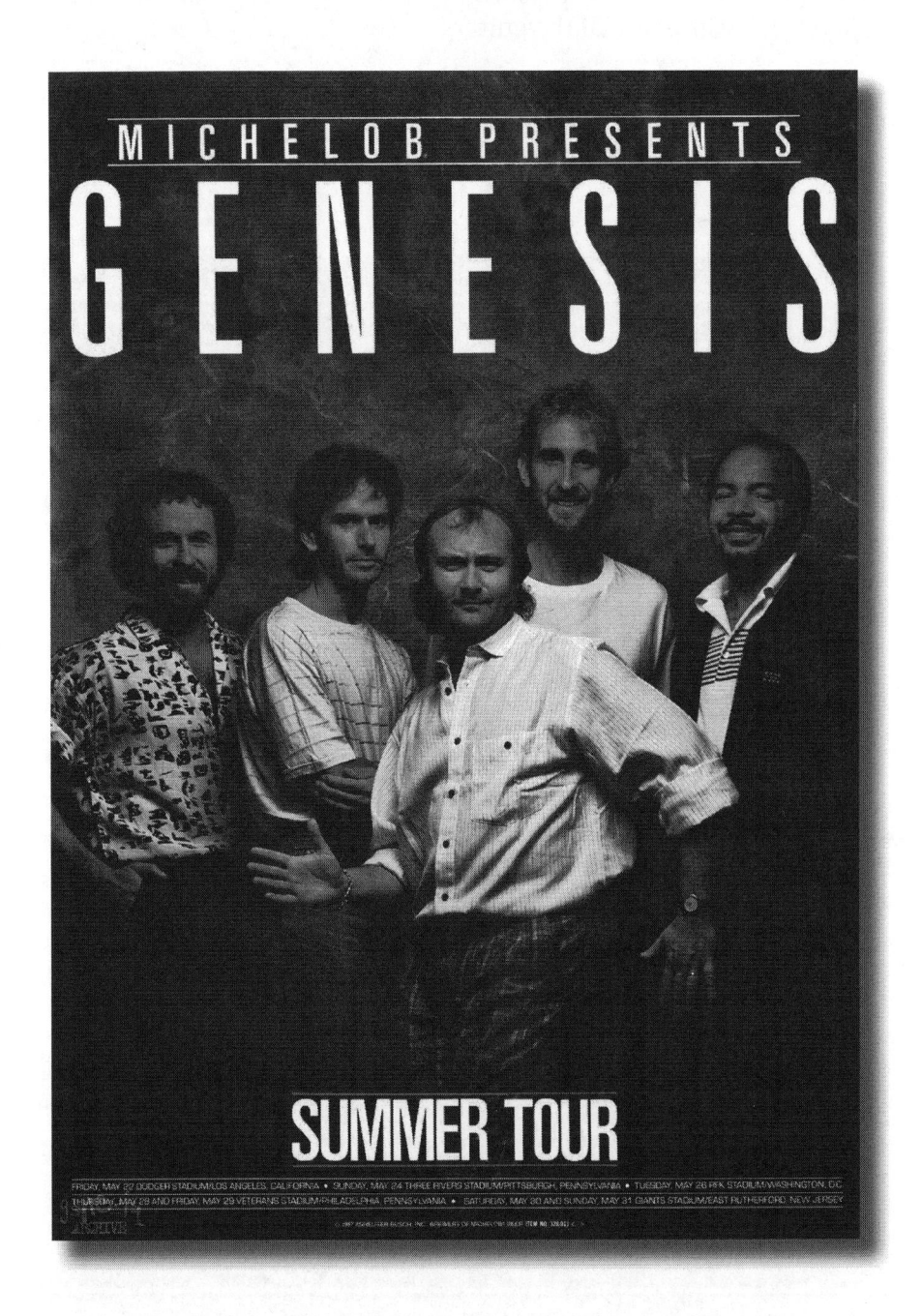

Martin talks to Ralph Chapman, Jamie Laszlo and Bill Schuster about *Invisible Touch*.

Martin Popoff: All right, Genesis bound into 1986 as a huge band with an even bigger frontman in Phil Collins, given his enormous solo career success. What do you guys think of their *Invisible Touch* proposition?

Ralph Chapman: Spiritually I look at *Invisible Touch* as the band's last album, their last real album. As a backdrop, contextually, '85 and '86 were amazing days to be a Genesis fan. But when I started in '81, it was an embarrassment of riches because all the members, and actually other prog bands as well, were all entering these interesting phases. But in '85 and '86, you had *No Jacket Required* and the first Mechanics record. I didn't feel that those records were as good as say, Rutherford's *Acting Strange* or Phil's *Hello, I Must Be Going* or *Face Value*. They were diminishing returns, but they were still fantastic pieces of work and my love was as strong as ever for what they were doing.

But '86 comes around and you get GTR with "When the Heart Rules the Mind," which didn't blow my mind. Max Bacon's voice was certainly something you had to acquire a taste for, I thought, but the record was good and they had "Toe the Line" and "The Hunter" and all these kinds of tracks.

And around the same time, "Invisible Touch," the single, comes out, and Peter Gabriel's *So* is out and you get "Sledgehammer" that April. "Sledgehammer" was such a departure from *Security*, the fourth album, and again unabashedly commercial in the best sense. It had brass on it and just an amazing groove. I didn't really understand that, that some of Peter's influences were Stax and soul records at that point. I just didn't know. But what was interesting—and this might have been partially due to Manu Katché's drums—but it sounded really grounded and alive and real. Not that it would have come from Muscle Shoals or anything, but it was a great song.

So unconsciously or consciously, there's an expectation. I'm sure I knew a new Genesis record was coming out. Hackett had reemerged in this new commercial context with Steve Howe and Geoff Downes producing, and then there's the *So* album. So to hear, first, the song "Invisible Touch," and to hear something that sounded so mechanical and so contrived and so tossed-off, was disconcerting. It was a short song as well. It made me kind of fearful of the full record that was to come.

And I can't remember whether I bought the single, which would have been very unusual. I may have looked at the single in the store and flipped it over. Because Genesis were one of these bands who would make great B-sides. In this case, the song on the B-side was from the album. So I thought not only are they ripping me off with the single, but they're not even giving me something new. At least that's my memory of them putting the second part of the "Domino" thing on the B-side.

Anyway, so I get the album, down at Sam the Record Man in downtown Toronto, and put on side one, which has this orange label. B-side is green label. So I put on side one, knowing what I'm going to hear with "Invisible Touch" and my opinion doesn't change. Stand by, because all of this eventually changes. But at this point, on my humble little Harman Kardon stereo and Dual turntable, I can hear it a lot better than the car radio.

And what I hear mostly, again, is I can't distinguish any contribution from Rutherford. I'm 20 at this point, and all I hear is these Simmons drums. Phil used them when he was touring with Robert Plant, and I know Robert Plant turned him on to Simmons drums. And then with the self-titled, they're used a lot on that record, although it's a lovely balance between acoustic drums and Simmons drums. And guys like Roger Taylor and Phil and Jerry Marotta were these experts at combining acoustic percussion with the new technology. But "Invisible Touch" just seemed like the drums were playing him instead of the other way around. It all felt easy and tossed-off, which was a ghastly feeling for me. But that is my first impression. Stand by for a lot more (laughs).

Martin: Oh, I will (laughs). Jamie, how about yourself? How has Genesis changed from the self-titled to *Invisible Touch*?

Jamie Laszlo: They change quite a bit, don't they? Now, here's the thing. This is six times platinum in the US—six million. And I'll tell you what, Phil was coming in hot from *No Jacket Required*. That was released on February 18, 1985. "Take Me Home" was in heavy rotation until August or September of that year. So just nine months later, we have a boatload more hits on the radio sung by Phil Collins. So this album was sort of an extension of *No Jacket Required*. And looking at the tracks on both albums, five tracks from *No Jacket Required* got played on the radio, and then another five from *Invisible Touch*. So that's ten radio songs in less than two years. No wonder I got tired of hearing Phil's voice. It took me decades to get over it. I was tired of his voice until about 2005, when I finally was able to take it again.

I want to add that dissecting this band's dense prog albums really intimidates me. That's why I chose to talk about these other more popular albums. But I also found it challenging to dissect their pop songs, because sometimes there's too much in the music to try to dissect and then sometimes there's not enough. But I started to think, six of the tracks on these albums were videos on MTV. And since 1986 and 1987 were the peak heyday years of the MTV era, I decided to watch all the videos for side one in the same sequence they showed up on the album. I didn't listen to the album. I watched each video and heard the songs that way, in the same order. And that's how I made my notes. And it quickly became apparent that side one plays out like a greatest hits album for the band.

Bill Schuster: I like *Invisible Touch* a lot more now than I used to. When it came out, I was not a full Genesis fan yet. I had been a fan of the previous album, the shapes album, but I didn't purchase *Invisible Touch* right away at the time. I had been getting more into metal, like Black Sabbath and Metallica, so this wasn't quite in my wheelhouse at that point in time. I heard most of the songs on the radio, because they were played incessantly, but I was not appreciating the creativity that went into the songs. I kind of bought the line at the time that these guys had sold out and they were just writing simple pop songs. As it turns out, it was, oh no, far from it. They still had their creativity fully intact. They were just doing something different with it.

Martin: How creative did you think they were being with that album cover?

Bill: I hadn't noticed until very recently that there were basically these four little cartoon silhouettes of people inside that green and yellow box. I was just seeing abstract colours and shapes there. I have no idea what that's supposed to represent. I assume this hand is supposed to represent the invisible touch. But why is it apparently getting ready to touch this entire family? It's like two adults and two kids. It's a cool-looking image and it's very '80s, so it fits for 1986. But the interior artwork drives me nuts when I'm trying to read the lyrics. especially on the green because the words get completely lost in the colours there. It's hard on older eyes.

Jamie: You can't get more '80s than that album cover, with those garish colours and the white background. You look at that album and you know it didn't come out yesterday.

Martin: It could be a Spandau Ballet or Human League or Duran Duran cover.

Jamie: Yeah, and that's the fanbase they're trying to reach with this album, that '80s pop or synth pop crowd. That's why it sold six million copies.

Martin: What are your thoughts on the overall production?

Bill: I think the production is good for what it is, but the only copy I have is the un-remastered original CD. I've never actually owned *Invisible Touch* in any other format. So I'm not sure if the vinyl might have sounded better or if the remaster was any sort of improvement. Overall, it has a nice, bright, pop production to it. To my ears, it's not quite as strong as the previous two albums, but it's all right.

Martin: Okay, the album opens with its title track. What is our assessment of this bouncy yet complicated song?

Ralph: Like I say, my first memory of "Invisible Touch" is hearing it as a single in the spring of '86. These things are imprinted in my mind. I was driving with my friend Rob, I think in his Honda Civic. Q107 played the title track and we pulled over. I believe they announced it first and we pulled over and listened to it. And at the end of the song, the DJ said, "That was the new Genesis single, a very slight tune," which was a funny thing to edit on air, for a Genesis song. But hey, certainly in the mid-'80s, there was a whole facet of the so-called rock intelligentsia at Q107 that were so fucking arrogant back then. I just loathed listening to them.

But nonetheless, that comment, as odious as it was, I couldn't and didn't dismiss it. Because I couldn't defend that song. It was a very strange feeling. Every Genesis song I'd heard up 'til that one, I could defend. Or I could see something that seemingly no one else was seeing. Even "Illegal Alien" or some of the songs that people were somehow Exhibit A of Phil destroying the band or something stupid like that. You know, there's a lot to love about the *Invisible Touch* album beyond its humour, its execution, its melody, its arrangement, all those things. The sound of that record is great.

But "Invisible Touch," with those heavy Simmons drums and on a little, tinny Honda radio, it just sounded like noise. And even on that radio, I could hear the reverb they piled on Phil's voice; the reverb is so outrageous on that song. So it was quietly dismaying. I don't think I spoke to my friend Rob about it, because I was uncomfortable. There was nobody in my circle that was a bigger Genesis fan than I was. So it quieted me, that song.

Jamie: Watching the "Invisible Touch" video, you see the charisma that Phil Collins had. He went from being the drummer for a weird little prog band, who was always stoned behind the drum kit, to this lovable character. So lovable that Hollywood put him in a movie called *Buster*. They thought he would have appeal in a movie. It's easy to forget just how much of a star he was. He was right up there with Madonna and Bruce Springsteen. And between his solo career and Genesis, he was everywhere.

I will tell you right now, ask a millennial on the street who Phil Collins is. They will not know, most of them. They'd never heard the name. And I remember the first time that happened to me, I was shocked. And then I just started asking millennials. If you tell them he did the music for *Tarzan*, they'll go, "Oh, that guy, the Disney movie, *Tarzan*." That's how they know, believe it or not.

And man, is he hamming it up for this video; he's almost overdoing it. But back then it worked. You'd seen videos like this a few times a day, every day for a few months. So we would have these videos memorised. Even today, I was still able to predict every camera angle and facial expression coming up next in this video.

Martin: Coud you describe a little more of what goes on in the video?

Jamie: Oh, they're just playing in a big warehouse or garage or something. Or is that a studio? And they're just hamming it up. You've got Phil Collins dancing around and singing into drumsticks. They're just using these very limited resources to do jokey things. Drumsticks? I'll just sing into them. I'll hit him in the head with these drumsticks. Stupid things. It's almost like a Three Stooges routine.

These videos were embedded into my head. A lot of people my age who were 15, 16, you'd come home from school and put on MTV. And a lot of people my age cannot forget him just dancing around, singing into those drumsticks. Things like that almost become part of the song itself. So in the '80s his songs now had another dimension to them, from the visuals in the videos. Because I don't know about you, but when I hear the song today, I'm still thinking of him singing into those drumsticks.

Look, we all get images in our minds when we listen to songs, and person to person, that can be very different. But in the '80s, many of us seemed to share the same exact image because of the MTV video, and that makes it part of the song. And I believe Phil's quoted in a book saying this is his favourite Genesis song. Do I think it's the best? No. And I don't think real Genesis fans would either. And we know what we mean when we say real—the prog fans. But it's a fine pop song. I'd even call it a pop rock song. The production on this album is dated, but a good song like this can overcome it.

Bill: Opening track, title track… if you're familiar at all with the Will Smith show *The Fresh Prince of Bel-Air*, I picture Carlton from that show dancing to this every time, his particular goofy dance. I can't help it, but every time the song opens up, that's what I see. I see Carlton doing his ridiculous dance. It's the only No.1 hit they had in the US. Tony's keys are so catchy and so at ease, but a bit annoying. Still, my head involuntarily bobs side-to-side while this is playing. I don't want to like it, but can't stop bobbing and bopping. It's irresistible. The keyboard break from 1:45 to 2:00 is pretty cool. It kind of breaks up the upbeat stuff there. It's really short, but nice. And Mike is doing some tasteful, understated stuff under all the hooks. How this was their only No.1 hit, I'll never understand. But I do like the song more than I used to, despite my own misgivings about liking it.

Martin: "Tonight, Tonight, Tonight" is pretty admirable, isn't it? It's futuristic *Abacab*-forward Genesis, to the point of nearly masquerading as a Peter Gabriel song.

Ralph: As I was looking at the record for the first time, I noticed that "Tonight, Tonight, Tonight" has this eight-minute or so running time and I'm thinking, thank Christ that "Invisible Touch" was just this single, the new "That's All" or whatever, which is actually a song I adore. Anyway, it's the pop song to lure us in. And then I listened to "Tonight, Tonight, Tonight" and it sounded half-finished, half-baked. It sounded like there was none of that journey that went

Invisible Touch

with Genesis, none of those melodies and textures. It sounded like a collection of like bleeps and blurps and weird jungle toms. It sounded tossed-off, and then stretched to an outrageous length.

I didn't know this at the time, but Phil had written those lyrics as just this grab bag of clichés. And then it sort of chugged along and didn't go anywhere. And I sat looking at that the cover, the Bill Smith cover, and it did nothing for me either. And I just thought, what has happened to this band? So as I got into the record for the first time—and again, stand by, because this all changes—the disappointment that was established with "Invisible Touch" just kept going. And the other thing about "Tonight, Tonight, Tonight" is it had that sin of having a chorus that went "Tonight, tonight, tonight, whoa!" Which of course, sticking in a "whoa!," that now has been a staple for 20 years for people in lieu of writing a good lyric. Just do a "whoa!" It sounded awful to me.

Jamie: "Tonight, Tonight, Tonight" was used in a 1986 Michelob commercial. See? You could not get away from Phil Collins' voice in the '80s. Even when you tried to watch a TV show, he appeared in the commercials. It's a cool, moody song that lies somewhere between "Mama" and "In the Air Tonight."

And the video is moody as well. There's lots of purples and mist and fog. They're silhouetted and in shadow most of the time and there's this chain link fence and they're set up in what looks like the bad part of town. I will say that it makes for an odd single. It's surprising that a song like this was such a hit. It's not a short song, although, granted, it's 4:32 for the single version, along with 6:18 for the music video version, oddly. You really can't dance to it. It has this whole synthesizer part in the middle that verges on prog and yet it still made it to No.3 on the American singles chart.

But you know, even these days I'm surprised at what becomes a hit. I hear a song by Billie Eilish and think why is this moody, depressing song so popular? So if you put me out there as a scout to tell you what could and what couldn't be a hit, I'd be the wrong person. I only know what's a hit in this house to my ears. One more thing, it's weird that in this song "Tonight, Tonight, Tonight," "in too deep" is part of the lyrics, when the actual song "In Too Deep" is two tracks away.

Bill: I like the sinister opening atmosphere of this song. It sounds to me like Phil's drumming on woodblocks at one point, but I'm sure it's electronic. It doesn't need to be so long, but I'm glad that it is. The single cut is an abomination to me. I'm not a big fan of single edits anyway, with some rare exceptions. But this is one of those that needs to have that long, slow build and that jam in the middle. It was interesting to me that this song, which is largely about addiction and trying to score drugs, was famously used in a Michelob beer commercial. Was that deliberate? Were they tone-deaf? Did they not realise what they were doing there? It reads like an inside joke. And Jamie's right; it's got the same kind of incessant drone that you get with "Mama."

Martin: Next we have "Land of Confusion," which is perky like "Just a Job to Do," and I guess, more adjacently, "Invisible Touch."

Ralph: Yes, and it's a serious song lyrically, but again, it also had a "whoa!" as part of the chorus. Plus it had a terrible video.

Jamie: Yes, like the first two songs, this song brings in that other dimension, the shared visuals in our minds of the video. I mean, who hears this song without thinking of those puppets in that video? I can't. They were done by a British TV series called *Spitting Image*. If you go to the Wikipedia page for this song, two paragraphs are about the song and ten paragraphs are about the video. Isn't that crazy? And the video starts off with Ronald and Nancy Reagan going to bed at 4:30 in the afternoon. And when Ronald lays down on his pillow, you hear a squeaking noise. So it's kind of funny. It was played nonstop in 1986 and '87 and we just could not take our eyes off this video as teenagers. But now I watch it, and in certain parts, it's creepy as hell. There's a YouTube comment that was so good, I just had to share it. "It's ironic that the Disturbed video is less disturbing than this one." Because Disturbed covered this song.

But as a song, it kicks at least a little bit of ass, even with the dated production, most notable through the electronic drums. It has a lot of things going against it, but somehow it rises above it all and still becomes this giant rock anthem without having any real aspects of actual rock music in it. It's like they pulled off some sort of magic trick. So like you said, it's a little bit like "Just a Job to Do"—it comes off as a rocker without any rock aspects to the song, although, granted, there's something of an edge. And the lyrics mean just as much today as they meant then. "There's not much love to go 'round" probably means even more today than it did then. So to everyone out there reading, let's try to do our part "to make it a place worth living in."

Martin: Anything else you can remember about the video?

Jamie: It ends with like a parody of USA for Africa. And there's the line, "Superman, where are you now?" In the song, I think they want the actual Superman to come and make this world a better place. But they got Ronald Reagan dressed up as Superman, like he's going to save the world. I don't know whether they're sincere about that or that's just kinda satire there. Those faces though, man, they looked like the California Raisins from the same era, you know, in that commercial (laughs). We used to think back then that the detail was so great on those puppets. Now I look at them and they're just creepy.

Bill: With "Land of Confusion," at this point it's easier to tell who is playing which instruments and making which sounds, unlike on the last album. Lyrically, it's a somewhat generic call-to-arms. It's like, sorry guys, your generation didn't put it right and you did make promises never kept. It's got sequenced bass from Tony, very electronic drums from Phil, simple guitar punctuations from Mike, and yet somehow this thing rocks pretty hard. It strikes me as a slowed-down, synthed-up version of "Just a Job to Do." It's the designated rock station track, basically. And of course this was covered by Disturbed in 2005. They had it on their third album, *Ten Thousand Fists*.

Martin: Next, wow, Genesis have done a lot of ballads in their time, and this is certainly one of them.

Ralph: "In Too Deep," at first glance just seemed like a bland ballad. The thing about "In Too Deep" that I want to say, at the time, Genesis created and sequenced these album sides with purpose. They were journeys, and also everything they did, they earned, if that makes any sense. So you had a piece of music and the next one built on the last one and it just crescendo-ed. On *A Trick of the Tail*, "Mad Man Moon" is in many ways a crescendo of the first side of that album. It collects everything that's great. So far, "In Too Deep," they didn't earn that ballad. It was tedious. I felt betrayed, which was, again, a very lonely feeling for someone like me.

Martin: So crudely speaking, we're zero for four so far.

Ralph: Yes, definitely zero for four. But I will revisit this at the end and try to do it as economically as possible. Because what I felt as a

20-year-old, I do not in any way feel now as a 58-year-old. But for a variety of reasons.

Jamie: Now I don't know if you're gonna want to include this or not, because you're not a movie guy. But there's a lot of movie fans out there. Now, Patrick Bateman in *American Psycho* is quoted as saying "In Too Deep" is the most moving pop song of the 1980s about monogamy and commitment. The song is extremely uplifting. The lyrics are as positive and affirmative as anything I've heard in rock. That's a character played by Christian Bale in *American Psycho*. He loved 1980s pop music, and he loved to dissect it and discuss it with his victims as he put on rubber gloves and lay down plastic to kill them. There's a lot of readers out there who know exactly what I'm talking about.

But here's the thing. Do I agree with Mr. Bateman? No. So I'd be killed even quicker. It gets a little too close to "A Groovy Kind of Love," which is Phil solo. This would have worked better on a Phil Collins solo record and it's probably the most poppy Genesis song of all time. I mean, there's not a lot to say about it. That's why I talked about the quote from *American Psycho* for so long, just so I had something to say about it. Even the video was kind of boring. Everyone is dressed in pinks and purples and it's very glossy and just not my favourite.

Martin: What do you think is the statement being made in *American Psycho* about this song?

Jamie: He does it with Huey Lewis as well. It's this contrast of how can this guy who's killing people love this peppy pop music at the same time? And love it so much that he loves to talk about it with his victims. It's like, is he really going to kill them? Doesn't he just want to continue to talk about music almost as a friend? Why would you kill these people that you want to have this nice conversation with about music? It creates this weird contrast in the movie.

Martin: Maybe this music is so horrible, that only the most horrible people in the world could like it.

Jamie: Or it's supposed to be horrible. And dated. Maybe. And he does one of the worst dances as he describes the music in the movie, to make it even more awful.

Martin: But it's like the least critically acclaimed music there is, right?

Jamie: Yes. The very least. So in a way, it kind of makes him a shallow person. That he would think this is as good as music gets. He doesn't have that personal connection with people or regular emotions.

Martin: Do you remember anything else about the band's own video for the song?

Jamie: They have these pink stairs and half the video is Phil walking up the stairs and back down the stairs. Everyone's moving very slow. There's not a lot going on.

Martin: That video is about as '80s as you can possibly get.

Jamie: Yeah, it has all the colours that they used in *Miami Vice*. You know the whites, the pinks, the purples, and they're all in these matching *Miami Vice* suits.

Bill: "In Too Deep" is another song from this album that I took for granted because it was played so much on the radio. But now I appreciate it a lot more. You get that, "Crying at the top of my voice" line where Phil does his high-pitched soul man vocal, which I think is quite lovely. The lyrics in the chorus are so generic, I can never remember the proper order to sing along with them. But it still somehow works for me. It's a pure pop gem, and very well-constructed. Mike plays some simple but effective guitar accents that remind me of David Gilmour and Mark Knopfler. From 3:08 to 3:34, Tony has this sweet keyboard bridge that nicely sets up the final verse and choruses. Phil effortlessly sells this vocal. No wonder every soccer mom in 1986 was swooning over the teddy bear. I don't think I really appreciated back then what a good singer Phil was; I took him for granted.

Martin: You know, you have *Invisible Touch* and *No Jacket Required*, and then suddenly there's Mike + The Mechanics with "Silent Running (On Dangerous Ground)" and "All I Need Is a Miracle." They really did rule the mid-'80s.

Bill: And then there's poor Tony.

Martin: Yeah, I guess he had *The Fugitive* in '83 and then *Bankstatement* way up into 1989. He never lit the world on fire with his solo career.

Bill: You're not alone in thinking that.

Martin: Next we have the perky and poppy "Anything She Does," which offers a number of interesting textures.

Ralph: Yes, and continuing with my first impression story, I remember that I flipped the record over and again, the label's green, which, unconsciously, it's just a nicer thing to look at. And a wave of a relief rolls over me as soon as the needle hits. It starts with real drums, a drum lick. And yeah, it's a synth horn line, but it's a cool synth horn line. But the whole thing has bottom end to it, and for the first time, it's a band jamming. I remember thinking, this is interesting, it's such a contrast and maybe there's a concept. I'm not sure what's happening.

But it doesn't matter because I'm loving this. Again, side one suffered from such banality in the lyrics. I didn't get that with "Land of Confusion," but the other three, maybe coincidentally, were Phil lyrics. It doesn't really matter. I won't blame him because it was a collective. I know at that point, as soon as everything became group-written, they would kind of hand out whoever felt... as Phil once put it, whoever was not exhausted with the song was chosen to do the lyric.

But with "Anything She Does," that first track on side two, the lyric is, "You know, you decorate the garage walls/Hang in people's halls/Live in secret drawers." What a lyric—just magical! It's an enigmatic, poetic, mysterious line that had just a trace of, "I'm talking to you, you know. And, you know I know." It's telling me that I know exactly what the singer is talking about. I'm completely immersed in the music because the music is authentic, and the lyric is drawing me in as well.

And then, during the chorus, one of the great moments is, "Or be the cause of anything she does," It's a Tony Banks lyric. A great poet or a great lyricist hits on an angle. There's so many angles that have been done over and over around the idea of yearning and sadness and the unachievable in the romance world. So when you hear a lyric that finds another angle, it's so inspiring. "I'll never get to know her/ Or be the cause of anything she does" is his way of saying I'll never be relevant to this person's life. And even if this person is a fantasy, it still relates to what you feel. When you imagine yourself with whoever you want to be with, it's heartbreaking to never be the cause of anything. You don't exist.

And I remember as a 20-year-old—and still now—thinking, that guy's a great lyricist. I don't know how long it took him to write that, but it's all wrapped up in this really tight, four-minute pop song. And to me that was Genesis correcting for the misfiring on side one and reclaiming themselves. Great structure, powerful tune. Again, Phil is throwing in cool drum things, like this great little flam on the snare at 3:32. Everyone's just feeling it, man, Mike's guitar, how they end that song, how it just kind of breaks down, it gives that sense that you're in the studio and that there was a jam. It's so entirely different from side one.

Bill: "Anything She Does" is much like the title track but even more so. I'm learning to reluctantly enjoy this song. For the longest time, it just annoyed me. I thought it was very awkward musically and vocally. But I'm learning to have fun with it. Like I mentioned earlier, it's basically another one where Tony is coming up with an imaginary woman, or an unattainable woman, an unknowable pinup model. But the music, especially the opening sequence, leaves me feeling assaulted. And they couldn't even bring in the Earth, Wind & Fire horns here; instead Tony does it all on his own. But I'm reluctantly coming around to it. It's getting its hooks in me against my will.

Jamie: Believe it or not, "Anything She Does" also got made into a video for MTV. And it featured Benny Hill as a security guard. He does this whole comedic bit that lasts for a minute-and-a-half before the song starts. And then he's hamming it up for the whole rest of the song as it plays. The video is actually better than the song itself. But here's the thing, when you have a good song, you can overcome thin, dated production. When you have a song that's not that great, all you're left with is the thin and dated production and I'd say that's what we have here. And those fake horns are a little too close to sounding like the horns in "Sussudio." I don't know anyone who likes that song. But if you watch the somewhat amusing video, it does make the pain a little better.

Martin: It's like they're making a bit of a statement using Benny Hill and the *Spitting Image* puppets. Those are two iconic British cultural references.

Jamie: Right. And you know what everyone thought when that video came out? Is Benny Hill still alive?!

Martin: Next the band indulge in their penchant for complicated song titles, with "Domino," which is split into two parts.

Ralph: Yes, and part one is called "In the Glow of the Night," which is one of those songs that makes me think this is the greatest band ever. It might be the immediacy of the vocal melody, it might be the arrangement, and it might be the sounds. There's what sounds like vibes, some percussion instrument, on that first verse. There's also the gentle keyboard that rolls along with the lyric, "Rain keeps running down the window pane/Time is running out for me." Again, it's a lyric that says so much. It's not bromides and it's not tossed-off. It's a suggestion. It paints a picture of what's going to happen, of expectation, of curiosity, like an amazing novel would do. It's so literary and it's so representative of Banks on top of his game.

And then the song just explodes, from an arrangement point of view. The drums come smashing in, and in tandem you get the full weight of Phil's vocals. You realise that he's hit a peak vocally. It leads into that drum break, which, like on "Invisible Touch," or even the self-titled album, demonstrates Phil's and the band's ability to seamlessly combine those technologies, the old world and the new world. So Phil starts with Simmons, and then he goes to that barking drum sound that just gives me chills every time. I don't know if it's the black Pearl kit he was using, but he's got that popping, barking tom sound, the concert tom sound. It's just an unbelievably thrilling moment on the back of the moody piece that just happened seconds before.

And it's tagged or hung together with this vaguely apocalyptic lyric from Tony that's delivered in this sort of fat vocal from Phil. As the song moves along and they find that section again, the second drum break is impossibly even more powerful than the first one. He's just hammering those drums. The sound that Hugh Padgham captures on those toms, I've just never heard that before and I've never heard it since; it's just masterful production.

The other thing I want to say about this song is that Phil's talked about that line, "Sheets of double glazing help to keep outside the night." He often complained about Tony's lyrics being hard to sing. Elvis always comes to mind, or Sinatra. Roger Daltrey would be another example. Like Phil, in the rock idiom, even if Roger has a tough time with the lyrics, he squeezes everything out of them. Both he and Phil are like brilliant actors. They just know how to get emotion out of lines that maybe even they don't understand.

And you never knew at that point. Phil got churlish in his later years, being critical of Tony, with "All in a Mouse's Night." "Burning Rope" was another one. But he sings those lines seamlessly, beautifully, melodiously, dramatically. "In the Glow of the Night" is Genesis in absolute full flight. It's as good as anything I ever heard them do. And when I heard that song for the first time, it was an absolutely joyous moment. It erased every single sin that I perceived to be present on side one. I though, man, these guys are absolutely on it.

And then the second part of "Domino," "The Last Domino," kicks in. At the time, it bothered me—and it still bothers me—that people during that period were claiming that Phil's solo material sounded like Genesis, which has always been so lazy and ignorant to me. One of the ways I would combat that is that I would tell people to listen to his vocal on "Domino." He never sings like that as a solo artist. He never even came close to singing with that kind of visceral power. He's so aggressive and yet he never loses the sense of being a melodic singer, which is what all the absolute greats can do. But that's why he was in Genesis, in part, so that he could use that side of himself.

The other thing about "The Last Domino" is the song's construction, how dynamic it is, and how the quiet bits demonstrate such a high degree of detail arrangement-wise. That's using a template of Genesis going right back. Certainly, you reach a high point with *The Lamb* in the Gabriel years, but it's all through the post-Gabriel years as well. For example, there's this kind of fluttering tambourine I couldn't help but hone in on; it's such a wonderful detail. You can get lost in a good tambourine part. It's worth its weight in gold.

Another thing that strikes me about "The Last Domino" is how he approaches the Simmons drums. In some ways, it's much like "Invisible Touch." I couldn't detect any acoustic drums in "The Last Domino," unlike "In the Glow of the Night." It's all Simmons. The difference between how he uses them in "The Last Domino" and how he uses them in "Invisible Touch" is that "Invisible Touch"... Phil used to talk about staccato drums. They were a type of drum that the guy in The Payolas used, I believe, and maybe even Alan White; I can't remember. But he was very dismissive of staccato drums. He was talking about new technology in drums, and he said, "They just leave me cold."

But how he used the Simmons on "Invisible Touch" left me cold, because it seemed like the technology was playing him, if that makes any sense. And with "The Last Domino," he's manhandling those Simmons drums. He's using all the great shit and the invention that was his stock and trade as an acoustic player. But he's doing it with Simmons drum. So all of a sudden, that makes sense to me. It was a bold and creative choice to do something as powerful as that, save for the artifice that is inevitably created by using an electronic instrument. So I was intoxicated by it. It was so bold and inventive and it was played by the guy who did "In the Air Tonight." It was that kind of creativity.

And it's not just creativity. Again, all great bands do this, but it's choosing the right tool for the job and going with it. "In the Air Tonight" is legendary. Phil always talks about how he did nine different fills and that was the one he liked best. All these great records by these great artists, you get to hear the process when you're allowed to hear some outtakes. But they know exactly what to do, or in this case, which performance is right.

And with his approach to the Simmons on "The Last Domino," he was saying, "I know how to deal with this technology. I'll sell you on how good this instrument can sound and how it makes sense for this song." And I don't know whether anyone else would approach that song that way. Check out his drumming at 8:55 to about 9:10 on "Domino;" it's just great playing. That was never reproduced live. Much like "In the Glow of the Night," a lot of Genesis songs suffered in the live environment, ironically. Not that they were necessarily slaves to production and arrangement, but the translation when Daryl and Chester got involved ended up somewhat lost. They are first-class players of course, but I never felt Chester really understood Phil. Or perhaps it was because he was given a lot more freedom as his tenure with Genesis continued, but I never felt that he did justice to what Phil was doing. Anyway, that's an aside, and no slight on him—Chester's brilliant.

Another thing about the "Domino" thing as a suite of songs is how the lyric perspective shifts from the first part, which is about fear and grief and vulnerability and sadness. It's a very emotional piece of work, very moving. "Domino" is all Banks' lyrics. It's got satire in it, plus humour and delusion and rage. So as much as it contrasts musically, I don't know how long it took him to write those lyrics, or how much of this was conscious or not. But that transition works, because there's a continuity—the story makes it continuous.

There's that double use of, "Do you know what you have done?/ Do you know what you've begun?" This is recorded in early '86, or late '85. It's the middle of the Cold War. The Russians had invaded Afghanistan and they also had shot down that Korean airliner. But this was still years before the wall came down. Maybe it's the early days of the emergence of glasnost and perestroika. In any event, this fear hung over the western world that it could end at any moment.

And why "Domino" is relevant to that line, that couplet in particular, "Do you know what you have done?/Do you know what you've begun?," I think of October 7 in Israel, I think of the invasion of Ukraine. Those words are evergreen. As long as there are humans, there's going to be war. And there are going to be troubadours, like Tony Banks, writing a set of lyrics that manage to capture not just the dread, but the enormous tragedy on a personal level of war, often done without the acquiescence of the population for scores settled from a thousand years before.

So in my world, that song would be played right now. Remember, during that period in the '80s, Mike + The Mechanics had done "Silent Running," Ultravox had done "Dancing with Tears in My Eyes" and Queen had done "Hammer to Fall." So there are writers talking about that existential dread of what could happen. All those songs should be played now, not least of which because they're also great songs.

Martin: Great stuff; thanks for that. Jamie, what are your thoughts on "Domino?"

Jamie: Okay, well, the first part of the song is called "In the Glow of the Night," and it combines pop rock and prog in a "Home by the Sea" sort of way. And this first part was the B-side to the "Tonight, Tonight, Tonight" single. And the second part is called "The Last Domino," and it was the B-side to the "Invisible Touch" single. Which is weird, since "Invisible Touch" was released first. So everyone who bought the two 45s got part two first.

My question is, did they do this song because they wanted to keep their prog reputation somewhat intact, or was it something that they really wanted to do? It seems to me that the people who came for the pop songs would be turned off by this and the people who appreciate this proggy song being on the album would be turned off by some of the pop songs. If they were going for the mostly pop direction on this album, they probably should have stuck with it. Because "Domino" feels a bit out of place. When it comes down to it, *Invisible Touch* is a bit disjointed because of this track. "Domino" doesn't seem like it belongs on the same album as "In Too Deep." But which of these is more out-of-place? Is it the more elaborate "Domino" or the more sappy "In Too Deep" or is it a tie?

I will say that the second half, "The Last Domino," sounds like prog being played on the wrong instruments and with the wrong production. Songs like "Dodo" and "Lurker" from *Abacab* and "Duke's Travels" and "Duke's End" from *Duke* still muster up a proggy edge even though they're both from the '80s. But this sounds too much like dated 1980s instruments along with quite egregious 1980s production, with the Simmons drums being one of the main culprits. You know what it reminds me of? It reminds me of that Jimmy Fallon bit, Classroom Instruments. He did it with The Who for "Won't Get Fooled Again" and Metallica with "Enter Sandman." They all crowd together and they play kids' instruments, along with the band, to these classic songs. It was funny, but it was definitely the wrong instruments used for those songs.

Bill: Like the other songs, I've gained a new appreciation for "Domino." Originally, I just focussed on the love song angle in it, but, of course, it goes a lot deeper than that. You've got the idea of dominoes. Tony was thinking about politicians and the actions that they take, and once they take those actions, how that sets off a chain of dominoes that fall everywhere that they no longer have control over. It's an anti-war song set in the nuclear age. Tony's lyric is vague enough to be surprising and universally effective.

As it progresses, the music becomes tense, with these keyboard stabs. Then there's a minute of peace and the "In silence and darkness" lyric, before the music becomes violent again, in tandem with the lyric, "Blood on the windows." Lyrically, this part of the song is a bit surreal. Is he dreaming? And then the violence-addicted audience tunes in to see the war on TV. They watch as each domino falls. That part where it first really starts speeding up, I can feel my heartbeat thumping, and that's kind of what the music sounds like. It's like someone's panicking. Someone's really afraid and nervous. It's an effective piece of music.

Martin: I'm just fascinated by the characters of Mike and Tony. I don't know; do you get the feeling that they're the quintessential kind of jerky aristocratic English rock stars? That they are the reason punk had to happen? That they are just detached or a few layers removed from their fan base, sort of thing? At the same time, I wonder if they even realise how talented they are. I don't think they get enough credit, which leads back to the first point, that they just don't seem like they are in the trenches, so they wind up sort of anonymous. I mean, even just lyrically, they write some pretty heavy stuff.

Bill: Well, yeah, I think of the two, Tony gets the reputation as the proper, upper class English guy that puts his nose in the air or that is above it all. But if anything, Mike's possibly a bit snobbier than Tony, from what I've seen. I think Tony is nicer than his reputation. One thing about him though, he does have a bit of that cut-throat attitude where he fights to get his material on the albums. But he apparently has a sense of humour too. If you check out some of his interviews, he's got that dry, English sense of humour. The way I see it, Tony's come a long way from the English schoolboy thing.

Martin: Phil can be quite cranky as well. Which is understandable, given what he's been through health-wise, relationship-wise, even with the critics, most notably when it comes to the solo stuff.

Bill: But everybody sees him as a big teddy bear too. Even on that last tour, where he was confined to a chair and was a shadow of his former self, he was still that loveable teddy bear. I've read his autobiography. He did a lot of sketchy stuff throughout his life and didn't always treat people well, including his wives. But he's still a likeable and even loveable guy. It's like, "Come on now. We've got a groovy kind of love, folks. It's me, Phil. You can't hate on me. Won't you forgive me?" (laughs).

Martin: The guys score yet another big hit from this album with "Throwing It All Away." Where does this one land with you guys?

Ralph: Okay, so I know I said with "In Too Deep" that they hadn't earned it. "Throwing It All Away," they earned this. It's an unabashed love song in a long, beautiful line of Mike Rutherford lyrics which include "Your Own Special Way," "Follow You Follow Me," "Alone Tonight," "Like It or Not" from *Abacab* and "Taking It All Too Hard" from the self-titled. I'm just picking a Rutherford lyric from each album, to show that there was a singular creative line of Mike Rutherford's work.

By this point, he'd hit a real purple patch, in terms of being able to write a nakedly vulnerable and beautiful set of lyrics that had enough poetry in them that you never must mistook them as just a tossed-off love song. Rutherford was easily as good as Collins, and some might say better. But he was on the same track as Phil was. At less than four minutes long, "Throwing It All Away" is perfectly sequenced on side two. You need that moment that this song brings. It never worked live for me, because it was stretched out into some kind of showpiece. Nothing beats the studio version. There's this economical and pure Ringo-style drumming from Phil where he plays completely without ego. There's no ego on that song at all. It's just what it is. It's one of the best love songs I've ever heard to this day.

Jamie: "Throwing It All Away" is the sixth song from *Invisible Touch* to get an MTV video—that's six out of eight. But again, people need reminding that it's not a Phil Collins solo song. I would call it a better "In Too Deep." This takes every dated '80s production trope and makes it work within the song. It's the opposite of "Domino," which suffers because of the production. Here it enhances the song. Since it's written as a good pop song in the '80s, it needs to have those '80s production values. It's just like the 1980s Madonna albums, where the '80s production on those albums enhances the pop songs. I don't want those Madonna songs to have the same production values as the 1990s Alanis Morissette album.

Bill: It's a simple but strong pop song with a lyric by Mike. Only one person wants to end this love affair. Tony's keys on Phil's vocals really milk those lyrics in the choruses. The final lyrics, where it gets into, "Late at night when you call my name/The only sound you'll hear is the sound of your voice calling, calling after me," that's brutal. That's a real kiss-off. Like, you had your chance, but it's too late now; see what you've done.

At the music end, Tony's keys on this one are much more traditional. He's not trying to do anything weird. It's just very lovely but only slightly more modern Tony. It's not like he's trying to resurrect the sounds of the '70s. It's very '80s, but not new wave. In fact it's almost adult contemporary, and I don't mean that as an insult. Yeah, this was a well-deserved hit. Who would have thought that these guys would be writing ballads like this?

Invisible Touch

Martin: We end with another tradition, a closing instrumental on a Genesis album. Is "The Brazilian" a successful one?

Bill: Absolutely. I love that we get this weird, Prince-like instrumental on what is otherwise a smash hit album of pop songs and even pretty conservative ballads. Can you imagine all the people that bought this because of "In Too Deep" and "Invisible Touch" and then they get confronted with "Domino" and "The Brazilian?" I wonder how many people got to the end of their cassette and fast-forwarded past "The Brazilian" to get back to "Invisible Touch" on the other side. It reads like the follow-up to "Second Home by the Sea." But seriously, go listen to "Darling Nikki" from Prince's *Purple Rain* and tell me these guys weren't listening. It's not a clone, but the sounds and vibe are there. A little more than a minute into the song, it definitely gets this "Darling Nikki" sound too it. It seems like Genesis, much like Rush, were absorbing influences, and timing-wise, this was exactly two years after *Purple Rain*, which was huge. But of course, despite the instrumental, this is the album that put Genesis in arenas. This is their most commercially successful era. And yet they've got a couple songs that are nine and 11 minutes long—that beats *A Trick of the Tail*, prog fans.

Ralph: Contrasting side two with side one, the album starts with "Invisible Touch," which is awash in technology. "The Brazilian," undoubtedly, is the same thing. It's so dense and drenched in this technology and these toys and these new keyboard sounds that Tony has brought in. So why does it work? Is it that the great guitar solo at the end? Is the melody provocative and interesting? Or is it merely the sequencing? With this song serving as the palate-cleanser of side two, which I don't mean in a negative sense.

Jamie: "The Brazilian" is a weird little track. It reminds you that there's a thin line between prog and quirkiness. Just because something is weird, it doesn't make it prog—see "Who Dunnit?." But sequencing it at the end of the album doesn't work for me. I would have put it after "Domino." That way, you have all the pop songs grouped-up, and then the album ends with these two proggy, quirky pieces. It would have saved the pop fans the act of having to skip "Domino" to get to "Throwing It All Away" and then get back up to eject it before this track starts. They could have just ejected the CD after the first six tracks and be done with it. Because there are girls—

and some guys—who just want to hear the hits and the songs that sounded like hits, and "The Brazilian" and "Domino" are getting in the way.

Martin: It's funny; every time a band ends an album with an instrumental, I think the singer's not really into the band, that he left the studio early.

Jamie: Or they had something unfinished that they just threw on at the end to fill out the time. Sort of like, okay, it's a wrap. Can we go home now?

Martin: All right, so Ralph, you've been promising. You say you came around on this album past those slightly negative initial reactions. Tell us more!

Ralph: Okay, well, we've been through this journey. We've had the frolic and fun of "Anything She Does" and the energy and the power of that. But then we've gone to another place. And then we've had the release with the love song. And now we're going to leave you with something to ruminate, which is a great place for an instrumental. I don't know why "The Brazilian" works. It just does. It's not a mere exercise, necessarily. Although the guitar solo is great, there's nothing flashy about it. It's all mood. That whole song is mood and melody. Again, that's what makes Genesis great.

So yes, to wrap up, I still have all those strong, positive thoughts I had about side two; those are as strong as they've ever been. But overall, I initially called *Invisible Touch* the final album. It feels like it's the end of an era for that band. It's the end of the arc with Hugh Padgham. He came on with *Abacab*, he'd done the self-titled and he did *Invisible Touch* and then he was gone. So there was that part of it. He shifted the band or he helped shift the band. Or he met a band that were so open to being musically, sonically and profoundly pushed in new directions, which, for a guy like me who hopped on board with *Abacab*, Hugh Padgham is a hero.

But it's broader than that. Obviously *Invisible Touch* is not literally the final album, but it represents a perfect moment. Genesis were very much a vibrant part of the music scene in the mid-'80s. There were always going to be negative people who only liked the Gabriel era or thought because these guys were in their mid-30s, that they were dinosaurs. I went to see Genesis on that tour at the CNE in September of '86. I was 20, so any reference I might have made to being 19, I was 20 when that came out. The crowd was all kids. That's my prevailing memory. Kids, a lot of girls too, a lot of smoking up and drinking, but not 30-year-olds, in my memory of it. I could tell, because when they did the "In the Cage" medley—and at that point on the early part of that tour, they went into "Apocalypse in 9/8," which was so thrilling—that's when everyone went for beer.

So the negative side is, oh, well, they just attracted a bunch of newer fair weather fans or whatever. But that's actually beside the point. The point is, they were part of the music scene as much as George Michael and Prince were, in my mind. They were in the thick of it.

And they had evolved. They didn't do Yes. They didn't bring in a young guitarist and then you have the repackaged Yes. And they didn't do an Emerson, Lake & Powell, where they brought in a new guy but didn't really change their approach. ELP was updated, but it was still very much the case that you could mistake Emerson, Lake & Powell, that album, for Emerson, Lake & Palmer. The distance wasn't that great.

And the other thing about *Invisible Touch* is, it was a reflection of this balance that they had created within Genesis against their solo careers. This used to get a lot of media attention. They'd ask Phil, especially, "Why are you still in Genesis?" But when Phil would say, "I get something out of Genesis that I don't get from my solo career," you believed it. And Rutherford now had Mike + The Mechanics. So there's a little more balance there. But it was the synergy, ideally, of everything you learned from your solo experiences that you'd put back into the band. That's what *Invisible Touch* felt like to me. And that was an amazing recipe.

I don't know if you know this, but the *Invisible Touch* tour was very, very long. It stretched, from... I saw them in September '86 and they basically went full-bore, I think, until July of '87 when they did a big stand at Wembley, which they made a video out of. And coincidentally, days after that tour ended, that's when I met Phil in front of his house. And he was just drained. He looked like a corpse. Anyway, that's an aside.

The thing is, something had changed at the end of that tour. This is my speculation borne out by how things played out. But if you look at the chronology of *Invisible Touch*, you had—bear with me—*Abacab, Three Sides Live, Acting Very Strange, Hello, I Must Be Going* and Tony Banks' album, *The Fugitive*. Then Phil explodes as a producer. "Easy

Lover" is a huge thing. Then he does *No Jacket Required*. Then we get Mike + The Mechanics and then we get *Invisible Touch*. So all this creativity and all this output is happening. I talked about this earlier, but it's an extraordinary time to be a Genesis fan. When the *Invisible Touch* tour ends, that's when Phil does *Buster*. That's when he kind of changes. We get a Mike + The Mechanics album in '88. Tony's solo career is just never gonna get off the ground. So by the time we get to *We Can't Dance*, Genesis now feels like a hobby. Are you following any of this? Does any of this makes sense?

So now these guys are in their 40s, like five years later, too, right? It's taken them five years to put that record together. You watch the energy of the interviews they did to promote *Invisible Touch* versus the energy surrounding the *We Can't Dance* album and that tour there, it's like an uncomfortable coda to me, not even thinking about *Calling All Stations* or the reunion stuff. *Invisible Touch* was the last time we met Genesis in full flight, where everyone was on board, everyone believed, everybody was collaborating,

You know, I don't negate the team spirit of *We Can't Dance*, but Banks acknowledged that *Invisible Touch* was a commercial peak, a creative peak, possibly a collaborative and friendship peak. That's why I think it's the final album. It was never the same after that. It's the last time you heard Phil sing like that. It was the last time you heard him play like that. Again, that doesn't negate his big band stuff in the late '90s. It doesn't negate some of the stuff he did on some of his later records, specifically *Dance into the Light*. But that fire was out. Everybody's fire was out after *Invisible Touch*. The visceral experience had changed.

Which brings us back to *From Genesis to Revelation*, the debut from '69. One of the other reasons why I think it's final is it reflects the perfection of where they started. Mike and Tony, specifically, started in the late '60s as a songwriting collective. They went from being those humble Charterhouse guys—not humble financially, but just kids—to ruling the world in 19 years. Now they had nothing more to say, nothing more to do as songwriters. That's it. That's the arc. That's the big arc.

The other thing that hindsight provides, looking back, is it's impossible for me to look at *Invisible Touch* without looking at the *Invisible Touch* sessions. So Genesis were like McCartney, as someone who often left off the record some of his best, most inspired work. And *Invisible Touch*, you can't help but wonder how this record would have been received if they left off "In Too Deep" and stuck on the instrumental "Do the Neurotic." And if they found a way to put "Feeding the Fire" on.

When I sequence that record now, when I stream it or whatever, I always put "Do the Neurotic" on as the side one closer, and I stick "Feeding the Fire" in between "Throwing It All Away" and "Do the Neurotic" and it changes the record. One of the few good things about streaming is that you can still enjoy *Invisible Touch*, but you can slightly augment it with this material that for whatever reason they didn't put on. So that's how I look at that period now. Those are two very progressive songs. "Feeding the Fire" has great lyrics and I think they come from Mike. And "Do the Neurotic" is just them jamming. I'm not going to mention "I'd Rather Be You" because it's just a little pop song that was probably inferior to everything else.

The other thing is, I've changed my mind on side one over the years and it's because context is everything. I'm not 20 years old. I now look at records, especially from my past, as statements, as cohesive statements. And I can project onto them reasons why the artists made the decisions they did. That doesn't mean I've suddenly gone soft in the head. But I understand things now, and I give benefit where I didn't give benefit as a 20-year-old.

So the darkness in the "Invisible Touch" lyric, or the production touches that were sort of an anathema to me, all of a sudden those things are interesting to me, for whatever reason. On "Tonight, Tonight, Tonight," I didn't really see that. I didn't understand how that might have been an exercise in the very act of dispelling expectation, of creating mood over jam and visceral impact, of experimenting with sounds, of just doing something entirely different and seeing if you could pull it off over eight minutes. And I embrace that now. And I embrace the little guitar parts and the mood of Banks' keyboards. Now I think it's a superb track.

"Land of Confusion," I now understand how hard it is to create a lyric that balances that sense of rage, frustration and powerlessness, and within the same lyric have a small vignette of a family possibly being pulled apart or decimated by the broader effects of war in the Atomic Age. It's a beautifully-balanced lyric idea. And it's very catchy, and I don't pay attention to the video. It's just a great song which, again, is not done very well live.

And finally, "In Too Deep," I know it was used in a film called *Mona Lisa*, which isn't really relevant to me. But now of course, when I hear "In Too Deep," and how it tumbles along and how those toms work the way they do, I just feel the storm clouds of old age around the corner. I'd give my left nut, almost, to write a song as melodic as that one was.

So I guess, to sum all that up, I see side one as Genesis flexing their muscles as taught and accomplished pop songwriters with three of those tracks, while "Tonight, Tonight, Tonight" deliberately confounds expectations. Which is why Genesis lasted so long and their records are so relevant. Side two always represented—and still does—classic Genesis to me. And that's the statement I see with *Invisible Touch*, from side one through to side two. I love the contrast. That's the path I took toward this record becoming one of my favourite albums of all time.

Finally, I want to add about *Invisible Touch* that if you look at chapter and verse, its legacy has been undone by the very things I celebrate. It's considered a pop album. It's kind of peak Phil in terms of when Phil talks about it, he's so self-deprecating, it makes you nauseous. He's so apologetic about how he was on stage that he cringes and is embarrassed by it. And I think that sentiment, plus the fact that that record was their commercial apex, has robbed it of a clinical and educated reappraisal. And that's what I wanted to get across here as best as I could in a conversation like this. I'd like to get people to listen to it without the massiveness of the baggage that surrounded it. As noted, the Patrick Bateman bit in *American Psycho* also stained the record. *Invisible Touch* is a very, very, very hard record to defend, because of everything around it, and not because of the music itself. But yes, Bret Easton Ellis indeed contributed to the album's miserable stained legacy, and truthfully, I don't think its reputation will ever be rebuilt.

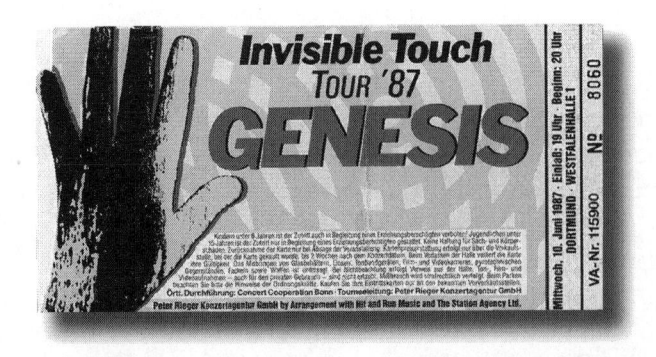

Invisible Touch

Behind The Lines: Genesis on Record 1978-1997

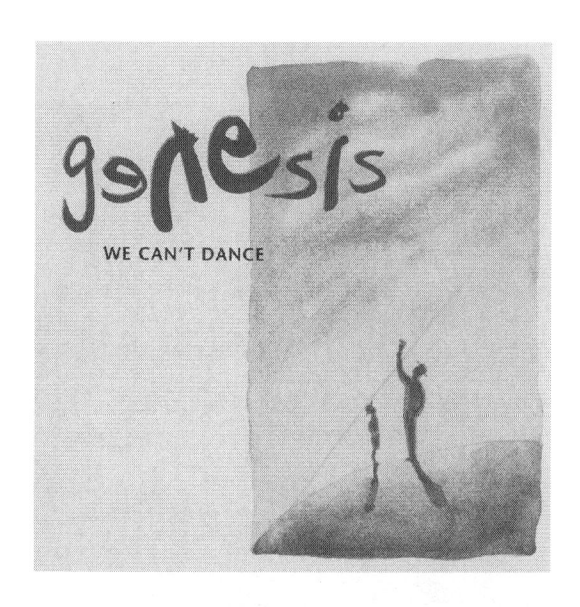

WE CAN'T DANCE

November 11, 1991
Virgin GEN CD3
Produced by Genesis and Nick Davis
Engineered by Nick Davis; assisted by Mark Robinson
Recorded at The Farm, Chiddingfold, Surrey, UK
Personnel: Phil Collins – drums, vocals, programming; Tony Banks – keyboards; Mike Rutherford – guitars, bass
All songs written by Genesis

1. No Son of Mine 6:39
2. Jesus He Knows Me 4:16
3. Driving the Last Spike 10:08
4. I Can't Dance 4:01
5. Never a Time 3:50
6. Dreaming While You Sleep 7:16
7. Tell Me Why 4:58
8. Living Forever 5:40
9. Hold on My Heart 4:38
10. Way of the World 5:39
11. Since I Lost You 4:09
12. Fading Lights 10:16

Entangled: Genesis on Record 1969-1976

A *We Can't Dance* Timeline

October 21, 1991. "No Son of Mine," backed with album track "Living Forever," is issued as an advance single from the forthcoming *We Can't Dance* album. It reaches No.6 in the UK and No.12 in the US.

November 11, 1991. Genesis issue *We Can't Dance*. By the end of the year, it is certified platinum and currently sits at four times platinum. The album becomes the band's fifth consecutive to reach No.1 on the UK charts and achieves a No.4 placement in the US.

December 30, 1991. "I Can't Dance" is issued as a single, backed with the non-LP "On the Shoreline." The track reaches No.7 on both the UK and US charts.

April 6, 1992. "Hold on My Heart" is issued as a single, backed with LP track "Way of the World." The A-side reaches No.16 in the UK and No.12 in the US.

April 16, 1992. *Invisible Touch* is certified five times platinum.

April 30 – June 25, 1992. The band tour the US and Canada in support of *We Can't Dance*.

June 28 – November 17, 1992. The band tour Europe, including Knebworth and Earls Court dates on home soil.

July 13, 1992. "Jesus He Knows Me" is issued as a single, backed with the non-LP "Hearts on Fire." It gets to No.20 in the UK and No.23 on Billboard.

August 11, 1992. *Genesis* is certified triple platinum.

September 15, 1992. *We Can't Dance* is certified three times platinum.

September 28, 1992. Peter Gabriel issues a sixth solo album, entitled *Us*, which certifies platinum.

October 19, 1992. "Never a Time" is issued as the fifth single from *We Can't Dance*.

November 16, 1992. Genesis issue a fourth live album, entitled *Live – The Way We Walk, Volume One: The Shorts*.

January 4, 1993. Genesis issue a fifth live album, entitled *Live – The Way We Walk, Volume Two: The Longs*.

February 8, 1993. "Tell Me Why" is issued as the final single from *We Can't Dance*, representing the last Genesis single with Phil Collins in the band. Royalties from the single went to the Save the Children and Red Cross charities.

February 24, 1993. "I Can't Dance" is nominated for a Grammy in the Best Pop Performance by a Duo or Group category but loses out to Celine Dion and Peabo Bryson's "Beauty and the Beast."

November 8, 1993. Phil Collins sees the release of a fifth studio album, entitled *Both Sides*, which certifies platinum.

April 25, 1994. Stiltskin perform on a song written by Peter Lawlor called "Inside." It's issued as a single on this day, having been used in a Levi Strauss & Co. commercial. The song becomes a No.1 hit in the UK and stays in the Top 100 for 11 weeks. It also makes the Top Ten is ten other countries. On lead vocals is future Genesis lead singer Ray Wilson.

October 17, 1994. Stiltskin, riding the fame of their single from earlier in the year, issue their debut album, *The Mind's Eye*.

March 6, 1995. Mike + The Mechanics issue a fourth album, called *Beggar on a Beach of Gold*.

September 11, 1995. Operating as Strictly Inc., Tony Banks and Wang Chung lead vocalist Jack Hues collaborate on a self-titled album.

March 4, 1996. Mike + The Mechanics see the release of a compilation called *Hits*. "All I Need Is a Miracle" is re-recorded for the occasion.

March, 29, 1996. Phil Collins announces he is leaving Genesis.

June 12, 1996. *Invisible Touch* is certified six times platinum. *Genesis* and *We Can't Dance* are certified four times platinum.

We Can't Dance

October 21, 1996. Phil Collins issues *Dance into the Light*, which goes gold.

December 5, 1996. Phil and Jill divorce, after ten years of marriage.

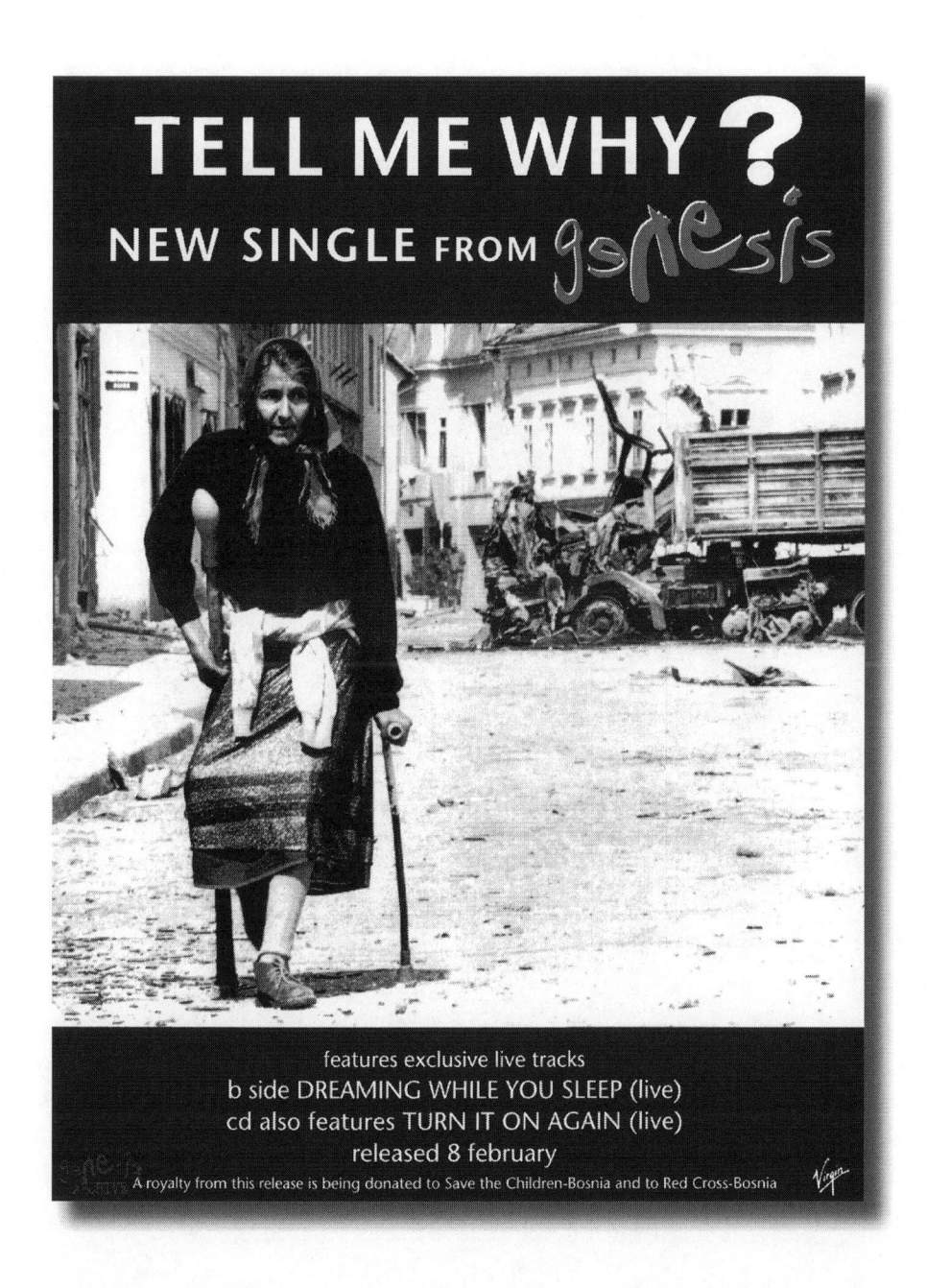

> **TELL ME WHY?**
> NEW SINGLE FROM genesis
>
> features exclusive live tracks
> b side DREAMING WHILE YOU SLEEP (live)
> cd also features TURN IT ON AGAIN (live)
> released 8 february
>
> A royalty from this release is being donated to Save the Children-Bosnia and to Red Cross-Bosnia

Behind The Lines: Genesis on Record 1978-1997

Martin talks to Todd Evans, David Gallagher and Douglas Maher about *We Can't Dance*.

Martin Popoff: Okay, now we're up to the last album with Phil Collins at the helm. Ralph's already declared *Invisible Touch* the final Genesis album of sorts, and I'm sure loads more people will call this the last album, given the messy end that is *Calling All Stations*. What are your views on *We Can't Dance*?

Todd Evans: Well, it's funny, because amongst Genesis fans, when this came out, or at least the Genesis fans that I knew and talked to, we were all in unanimous agreement that it was an improvement over *Invisible Touch*. *We Can't Dance*—and I actually think *Calling All Stations* as well—suffer from the whole, we can put 75 minutes on a CD, so let's make the album 75 minutes long. *We Can't Dance* is probably two tracks too long, which makes it difficult to learn. And for the casual fan, it makes it difficult for it to make much of an impression. I think that's its biggest weakness. But it's a departure, because they use Nick Davis instead of Hugh Padgham. And Nick Davis is very good; he gets the whole '80s gated drum sound absolutely perfect. It sounds like Hugh Padgham is there. So that was something I think they learned how to do on their own. But there's a big chunk of this album that has just regular drums on it, and I think that's really cool. But I would have left a couple of things off of it, and we'll get to what those are.

David Gallagher: I have to do a caveat here. My goal in preparation to talk to you was to listen to this record 25 times. And I'm going to imagine that I am not a muso, that I am not someone who knows the Crimson catalogue up and down, knows and loves most of Yes, knows Tull, knows all these classic bands. I'm going to imagine that I am 25 years old in 1991 and the last three albums I bought were Genesis, Bryan Adams and Enya, because I looked at what was selling in 1991. So I'm only buying the most popular of popular music essentially.

And Genesis, at this point, are just the epitome of popular mainstream music, and past their peak in a lot of ways. But for the mainstream, this is still that period where guys in their mid-40s could have massive hits. And how bizarre is it that guys in their mid-40s were considered old and past it, just a few decades ago (laughs). So that was the mindset I had for this. To reiterate, I'm going to imagine that I'm not a muso, but instead, the most casual fan. I'm the person who keeps up with music by who plays at the Super Bowl every year. And even then, I still struggle with most of this record. It's certainly going to be the most negative of anything I've given you in these books so far.

Martin: All right; I can't wait (laughs). Doug, any opening remarks before we get into individual songs? Well, let me ask you this. What is the personality dynamic of the band at this point? Have Mike, Tony and Phil risen to the top of the UK rock aristocracy? And if so, is it a stodgy, stuffy gathering of people in that room?

Doug Maher: Yeah, now that you mention it, I suppose there's an unbelievable amount of snootiness and arrogance in that room (laughs). I used to think that Bill Bruford had that kind of personality. He had that look on him like he was quietly judging you all the time. But he's not. Bill Bruford is actually a really nice man. He's a very intelligent man and he's a teacher, too. And wasn't Tony Banks also very well educated himself?

Martin: I'm not sure how that is possible. He became a full-time, working musician with records right out of high school.

Doug: No, I'm talking about musical background, a musical education. There's a progressive rock arrogance that exists. Anybody who's in progressive rock is intimidating. People approach musicians who are in these bands, and it always seems a chore for them to talk to you. They're not humble. There's a difference between the UK and the US. I don't know if there's a humbleness that doesn't exist in British musicians themselves or what. There's this dry, sarcastic wit that nobody else understands or grasps unless you live there. Unless you have a full appreciation and understanding of growing up with or living with people from there, you might take offense to it. But there's a highbrow level to that dynamic.

They were doing a documentary on Phil Collins. It's on YouTube. It's in like seven parts and it's just interviewing him. It's just him sitting in different rooms and different locations at various different times. I think it was done by a British producer. It looks like unused footage for a documentary. And Phil Collins gets into the most interesting conversations.

But what I noticed about it is that Phil Collins is completely approachable, because he has humility. He recognises his own faults and his own failures in life. Whereas Mike Rutherford and Banks, they're not the public eyes, they're not the public figures, to the extent that Phil Collins was. And there really is an arrogance about performers who stand in place and don't do anything other than just play their instrument, because they're so locked in.

Jordan Rudess is kinda like that. Jordan Rudess has this personality of where he tries to reach out and have a communication with his fan base, or the Dream Theatre fan base, what have you, and at the same time, I've been in the same room with him a number of times and it's like he's staring through you. Because the guy's brain is working 24 hours a day on what he can create next. You know, oh, I just heard something, I gotta go, I gotta create something. So he's constantly creating.

As far as Banks and Rutherford are concerned, I think that they wanted to play live a lot more. I think that they wanted to record a lot more, I think they wanted a lot more out of Genesis that they knew they weren't gonna get. Phil Collins wasn't gonna allow it. They eventually wound up knowing that without Phil, this just isn't going to work. And what are we going to do? Peter's not going to come back. We're not going to redo this whole thing.

So, in that respect, it's kind of like, look at what we've accomplished. Look what we put out and who we've influenced. Look who looks up to us. And at the same time, we were just kids back then. As adults, you have no idea the level that we're at now. So I understand that kind of thing. There's a British classism thing that goes on there. But I think a lot of it is early accomplishment, early achievement, Neil Peart had an arrogance about him with that. Now, look, I only met him once for 30 seconds—that was it; that was my whole interaction with Neil. But it was, you know, acknowledgement of my presence, can I get the door, and that was pretty much it, and a shake of a hand. I'd gone into a tuning room. I knew that was my only chance that I was ever going to meet that guy. Very difficult to me.

So the thing is, with people like that, they don't hear the word no in their life. They don't. And everybody starts saying yes to everything you propose as well, no matter what it is. You could probably agree with me on this. That Tony Banks album, *Still*, with "Angel Face;" nobody would have signed that shit—nobody. I mean, there's some really unlistenable stuff and there's some good stuff that falls in between the cracks. Or is anybody ever really going to just take Mike Rutherford by himself and say, "Oh yeah, let's run with this guy." No way. That's why Rush works. That's why The Police worked. That's why all of these legacy acts worked. They had the magic, but only as a set, only together. You talk about arrogance; every guy in The Police is absolutely in his own zone. The Police are one of the most arrogant bands in history.

Martin: I feel like that stodginess or conservativeness carries over to the cover art, yet again. But it's funny; the *We Can't Dance* cover uses the same yellow backdrop of *Selling England by the Pound*, and even the painting uses the same hues.

David: You'll note as well that they both feature a rectangular inset illustration too. Although, I'm tempted to suggest that *Selling England* is organic for that yellow colour, whereas *We Can't Dance* has probably just been left in the sun too long by the producers.

Martin: Okay, into the record—the band's first without a side one and a side two—and it's "No Son of Mine" to begin the show. Up-tempo, a bit of a rocker, but a heartbreaking story.

Doug: First, let me back up a bit. When you asked me if I'd be okay talking about *We Can't Dance*, I thought, would I rather be talking about *Invisible Touch* or even the '83 record? Yeah. But whatever. I know this album like the back of my hand, because I was so looking forward to a Genesis record for so long, because of how long it was since *Invisible Touch* to this point. And for *We Can't Dance* to be the result, it's like, how is it that *Invisible Touch* was such a hit factory and yet that second side still showed their progressive rock bonafides? They had that in check and in place and could pull that off no problem. That was so cool to me.

I didn't like the song, "Invisible Touch," so when it came time for this album, and I saw that "No Son of Mine" was coming out as an advance single, I was like, okay, hopefully it's a better first single than "Invisible Touch." And "No Son of Mine" turned out to be very dark song. And then the video hits you like a hammer, if you come from a place with any form of abuse in your life, whether it's from a parent or a sibling or a stranger, or just abuse in general.

And I disagree with the context that people take it in. A lot of people take it in the context that the song is completely about child abuse. It's not completely about child abuse. It's about abuse period, in the home setting, you know, with the mother getting beaten, and he's watching that cycle repeat itself. And he runs from this, abandons the family. And the family is more or less turning on him because he didn't stand up for himself. He didn't stand up for his own convictions. In a lot of tough households in America, you still see that embedded. It's in our DNA, it's in our culture, with homes that do have the father figure present. They want to build this character in a son that is tough enough to handle seeing the worst shit, taking the hits, taking the beatings.

And that's a generational thing. You know, my mom got beat every day of her life by her mother until she moved out, when she was almost 18. She'd go to school with black eyes and a cracked rib. And she's paid for it physically her whole life, and mentally, emotionally. And I think if you run away to escape the violence, whether it's directed at the mom or siblings and stuff, this character still felt the need to go back twice and get closure. And it explores issues of control, and how that carries on into relationships and marriages. People wind up getting stuck in these things. And then it becomes a cyclical nightmare amongst families. And that clock, the hypnotic clock that starts the song and keeps it going, to me that is... I'm not saying that was the point, but I'm taking from the song that this cycle of violence and control is nonstop.

Martin: It's an actual metronome, right?

Doug: Yes, it is. But it didn't have to be there on the song. It represents a ticking clock, which sort of says to me that this goes on forever. So the father is violent to the mother, and emotionally abusive to both. Maybe the father doesn't want a cowardly son at the end of this. It's maybe just that simple. Yet, I appreciate the way that it's written. It's left open to interpretation. You're able to see in the scenario what you want.

Chart-wise, "No Son of Mine" was almost a Top Ten hit. Adult Contemporary and Mainstream Rock, those were, what? No.8 and No.3. It was No.12 on the Billboard Hot 100 and No 6 in Cashbox. You know, this song connected. The video was on obnoxiously, on repeat cycles. So yeah, it's a song that stands the test of time. If it wasn't for "No Son of Mine," *We Can't Dance* would have major, major problems as far as quality and substance. I think the song saves the record because of the message. You started to feel like Phil was getting even darker. Because two years previously, his lead-off was "Another Day in Paradise" off *...But Seriously*. When people hear an opening track, you know, first track from a record, they're not expecting something to be serious and dour. U2 doesn't even do that. U2 puts out singles that sound like celebrations or rallying cries. They just know the formula.

So, the song definitely set the tone that this was a different record than we imagined we were getting. Because it's totally different from "Invisible Touch." Even from a synth and drumming point of view. And there is this organic, authentic approach that Rutherford is trying to execute, even though he never emerges as a standout guitarist. It's really difficult to have that transfer over to rock radio when you're used to these driving riffs in every song and then boom, Genesis comes on. Alex Lifeson at least gave you riffs. Or if they weren't riffs, there were at least driving chords that would keep you reminded that guitar was being used.

Todd: "No Son of Mine" is one of the best examples of what's good about this album, which is that the lyrics are dark. But it's written really well and it's sung well and it doesn't bog you down too much in the sadness of it. I think it's done just right. It's a bit more straightforward than some of the singles off of *Invisible Touch*. It's Genesis playing with not a lot of gimmicks. It's got that little growling thing that I'm pretty sure is Mike's guitar. You're not sure whether it's Mike or whether it's Tony; could be either, which I think is cool. In the end, "No Son of Mine" is effective but maybe too long. It could have had a minute or so trimmed off of it. He kind of vamps on the whole "No son of mine" thing more times than he needs to. But it's a really strong track, and not particularly commercial.

David: The victim of the abuse in the lyrics may be the boy, may be the mother. But for me, straight away, the real victim is the sound, the insipid production from Nick Davis. What we might have is another victim of what is know as the loudness wars, where CDs were just awfully produced at this point in time in terms of the mix and this idea of brick-walling, where everything was put loud in the mix sort of equally. It was one of these horrendous techniques going on in the early '90s that causes ear fatigue, although you don't really know why you are suddenly feeling tired and cranky at the album.

But yes, "No Son of Mine" is the epitome of that kind of thing. It opens with this sound that Mike called elephantus, which was Mike's guitar recorded through Tony's keys for that bizarre noise that opens the track. That gives way to a vibe sounding like a slick update of Phil's "In the Air Tonight." It hurts me to know that Phil Collins is in this band. When the drums sound like a dustman taking the bins out at five o'clock in the morning, all I think is what a waste of what many consider to be one of the greatest drummers of all time. It really seems like someone's crashed down into Oscar the Grouch and made a terrible mess, because the drums are horrendous. I don't understand why drummers seemed to lose their own sense of hearing in the '80s and '90s. But they did as a community. Must have been something going on. Because you're a drummer. You must have been pulling your hair out at some point going why aren't they playing drums?! Why are they using computers for all this? It's a true din.

And these sort of dark, introspective lyric themes, this may connect with some people, but I think they handled it better on things like "Mama" and "Tonight, Tonight, Tonight." And it's a form of boomer bait, where the casual boomer fan would go, "Oh, that's sad, isn't it? I'll buy that Phil Collins record." Because for them, this wasn't consciously a Genesis record; rather, it's Phil Collins. It was all one and the same at this point in time, really. I mean, it's not as preachy as something like Phil's own "Another Day in Paradise," but then not much is.

Martin: Next is "Jesus He Knows Me," which percolates along like The Police's "Synchronicity I." I'm quite happy to hear that the *Abacab* drums are back, especially in the cymbal department.

Todd: Yeah, I swear that "Jesus, He Knows Me" gets a bad reputation based on the fact that it's got the word Jesus in it, but as a song, it's super-bold. I mean, not only did they address the whole thing that organised religion can be—and televangelists certainly are—complete frauds. But it commits to that and it doesn't pull any punches. I don't think it gets enough credit for being as bold and as scathing as it is. The line, "But she don't know about my girlfriend/Or the man I met last night" is bold (laughs). That was a risk. But it completely sells the idea of the hypocrisy of religious figures, plus the whole thing about not having to go anywhere. You just "get on your knees and start paying." There are so many lines in this song that are dark and bold and gutsy. The music's kind of bouncy, and maybe that discredits it a little bit. Maybe that's what people don't like about it, that it's kind of pop-sounding.

Martin: It's quite jaunty and synth-pop too, to the point where an arrangement like this might sound out-of-date in 1991. For all the band's stark evolution through the years, they've been making this kind of music since *Abacab*.

Todd: Yes, and in fact even the whole televangelist controversy is six or seven years old at this point (laughs). It was still going on, though. Seniors were still giving their money away to these guys at this point.

David: I'll surprise ya—I quite like this one. I like the iconoclast aspect of it more than anything else. It's much more cynical and on-the-nose than pretty much anything Phil Collins would produce in this period, or pretty much any period, to be honest. The atheist in me wishes that the sentiment would be directed more towards the pious theists rather than televangelists. I wish it was directed at maybe organised religion in general. But I appreciate they are trying to aim this at the most popular audience, and especially America. They don't want to alienate absolutely everybody south of the Mason Dixon Line, which is probably a smart move commercially. So just going after one group? Okay, I'll accept that. If you're going to take on Jimmy Swaggart and Billy Graham and that world, that's not too bad as a starting point. Iconoclasm and Genesis aren't something you'd normally put together, but hey, why not?

The music carries on with quite a bit of anger and crunch. I suppose it's got a little twinkle or gleam in the eye because they know they're being a little bit cheeky, that this isn't the kind of thing people expect from us. I very much admire that. I guess the word would be chutzpah, in Yiddish.

As for the video, despite its primary colours, remember that Phil started out as a child actor, and he was in a film called *Buster* in the '80s, which was a big hit in the UK, about The Great Train Robbery. Tony and Mike have never acted, which becomes painfully apparent because they are stiff as cardboard and Phil lights up the screen. He's magnetic, he's interesting to watch, he does little things, he demonstrates in the music video for this song why Phil was everywhere for so long. He just has a magnetism to him. Even as someone who, if Phil Collins came on my screen right now, I'd go, "Oh God, Phil Collins," for a few minutes, he makes me forget that attitude. It's a wonderful illustration of why Phil's such a charismatic personality. I wish his politics were always as progressive as that. Unfortunately, they wouldn't be.

Doug: Having six singles released from *We Can't Dance* is something that surprised me. Because after "Jesus He Knows Me" had been released, I was like, okay, that's enough of that. You asked my thoughts on the album now, after all these years. I think exactly the same thing as I did in 1991, as with the other one like this, which is *Roll the Bones*. Why? Why are we putting out cringe material like "Jesus He Knows Me?" The video is so uncomfortable to watch. I've hated it since day one, and I hate the song.

But to step back and look at the wider album, it comes out at the same time as *Roll the Bones* and, somewhat oddly, they're both commercially successful. They're both being played on the radio nonstop. Why? Why weren't some of these other records getting the attention? It's such a weird time too, because *We Can't Dance* rainbows over into the grunge era, with '91 and '92 being the biggest years of that scene. And you've got the hair rockers still fighting on, you've got hip-hop and rap really starting to rise up. You're starting to see all of these things, and fucking Genesis and Rush put out the two most awkward albums of their careers. "Fuck yeah! I want to put this up against the Chili Peppers and 'Enter Sandman!'" You want to what?! How does this album happen at this time? What are we doing?! I don't know if it was a payola thing. I don't know if Val Azzoli and Ahmet were filling program directors' bank accounts, you know, across the country, just saying, "Hey, there's an envelope of cash sitting out on your front left tire. Keep 'Jesus He Knows Me' in heavy rotation." You know, are you kidding me?!

To me, it's one of the worst songs Genesis ever wrote. It's fucking horrible across the board. As an American and as a Christian, a Catholic, we were inundated forever on a lot of channels with televangelists like Jim Bakker and Jimmy Swaggart and Pat Robertson. I could go down the whole list of them. There were some good ones too. Billy Graham was an honest one. Each person, it's between them and God, what they do.

But look, the video itself was just very uninviting to me. It just seemed goofy and cringey. It wasn't a very exciting topic to begin with. It was shit that we had all lived through. It still goes on today. You still see televangelism and you still see it online. Some of it comes from a legitimate place, and others it really doesn't. It's horrible, the bastardization of the Bible and the using and bilking of seniors. Americans have gone through this and I don't think we needed a song for it, especially from a British band. And I don't think we needed the video, because we lived it, we saw it and it was on the news constantly and in the tabloids. Again, it's an absolutely awful, awful song and the fact that it's at track two, there's an audacity there. You know, that song's like a track ten.

Martin: What do you make of "Driving the Last Spike?" It's baffling to me that this is ten minutes long, but equally curious is how it sounds like a very commercial version of "In Your Eyes," by Peter Gabriel, basically a Peter Gabriel ballad with all the personality missing.

Todd: In the whole realm of prog or prog-esque songs on later Genesis albums, there's "Domino" and "Home by the Sea," but I think "Driving the Last Spike" is the best one. I think it's got some of Tony's best melodies. The little part that he plays relatively close to the beginning, it's just a very simple instrumental part, and that's one of the things that Tony was really good at. He plays these little melodies that are pure and simple—they're almost nursery rhymes. But he puts them in there, and then they reprise back to it. And that song is beautifully sung by Phil.

Lyrically, it's just very moving. It's an interesting subject that I don't think anybody's ever tackled before. For him to talk about people getting hurt building the railroad, it's almost a precursor to Phil being really interested in the Alamo and collecting all those Alamo artifacts. He was becoming really interested in, not just historical things, but historical things that happened in the US, although this song is specifically about Irish workers building the railway in the UK. But it's still that whole historical thing that he got into.

I believe Tony wrote most of the melodies on this song, but there's some Phil in there too, and the lyrics definitely come from Phil. It's intense and effective, but it might be a bit long. There's some nice, jangly guitar effects as well. It rarely gets much notice. It comes after "Jesus He Knows Me" and I think that some people had already decided they don't like modern Genesis. They put this album on and they heard "Jesus He Knows Me" and they didn't necessarily want to go on.

Martin: Are Genesis sounding dated in 1991?

Todd: You could say that, yeah. I got that impression somewhat. But 1989, '90, '91 is a weird time because some bands were still doing the same things they were doing in the mid-'80s. The grunge thing was about to happen, or had already started to happen. So it's yes and no. I don't notice it as dated, but if somebody else said it was dated, I'd be like, yeah, I guess it is (laughs).

David: "Driving the Last Spike" represents the point where I think too many Genesis fans are searching for solace in their releases. They start to say, "That's a bit proggy," when actually, it's just ten minutes long. And that's not the same thing at all. The same band are making a ten-minute epic, but it does not remotely mean that it's progressing anything. It's regressive if anything. There's nothing that's progressive here. This is at the point—and loads of the major bands were guilty of it in the prog scene—where prog and progressive were not synonyms anymore. The idea of progressing stopped for most of these bands in the '80s and '90s. I'd say King Crimson were one of the only ones who kept saying, "What next?" Yes, Genesis, Tull… they all started saying, "What worked before?" which is regressive rock, as I like to call it.

"Driving the Last Spike" has some lovely melodies from Tony throughout, but it has that early '90s dull ambience in place of atmosphere and tension. Writing about the working conditions of Irish navvies in the 18th century is an esoteric choice indeed. The lyrics are strong and it's a compelling story, but I think I'd rather watch a six-part BBC miniseries about the story than listen to a bunch of millionaires singing about it and playing quite flat music. And I have no idea why it needs to be ten minutes long. Because there are no dynamic shifts in it. There's no intensity at certain points. There's no poignancy. There's nothing about it that justifies even half that length of time.

Doug: "Driving the Last Spike" comes off as a lyrical masterpiece, especially coming after such insane garbage (laughs). Being an Irishman myself—and I'm only two generations removed from my family that all emigrated here—when you look at the lyrics to this, this could be some of Phil Collins' best songwriting ever. And I'm not even kidding about that. Yes, I know he took stories from the railway navvies that were in a book he was reading at the time about the post-war construction of the British Rail System. He's sourcing it from the common stories told by the Irish workers that were recounted in that book.

And I don't know if you can hear it, but towards the middle and the ending of the song, it almost sounds like an Irish band is playing this song. I hear some Irish rock chords that you hear in a lot of the Celtic rock and those almost pub bands. They manage to do this song right. This is the work of a band that has the ability to tap into something that comes from the heart, that is addressing stuff from the point of view of a workman who took part in the process. I think that history is going to look very kind on this song 20 years from now, 30 years from now, when it comes to Genesis. I think it's highly underrated and under-discussed. It would be better to talk about this song with people who live in Britain and have ancestors from Ireland who were involved in the construction job. Because I know Genesis fans that I'm friends with who are Brits, and they connect to this song more than anything on the record.

There are three bands I can think of who operate in this space and do it well. One is Big Country. Stuart Adamson—storyteller. His suicide disturbed me, when that happened. I was just so taken aback. There are so many Big Country songs that literally dig into your soul, but I get why they didn't carry over past, really, that debut, in the United States. It's absolutely nationalistic music; there's just no question about that. But yes, the three are Big Country, The Alarm and Simple Minds. Their fans could potentially sit down and have an appreciation for "Driving the Last Spike." American listeners, American Genesis fans, can sit back and go, "That's a good song; that's well written." But I don't know if they have the attention span for the depth of it. But for however many fans of it there are, that's a song that is appreciated more by those in the UK and Ireland.

Martin: Next is "I Can't Dance," which I always looked at as a sort of nothing burger, a novelty song, and something I imagine buskers doing on the street with some upturned plastic pails and a little guitar amp and microphone.

Doug: As my notes say, "This is the worst Genesis song ever written."

Martin: You know, Doug, it always reminded me of Dire Straits' "Money for Nothing," because of the unexpected use of fuzzy guitars. But just like Dire Straits, it's like the most fuddy-duddy senior citizen riff ever. And then I'm additionally riled by the dissonance between the song title and the album title.

Doug: And then you have them marching along to it in the video. Why are you fucking this up for us even more? It's a horrible enough song as it is.

Martin: It's like a send-up of the iconic ZZ Top *Eliminator* videos, right?

Doug: Yes, yes! So here's the other thing that's a problem with this song. Other than the fact that it's absolutely atrocious on every level, there's nothing redeeming about it and it's just beyond unacceptable. It's the sheer audacity that it is as popular as it is, and that they keep it in their setlist not only in '07, but on the final tour.

And the fact that people like it, it's the "Roll the Bones" syndrome. My daughter and I laugh about this. She loves the song. She's 16. She's loved it for like two years. I told her when I first time I heard "Roll the Bones," I heard it inside of the studio at the radio station and I fucking ran outside and I yelled, "What happened to my fucking band?!" And then I went back in and listened to the rest of the record. I didn't want to disrupt anything that might have been going on in production rooms or anything else. I literally went out into the parking lot and yelled at the sky on that. What is going on here?! And when I see the crowd reactions to "Roll the Bones" and "I Can't Dance" and then I see the streaming numbers of them on all these platforms, oh God, it just doesn't make any sense! It doesn't.

Martin: Nothing happens in the song.

Doug: Nothing!

Martin: There's just no arrangement. There's no anything.

Doug: It's so bad. And yet somehow it was marketed like crazy. And they had the audacity to put them walking like that on the live albums, the two *The Way We Walk* albums. Look, that wasn't appealing in 1991 and '92 and it's not appealing now. Nobody that I know sits around and wants to turn that song on. I just want to know who these people are that like it. They're the same people that love when the rap part comes on in "Roll the Bones." Or when we start getting church organ sounds and the repetitive "Why are we here? Because we're here. Roll the bones" bit. It's the same thing with the "I can't dance" line. It's repetitively annoying; it's atrocious. And yet it went to No.7 on Billboard and No.7 in the UK.

Martin: You know why it's a hit, Doug, outside of the goofy music? It's that guys love to get out of dancing by saying "I can't dance."

Doug: Well, if that's the excuse you want to run with, then we'll use it, because it at least excuses something. Because I've never been able to find an excuse for it. It's just terrible. When I initially saw that title, I thought it was a tongue-in-cheek dig at progressive rock. Okay, so the song is going to be in an odd time signature and that's what it's going to be about. No! There's actually a lot of this album that you can dance to—except this song. It's fucking stupid.

Todd: I don't think "I Can't Dance" should have ever happened. I feel like this is one of those situations where they made themselves laugh in the studio by doing it, and then decided that it was so much fun that everybody else will think it's fun, too. I think it's the number one reason why people don't like this record. But they wrote that song "I Can't Dance," which is basically about a guy selling cheap crap at a market, and just wanting to get the attention of the ladies, which is really oddly specific.

They spent a lot of time in interviews when they were promoting this album trying to explain what "I Can't Dance" was about and I think that was a waste of time. And even when you look at the front cover art and the matching illustrations in the booklet, that really kind of represents what's going on through most of this album really well. And then right there on the front you've got the title, *We Can't Dance*, which implies that it's kind of a light album and it's not. But I'm wrong sometimes and maybe most often, because when you go to see them play, they always play "I Can't Dance" and everybody goes absolutely nuts. So somebody likes it.

It's funny, because they got a lot of crap for "That's All" at the time for being too lightweight and pop and stuff like that. But I go back now and listen to that song and I think it's really cool. It's got a lot of interesting things happening in it. But I don't do that for "I Can't Dance."

Martin: Well, they manage to turn the title refrain into a hook, an earworm, as irritating as it is. Plus playing that minimally, especially for Genesis, constitutes novelty.

Todd: Yeah, I think you're right. And I think if the sequencing had gone from "Driving the Last Spike" to "Never a Time" to "Dreaming

While You Sleep" and "I Can't Dance" wasn't in there, that would be a really killer side one. It would make the album sound and feel like this album cover, instead of having your brain go, "Well, what do I do with 'I Can't Dance?'"

Martin: All right, David, what do *you* do with "I Can't Dance?"

David: Well, I'm being a bit iconoclastic in reverse here, by saying I think there's a little bit of nailed genius to it. Because it's obviously a parody of how unhip Genesis were at this point in the music scene. They're making a crunchy blues rocker with the most basic riff possible, and with none of the band's usual histrionics. Even though the histrionics by this point in their catalogue had been sanded down by time and commerciality anyway, there's none of even the mistakenly progressive aspect to it that some people point to in some of the longer modern songs. Everything presented to us is just the most basic version of blues rock possibly imagined. George Thorogood might even consider this to be too lightweight, and that says something.

But they create a song which could be used in one of the Levi's adverts that they're kind of parodying here. Not really sure why they took such umbrage at songs being used commercially, but this could easily fit into one of those ads. And it's a song that yes, it's easy to mock, but again, they're mocking themselves at the same time. You see the video where Phil's pointing at himself saying, "A perfect body with a perfect face." Again, when he does that, he's very punch-able because it's early '90s Phil Collins, but he's doing it with a sense of irony. It's hard to criticise when the person is already mocking themselves. It's almost like they've developed a defence mechanism against criticism at this point, to defend themselves from any kind of criticism. And the ultimate validation of that has been massive sales, which of course, they consistently got to this point.

I like your "Money for Nothing" reference, although what helps that song is Sting showing up and doing the "I want my MTV" bit and the backing vocals. You don't have anything to latch onto like that here in terms of interest—nothing at all. It's nothing but a riff, and a slight idea that doesn't take its own notions far enough to be particularly interesting satire.

However, they're almost parodying the kind of music, again, that the trucker or the soccer mom can hear and bop their heads to. So while objectively I dislike it immensely, it's almost Machiavellian in terms of its sales techniques. They're coming up with something making fun of commercial music, and it comes out as the most commercial thing they've released in a long time. And then people listen to it with no sense of irony whatsoever and just go, "That's good." It's the type of people who own five CDs, and probably buy one every other Christmas. So in that regard it works. As a piece of music, it makes me want to vomit. But regardless, I'd have to admire that the compelling nature of it operates on an almost meta level.

Martin: And is Phil also telegraphing that he's old and comes from the prog world?

David: I wonder if at this point, they would even bother mentioning that second part, because their audience will probably go "Prog?" So probably just old—stick with that. Most of the buyers at this point probably started with "Follow You Follow Me" or more likely "Turn It On Again." In fact even more people probably started with *Invisible Touch*. And a depressing thought is that an equal amount of people probably started with Phil Collins. They started with their debut album, *Face Value*, the first Genesis album (laughs).

Martin: Now we whiplash back to the world of pop ballads, with "Never a Time" being one of those that could have been on a Phil Collins solo album.

Todd: Yes, but I think it deserves more credit, that it's somewhat underrated. There's a cool part of the documentary of the making of this album where Phil talks about having a bear of a time trying to sing it. And when you listen to it, you can understand why it would be hard to sing. You don't get that impression first off, but when you listen to the vocal melody of it, it really would be a challenge to get all of those pitches just absolutely perfectly. I don't remember exactly what happens, but I think Phil throws the microphone down and walks out because he can't get it right, and they have to take a break and reconvene.

Martin: Would you agree that it sounds like a solo career song?

Todd: It certainly does, but his reaction to trying to sing it betrays the fact that it's not one of his, that it was actually written by Mike. But yeah, I agree. Ther are better examples of that as we get further along in the album, but sure.

David: With "Never a Time," what enters my ears is perfectly pleasant, but I'm struggling to think, what about it makes this Genesis? In any sense of the word. And that's not the person in me saying there's no prog here. There's no searching here. There's no ideas here. I just can't get a sense of any real identity that's been formed here. Like say, Dire Straits were doing in the '80s. There's no sense of that newness that a lot of acts developed in the '90s. And frankly, it's the sort of track that could be from so many aging acts that were stuck in the middle of the road with no way out whatsoever, there in the early '90s.

On the embankments where interesting things still happen, you have the likes of Springsteen, Dylan and Neil Young. You have people who can still challenge musically and try different things. But in the middle, in the ditch, you have Eric Clapton, Steve Winwood and Billy Joel who are just trapped by their own commercial success and now can't really say anything interesting because their audience don't care for interesting. They care for, "Just do that again, please." And that's very much the "Never a Time" aesthetic: "It's just the kind of thing we do now."

Doug: "Never a Time" is like, huh? This charted?! It peaked at No.4 on the US Billboard Hot Adult Contemporary Tracks chart and was No.21 on the Billboard Hot 100. So that's pretty high. Jesus Christ. It's another lonely breakup song from Rutherford. Sorry, absolutely forgettable. "So sad, oh, so sad." so bad, so very bad, to play off the lyrics there (laughs). And to use an Eddie Trunk term, I was checked out on the record when this was a single. I didn't even know that this thing was getting that kind of traction at the time, mostly because so much was going on in music, that this wasn't a song that was being played on the hard rock stations. This was adult contemporary pop. And rock radio was not playing the song in rotation like it was the other initial tracks that had come out.

Martin: Would you say that a good chunk of the success of this album is due to the long wait since the last album?

Doug: Yeah, sure. It's not at *Chinese Democracy* levels or anything crazy, but the anticipation I think was tempered because there were so many Phil Collins singles and solo albums and tours, to where it's like, okay, that voice is still there. But people loved Genesis and they wanted to see what they were going to come up with next. Because it had been so long.

Martin: With "Dreaming While You Sleep," again, we're back in the commercial Peter Gabriel zone, although to be fair, Phil was part of that original sound with Peter and then Genesis themselves have been exploring these sound collage songs since *Abacab* as well.

Todd: Yes, I feel like "Dreaming While You Sleep" was a conscious attempt to make something like "Tonight, Tonight, Tonight." The lyrical theme is pretty cool, and oddly specific. It's kind of like "In the Air Tonight." It's about somebody thinking that there was an accident and I think I probably caused it and I hope that person didn't die. It's a compelling story. It's cool how it starts with the drum machine and then goes into the gated drum thing. So yeah, I feel like they were trying to do that "Tonight, Tonight, Tonight" thing, but I think they did it a little better here. It didn't get much attention. I don't remember whether they played it live. But I think it's pretty good. And I like your Peter Gabriel comparison. I think this is a good example of that. The feel of the song, especially the first half of it, is somewhat Gabriel-esque, I suppose more in relation to his later work.

David: Dated synths aside, which, again, it's just a product of the times—I try not to focus too much on that kind of thing—I like this one a fair bit. And you can say this for a lot of the album. This is obviously an album of the early '90s, where the CD has completely replaced the LP, especially in America where you didn't really have LPs by '91. As I discovered, Prince stopped releasing LPs in 1990 in America. Whereas that switchover didn't happen until the mid-'90s in the UK. But at this point, the CD tops out at about 77 minutes, and was eventually pushed to 80. And there's this bizarre need to say, well, we better put 70 or 75 minutes of music on these things then. I've never quite understood why anybody felt that need to keep pushing the runtime of these things when clearly they didn't have the material.

And a lot of the songs were just extended, because that's exactly what happens with something like "Dreaming While You Sleep." How many albums are there like this that we would never think of as double albums, but on LP, they definitely would be? It would really change your view of some of these albums, if that happened, because, for one, we take double albums quite seriously.

And that's a shame because this is actually a decent song, a story of someone getting in a car accident that they caused. There's a broodiness to the music for once. For once in this album, the music is telling me something, that something's wrong, something's happened, somebody's feeling bad. I can tell that without hearing a single word of the lyrics, which is great. It's one of the few cases in this part of the catalogue where you can actually say that at all. Much of the album is just generic. My only quibble with this, apart from the length, is that the volume of this track is all over the place in terms of the mixing. Again, we're in the loudness wars at the same time that we're in the CD length wars. We're also in the era that if something needs to be epic, it also needs to be loud at the same time. So things are just produced loudly to give that sense of danger and climax, rather than, "No, just leave it to the players; they'll guide you."

Martin: What's your opinion with respect to any Peter Gabriel comparisons it might conjure?

David: Yes, I think that's a good point. It's just a more dense and interesting track from them that, again, isn't progressive, but neither was Peter Gabriel at this point in terms of prog as we know it. But when you realise that Peter Gabriel's contemporaneous album would be *Us* in '92—I always remember, *So*, *Us*, *Up*, as in "sew us up"—Peter was so far ahead of anything they've got here in terms of ideas, in terms of dynamic shifts. And part of that is the sense of authorship for Peter Gabriel not wanting to put his name on any old thing.

But also he has musicians in his band who are interested in pushing boundaries at that point. Tony Levin and Manu Katché, who are still playing organically and are still playing interesting things, are saying, "What's new? Oh, world music." Or "R&B music; let's try it in a '90s sense rather than a '70s sense." There's rap music and the like. And sometimes that would lead to bizarre things and things that haven't dated well, if you like, in terms of cultural appropriation. Perhaps the most progressive idea of all was just the fusion, the melting pot of music. Whereas at this point, Genesis aren't really doing that apart from tiny little glimpses, like we see here in "Dreaming While You Sleep" for mere moments. And then it's gone.

Doug: "Dreaming While You Sleep" makes me think of Harold Faltermeyer, who did the music for *Beverly Hills Cop*. That whole beginning sequence is like Axel Foley in that movie. The figure in the song gets nervous and guilty for a hit-and-run accident. The girl's in a coma and they're running. They don't want to confess if they don't have to. It's somebody with a guilty conscience. It's a good song, slapping drums. There seems to be a pattern, where we're going with constructive criticism, sort of good song, bad song, good song, or maybe just mediocre song, with this record.

Martin: "Tell Me Why" is different for them, with the rainy, jangly guitars and even the chord changes, which are melancholic and R&B, even though it's not an R&B song.

David: It's nice to get Mike's 12-string Rickenbacker out of storage and use that for a change. It gives this song something of a dynamic shift. I'm not sure that at this point these are the guys and Phil Collins is the frontman to talk about the state of the world, when he's pretty much the epitome of the guy who's made good from capitalism and everything that entails within the western world. So singing and raising awareness about the Gulf War and Kurdistan as this song does, it probably needs to be more overt, and it probably needs to be a stand-alone charity single or something.

And even then it needs to be more interesting to catch on with the mainstream. Because an album track about that, it's doing absolutely nothing for nobody. And most of your audience, again, is so casual at this point that they're not really going to read the lyrics to think about the plight of the Kurdish people. They're just hearing a nice melody and thinking, oh, what's that instrument? That sounds a bit like... what were they called? The Byrds? That Roger McGuinn guy. They're not really gonna think about it that deeply.

I just don't think that this is the kind of mission statement Genesis needed at this point to establish any kind of relevance. Again, I don't know if it's a genuine thing or not, but Phil's got this part of his career where he's doing things like "Another Day in Paradise" and he's on any charity record that'll take him. He's never off TV doing appeals for this, that and the other, like Bono, like Tracy Chapman, like Sting, like Springsteen. And most of those people are just better writers, is the honest truth, and able to succinctly and poignantly write about issues and maybe see it from one person's point of view. Phil is just not that kind of writer at all. So for Phil to write a song like "Tell Me Why," it's just not pointed enough. It's not interesting enough to raise awareness, the very issue that he's trying to drum up. And that's a real problem. That's more disappointing than most things with the record because it's coming from a good place. But he's stifling himself by not being that good of a writer, unfortunately.

Doug: "Tell Me Why" was a total commercial failure. Didn't even know the video existed. Never saw it. Never saw it on VH1 or MTV. Might have aired at some point, but again, this seems to be more of an afterthought thing. It has a bit of a Beatles or Byrds guitar riff, and of course "Roll the Bones" is out at the same time asking similar questions. Literally, lyrically, if you took them apart, they're very similar. It's not like they were hanging out with each other while they were writing of their albums, but I found that interesting.

Todd: "Tell Me Why" could have been on a Phil Collins solo album. It came after "Another Day in Paradise," which was '89, and I feel like it's more of the same. I like the lyrical content of it, but it kind of opens you up to, "Well, you're a pretty rich guy; what are you doing about it?" That's kind of unfair, but at the same time, you wonder. It's worthwhile lyrically, but I think you could skip it. It could have come off the album and then you don't open yourself up to the criticisms of, you know, this is the second time that you've talked about a social cultural phenomenon that nobody's doing enough to help with. It's going to put a spotlight on you. And people who don't like it—or people that don't like you—are going to start saying, "Phil's always talking about homeless people and people who are poor and don't have anywhere to live, but he's a big, rich rock star."

It's not particularly controversial or fresh as a subject, but it's good that if you feel strongly about a social injustice and you feel compelled to talk about it, you should do it. But it almost feels like they set out to do that, like, on purpose, because they thought it would be good to do it, rather than somebody really having a personal conviction that this is something I really want to solve, or I really feel like should be solved. The way he sort of gives a laundry list of all the injustices that are going on... I almost hate to do this, but I gotta be honest, it almost feels like it's forced. I don't feel real conviction when I hear it.

Martin: "Living Forever" is a cool, dark horse track, I find, pretty forgotten on this record as we get deep into the CD-era track sequence of it all. It's Genesis applying a sense of craft to one of their pop songs, no?

Todd: Absolutely; "Living Forever" is super-underrated. It was actually the B-side of the single of "No Son of Mine," and that's the first time I heard it, because that was an advance single. It's got a lot of really interesting things happening in it, although it's kind of lightweight as far as the lyrical content goes. I don't think it's particularly deep and the lyrics don't make much of an impression on me. But "Living Forever" starts this little section of the album where you get a bunch of songs in a row that don't have the gated drums, and I think that's really cool. There's this really kind of laid-back groove they get into in the middle of this song that's got Tony's keyboard solo over it. It's not a flashy solo, and suddenly there's this groove and this very wet drum sound.

Martin: It sounds like Phil might be using some brushes there, or if not, he's good with the grace notes.

Todd: Yeah, it might be. Not being a drummer, I'm not sure. But I really like that. I can remember that making an impression on me the first time I heard it. It's like, oh, it's Phil playing the drums, and without the big effects. So I think "Living Forever" is really good. It's not one of the ones that I would take off the album.

Martin: Yeah, it's inspiring. They are being sonic explorers and it's a thoughtful arrangement with quirky textures.

David: Yes, musically, performance-wise and in sound, it's one of the strongest tracks on the record. There's layered vocals and a very contemporary drum machine style, with Phil's vocals matching the kind of droning beat that goes on. He's changing his vocal style up for this, for once, which is great. Mike's doing these guitar stabs, which is not something they've been playing with a lot, i.e. different guitar styles and how to incorporate them. It's a cousin of something like—and this is a bizarre song nobody will know—Robert Palmer's "Woke Up Laughing," where it incorporates different rhythms that are vaguely Afro sound or Afro sound-adjacent, without being too obvious about it. Unlike, say, Paul Simon's *Graceland*, which is overtly Afro-inspired, this is just addressing the idea of different beats, different styles.

But you know, I don't imagine the word analogue even existed in the studio at this point. Digital's the way forward—we all know that. Everything here is varying degrees of that. But there's a slightly more organic sense to this one, in terms of the ideas. It's like they've been listening to something else, or they've been inspired by something else, and it doesn't sound like everything else they're releasing at this point, with these reasonably interchangeable handfuls of different styles.

Doug: "Living Forever." Holy shit, what are we doing here? Diet fad songs. Fuck this. That was my reaction at that age. I was 17 when this record came out. Look, there's some truth to it. You hear something's bad for you for three years and then you see a study come out that says, actually, it's not bad. It's actually good for you. We heard this about eggs. We heard this about cholesterol. We heard this about bacon. You hear it about carcinogens and all the chemicals that are in processed foods, and yet they still get the FDA stamp on it. There's the food pyramid. This is good for you; this is bad for you. Fruit is good for you, but then you find out, well, no, this one actually destroys your kidney or eating this too much destroys your liver.

Yeah, I get it. It's that back-and-forth thing with fad diets and what have you. There's truth to it, absolutely. Do we need a fucking song for it? Absolutely not. This was written by Banks. You expect more from Genesis, as well as from a song title like that. Sometimes you look at a track listing before an album comes out, and you're like, that's a great title. You're imagining in your head, this is gonna be a great song; I can feel it. Then you listen to it and it's absolutely nothing like you thought it would be. You go, what a waste of a song title. I remember thinking that with "The Speed of Love" on *Counterparts*, seeing that title like four months before the record came out. I remember saying to everybody, that's gonna be it, that song is gonna be fantastic. That's the song I don't listen to at all on the record.

Martin: All right, things get quiet again for "Hold on My Heart."

Todd: Yeah, "Hold on My Heart" I would take off the album. I think it sounds too much like a Phil song. YouTube music has this thing where people can comment on every track, and all the comments were like, what a beautiful, heartfelt lyric, it reminds me of this, it makes me feel like this, it reminds me of my pet that I lost and all this kind of stuff. And it's like, he obviously did something right. People love this song. But whenever they played it in concert—they played it in 2007 and they played it this last time—I'm always thinking, oh, now I gotta sit through "Hold on My Heart" to get to whatever they're gonna play next. I think that "Since I Lost You," which we'll talk about in a minute, is far superior as far as ballads go. But "Hold on My Heart" is okay. If anybody was to ever say, "I have a hard time telling what's a Genesis song and what's a Phil Collins song," that's Exhibit A (laughs).

David: I'm tempted to just say no. It's an absolutely awful, insipid ballad that shows the most mawkish side of Phil, pretty much at his most cloying and annoying for me. As for any admirable performance points, which there are, Mike is playing some nice arpeggiated guitar. Mike's never been a great guitarist, but he's a solid player and a good rhythm player, which lends itself well. But that's the icing on a very distasteful cake. And frankly, it's just too much Phil Collins mawkishness. When you close your eyes and think of what a bad Phil Collins ballad sounds like, this is kind of 101 for that, along with "One More Night." If Mike on guitar is stealing the show, it's petty theft, to be honest.

Doug: I'd put "Hold on My Heart" in my top three for best Genesis love ballads ever. I was addicted to that song for many years later. I had gotten engaged really young, as a kid. I got engaged right out of high school, in college, and I was in a three-year relationship and I ended it. And then I went through a long period of regret at ending it. Because you go over things in your head, revising things that you should and shouldn't have said or shouldn't have done, jumping the gun on a lot of issues and whatever. That's all part of growing up. But the dynamics of relationships don't really change. I was like, that was my soulmate. I was convinced at the time.

So it's a simple song about the fear of taking the next step in a relationship. He's very in love. The last time he felt this way, he was hurt, or disappointed. It's a relatable track. From a male perspective, I think this connects harder than it does for women. And knowing what Phil's background was at this point, being in marriage number two and nearing the end of marriage number two, this guy had mastered the ability to diagnose, dissect, and lay out exactly how to speak to women, and how to speak about what that natural fear is when you fail in a relationship or you've been hurt in a relationship and been burned by giving trust to another human being.

And Phil just... God, he just knows how to do it. He's an absolute master at songwriting. It's what Phil Collins is. And the soft cymbal splashes that are there after that middle part, it's like an interlude, if you will. Those little splashes are coming down and introducing the idea of having this woman to hold onto his heart. What a hit. It deserved every bit of acclaim that it got.

Martin: Again, it's another ballad with a hint of R&B to it.

Doug: Yeah, it's something that could have worked just as well on *Invisible Touch*. At this point Rutherford has found his place in Genesis. He really doesn't have to do anything but serve that song with the right tone and that's it. He just needs to hold it. "Hold on Your Heart" lived on adult contemporary rock radio. It lived on those… I don't even call them Hot 100 channels anymore; I don't know what they are. But this was really it for them when it comes to the hits. I don't have the numbers in front of me, but I just know that it was big at the time here in America. This song resonated like it came off of *Invisible Touch*, that hit machine. But at the same time, it was pretty much it for them, their last massive charting song.

Martin: With "Way of the World," we're back to the same sort of zesty activity level as two tracks previous, on "Living Forever." Included is a little INXS-style guitar.

Todd: Yes, "Way of the World" I like because it's something bouncy in that position of the album, where it's about to get… what's the word I'm looking for? I don't want to use a negative word. It's about to get a little sad or a little more reflective. But it's kind of a generic lyric about, oh, the world's changing and I'm not sure what I'm gonna do about it. It doesn't bother me as much as "Tell Me Why" does. It's a little lighter. I don't think there's a lot happening in it. It sounds a lot like Mike Rutherford, like it could have been a Mechanics song. It's a group credit across this whole album, but usually these songs that are credited to the three of them have a main guy, and sometimes they reveal that in interviews. This is a Mike Rutherford song. But I like "Way of the World." The album needs something like this to keep it from being too sad.

Martin: So what is Mike's personality in this band? Is he essentially the same Mike as the one we get in Mike + The Mechanics?

Todd: Well, it's weird. I was thinking about this a lot when I was going through *Calling All Stations*, because it seems like he doesn't do a lot of what is considered to be conventional rhythm guitar. I mean, sometimes he does it, like on "…In That Quiet Earth" and the title track to *Calling All Stations*. But it's a lot of flourishes. It's a lot of little rhythmic things that are not, you know, power chords. I'm not quite sure how to describe it; maybe percussive sounds, licks, sound effects. This comes across in "Since I Lost You" a lot, where there are slightly bluesy little riffs that are put on top of things.

Martin: He plays guitar like a bass player and he also plays guitar like a keyboardist or even more so like a synthesizer player. And he also plays guitar like a drummer! Tony and him both, more than anything, they put on their hard hats and just build songs.

Todd: Yeah, I think that's really accurate. It would be easy to think, well, if anybody could be subtracted from this band, it would be Rutherford. But I don't know if that's true. Because he's really serving the song like 100% of the time, almost to the point where I feel like it would be better for him to have more solos. I don't usually say that, but it would have done these later albums some good, I think, for the arrangements. Rather than just every once in a while. I was gonna talk about that when I got to "Fading Lights." As much as I love it, if they had just structured that a little bit more like a prog song, I think it would have made a bigger impression on fans that only liked the prog songs (laughs).

David: "Way of the World?" is a bit more up-tempo and catchy than most songs that are this existential crisis-related in terms of the lyrics. It's unremarkable but it's not dull. It's not cloying and it's not jarring, and perhaps that's because it's following "Hold on My Heart." So again, my common complaint about them in this era is just more sonics please, more dynamics, change a tempo now and then, please. To hear them just go to verse, chorus, verse, chorus so often is leaving me cold. And quite often the verse and chorus are reasonably interchangeable, apart from just volume, which is just so depressing for me.

Doug: "Way of the World" give us more fear about the fate of humanity and maybe even global warming. Again, you could slot half the lyrics of "Roll the Bones" right in there with these ones.
Martin: And what's your opinion of Mike + The Mechanics?

Doug: Well, I got that first record. It was just one of those records you bought at the time. And I'm being completely straight with that, because that's exactly what it was.

Martin: Are they literally the most '80s band of all time?

Doug: I think you could throw The Hooters in there. The Hooters are pretty damn '80s.

Martin: They're a lot more analogue, though. I was referring more to technology. Every '80s technological trope known to man existed on those albums.

Doug: Oh, with Mike + The Mechanics? It's so easy to generalise something like that right now, because I know I could go down a list and go, we forgot about these guys. But it's true. That band was built for commercial radio. That's what that whole project existed for. It's Mike Rutherford taking a stand against Phil Collins, saying, hey, I can do something too. Can you? How long can this last for? But hey, when you see "Silent Running," "All I Need Is a Miracle" and "The Living Years," you've got three bonafide giant hits that are still regularly played on radio today all these decades later.

Martin: Even "Since I Lost You" sounds like a ballad on an R&B album, which might also derive, in part, from its 3/4 time waltz structure.

Todd: Yeah, and there's this really wet kind of Phil Spector wall of sound thing happening too, which I normally don't like. But it serves the song well—"Since I Lost You" is just absolutely beautiful. The lyrics are inspired by what happened to Eric Clapton's son. And the way that Rutherford plays leans a little toward Eric Clapton, especially the solo, which is really classy and cool.

When this album came out, on their press tours, they were often asked about a favourite song from the album, and just about every time they would pick "Since I Lost You." And the reason they always gave was that they did it so quickly. I believe Tony and Mike started it while Phil was at lunch. And Phil came in and heard it and loved it and wrote the lyrics really fast. And they wrapped it by like the end of the day, which is not usually how quickly they work. They're all really fond of it. What's always surprised me is how it's thought of as an afterthought after "Hold on My Heart." But I think it's much better. If it had been pushed, it might have been a much bigger song for them.

Doug: There's an intro on "Since I Lost You" that instantly gives me chills. It's a snare roll followed quickly by an epic entrance, and the whole sequence represents for me the farewell of Genesis as a recording act. Phil Collins wrote the song following the death of Eric Clapton's son Conor—it's about Conor. It's an absolutely gut-wrenching piece of music. And I don't know why it wasn't released as a single. It might have been too personal. Still, you had "Tears in Heaven" and everything that wound up happening with the *Rush* soundtrack. But man, what a song. It deserved so much more than it got.

But that introductory flourish has so much impact. It reminds me of "Innuendo" by Queen. It's like the final part of a play or an opera that you're watching, and you're hearing the orchestra in the pit perform this music. You feel like you're going into the grand finale of something. If you take three songs off the album and you put this last—I'll get to "Fading Lights" in a second—then you're looking at a completely different record. In my opinion, there are too many songs. If they had narrowed it down somewhat, you might have been able to save face on this thing. Of course, that means taking off the ones I told them to (laughs). You would have had to have cut "Jesus He Knows Me" and "I Can't Dance" in order for that to happen. And that's something that the label wasn't ever going to dream of doing. Because that's what they pushed. But I love that song.

Martin: We close with "Fading Lights," which of course is the most proggy thing on the record, even if that applies only to the loud jam in the middle. Elsewhere, it's another excursion into that whole hypnotic space of songs like "Biko," "In the Air Tonight" and earlier on this record, "Dreaming While You Sleep." My favourite music on the whole album is that massive guitar and drum sequence at 3:38. But as soon as Tony starts playing, it becomes lesser, although he redeems himself once he starts soloing. Then that whole section from there on to the end of it is my second favourite part.

Todd: Yes, with "Fading Lights," there's the beginning part with the drum machine. And then the second part of it is where you get hit with the gated drums again. They've given you a break from that, but then they hit you really hard with the gated drums, which I think is to really good effect. "Fading Lights," I think, is one of the reasons why we've not gotten another recording from these three guys. Because I feel like they intended it to be the last song. Or they might have suspected it would be the last song and I think they wrote it that way.

I feel kind of bad for the people that didn't go to the most recent tour because they thought, you know, I don't want to remember Genesis this way. I don't want to remember them old. And I don't want to remember Phil sitting in a chair. But they played the first half of this song as a trio in the show and it was incredibly moving. You could tell that it was them saying goodbye. I wouldn't have missed that for anything. So I think this song is really beautiful. Other than Tony's kind of crazy solo in the second half, it's pretty simple and kind of laid-back. It's powerful, but not complicated.

Martin: Was it incredibly moving because the fans recognised that it was the last song of this lineup? Is that what you mean?

Todd: I think some of them did. Maybe it was just moving for me (laughs). I think for most people, it was just one of the songs that they did acoustically as a trio. But for me, it was because I felt like it was them saying goodbye. And I think it's a great song. Those who dismiss this album, they're forgetting about how good "Fading Lights" is. It's a remarkable track. It would have done them some good to put a guitar solo in it instead of a keyboard solo, because just about every song on these last three or four albums has a keyboard solo in it. Of course, as somebody who loves Tony Banks, I love that. But I think it would have been maybe more memorable to more people had it been more conventionally structured, with a guitar solo instead of yet another keyboard solo.

Martin: Just to focus on your point there, to what extent do you feel the band themselves thought *We Can't Dance* would be their last album?

Todd: Tony Banks has said that he felt like maybe this would be the last. Every time they did an album, it was harder and harder to get their schedules matched. And he felt like this time, 1991, might be the last time that they would ever do that. I personally think that when they toured in 2007, they should have made an album. It's too late now, but they could have done that. But "Fading Lights" is a really good send-off, and maybe also a good transition to what we're about to talk about next.

David: Thank *The Lamb* that they go out with something better than anything else on the record, I suppose. The quieter, ambient feel adds greatly to affairs, I think, here. And it's very much a goodbye song, isn't it? It's a goodbye to this album. It's perhaps the only place on the record where it feels like this was always going to be the last track. This was the only one positioned to go directly against my previous statements. This is the only one where they said this needs to be the closer. This couldn't be track three.

And in a lot of ways, it's a goodbye to Genesis, isn't it? Obviously they would have *Calling All Stations* in 1997, but let's be honest, that's a Mike + The Mechanics album that changed its name to try and sell more copies. Ray Wilson for me is a Mike + The Mechanics Paul Carrack replacement more than he is a Phil Collins replacement for Genesis. There's nothing Genesis about that record whatsoever. For this band, this is the, "Thanks for all the memories and we'll see you on the reunion tour when we need a few million," as has happened twice now.

I do wonder if "Fading Lights" would have been better if it was half the length. At ten minutes, it's too long for the most casual of audiences, who are probably the ones following you at this point. But again, so many in that casual audience are probably just driving in the truck or doing the ironing that they might not notice the length. There's a lot of guitar and synth in the second half. I'm kind of being hypocritical here because I'm complaining about the length, but I've also said this has got different parts. And I have said I wished that there would be more dynamism on this album. And then when we finally get that, I'm saying I wish the song was half the length.

But having the guys come up with all sorts of ideas and stitching them together one more time kinda gives me the warm and fuzzies. It's the first time on this whole record that it feels like three or four ideas have been put together, in the old style, and that they've come up with something grander than any one of the ideas, any one of the constituent parts. The whole is greater than the sum of the parts. And in ye olde Genesis style for the first time on this record, certainly. And in the catalogue for the first time in an awfully long time, really, probably since as far back as *Duke* or *Abacab* at least, and I'm being charitable now. So yes, it's almost a trip around the three-piece one more time, and then it goes right back to the subdued opening, the very patient opening it starts with. Quiet, loud, quiet isn't revelatory in any sense of the word, but at this point in Genesis' catalogue, anything is better than nothing. And this isn't just anything; it's something.

Doug: Man, with "Fading Lights," ladies and gentlemen, this is how you close out a recording career. Perfection. Nobody realistically thought this was goodbye in 1991, but it was. Still is and always will be. It drove me insane on the farewell tour that they only played it up until they were about to launch into that epic jam at 3:39 in the song. I'll offer my last comparison with Rush, because those guys closed out their career with "The Garden" to perfection. Genesis closed out theirs, unintentionally or intentionally, also with perfection. Not a single second is wasted here. It's an absolutely perfect song that gives me chills and tears and everything to this day.

Banks can deny that it was about the end of the band, but until they release another album, prove me wrong. I don't want another Genesis album just like I didn't want another Rush album. Once you heard "The Garden," Neil dies, that's it. You walk. And Genesis chose to not make any more records together after this. They could have, in 2007, before this farewell thing. They could have gotten together in a studio and worked for six months. I know Phil still has a brain. He still could have his son play drums. He can still write. So I really think that this was intentional. And I'm not alone in that, because Phil wasted so much time on really mediocre records in the '90s into the 2000s that were nowhere near what he was doing here.

But the output of work that he did with Genesis, his solo work and the soundtrack stuff, that will wipe a human being out. And then you risk getting into vanilla stale territory. That's what happened to Phil. Remember, he was on *Oprah* with *Dance into the Light*. He was on *Oprah* pitching that thing for an hour. I'm like watching it and I'm going, okay, I'm hearing nothing here. This is not the same guy that was handing me, you know, *Abacab*. What happened here? And I get it. People mature and they hit different points in their life and they're gonna write about different things and whatever. But "Fading Lights" is how you close out a progressive rock career.

How many bands can say they did 14 records—15 counting *Calling All Stations*—and have a legendary career and sold 100 million albums as a band worldwide and they haven't released an album since 1991? My point is, it didn't take them more decades to get to 14 albums. There's very few bands that have done that. Even AC/DC still put stuff out. But Pink Floyd managed to do that. They were able to get away with *A Momentary Lapse of Reason* in '87 and *The Division Bell* way up into 1994. But there are few bands that have done that. I know Journey's out there putting out new records, but again, it's quite a compromised lineup and it's not good stuff. There's Styx with

Crashing the Crown. I listened to that. Are people really gonna think of that as, oh yeah, that's the way to sign off; that's the way to go out? No, there are very few bands that have had the opportunity to go out on such unbelievably high notes.

Martin: And "Fading Lights" even has this quiet and quite prescient final two minutes, right? It's actually kind of haunting.

Doug: Absolutely, but they blew it on the final tour. As far as I'm concerned, that should have been the last song, you know, just bringing the curtain down, drawing it to a close. Production-wise, all these things come into my head when I'm seeing a band. I'm like, how are you not seeing this? Just like Rush did with R40, you could take it back to the early '70s to close it out. I know Hackett was there. I know Gabriel was there. And you're giving the nod to the more progressive-loving British crowd who swears by the Gabriel era more than the Americans do.

So from a production standpoint, I'm looking at everybody and I'm going only "Fading Lights" makes sense. It was the last song we recorded. It's the last song on our last record. It should be the last song. It's about the lights fading. And the fact that Phil even says, "We're not playing anymore—this is it." You know, he says it at the last show. So whatever. That's just me being a fan. I'm not a production master. I know that you'd have to change a whole bunch of shit around. But that just makes sense to me.

But at least with *We Can't Dance*, Genesis can be remembered for the fact that they closed out their final album with two masterpieces that were genuine Genesis songs that you could have heard earlier in their career. They managed to pull that off, mind you, after having a lot of garbage packed in, a lot of empty calories.

Martin: So ultimately, how did they close out that last concert?

Doug: That was in London, over there at the O2. They did a homestand stretch there. They played all their final shows in England. And then Peter Gabriel and Steve Hackett showed up for the final show, to sit right there in the front. And Phil told them before the show started, you know, this is it. Because Gabriel had said to him, "You're not looking well. You shouldn't be out here doing this. You're killing yourself doing this." And Hackett said the same thing. He's like, "You don't need to do this anymore. You don't have to be doing this."

And it makes you kind of wonder, was it all really pushed as much as it was because of Phil's divorce? Was it because he had his clock cleaned? She's still trying to pull scams off down in Miami here selling all this crap. And it's just, you feel so bad for what Phil Collins has gone through in his life, with the health scares and everything else.

Those interviews on YouTube are priceless. He's so honest about, look, I was near death, a handful of times. He's like, I would just go in and lock myself in. And this is in the 2000s! In the 2010s! Just collapsing, drinking bottles and bottles of wine all day, all night, being completely incoherent. He had physically done so much damage to himself, not only through decades of abuse on tour, but his drinking had gotten so out of control that he was falling all the time. He was physically hurting himself to the point where he was constantly having surgeries.

That's one of the untold things. He went to have this corrective spine surgery, and it affected his hands and his feet and then he got club foot and all this other stuff. And then they wheel him out there in a chair that looks like it's from like OfficeMax. It was humiliating to see this icon like that. At least when Dave Grohl broke his leg, he had this throne he sat on. Phil Collins was in like a members-only jacket and a pair of khakis and he's sitting in this basic chair that has rollers on it. It's like, what?! What am I seeing here?! And he did that on a solo tour too. But he did the announcement there at that final show and said this is it; you are seeing the final Genesis concert. We are ending this tonight.

That was March 26, 2022, at the O2 Arena, and as the set list went, a lot of the classic songs were made into medleys. without any lyrical context to them. It was just the band jamming. So you had Phil sitting in a chair as the band's playing for like fucking ten minutes. He's just sitting in a chair staring at them, you know, looking back at his son, looking at the band. And it's like, how are these things not thought out in advance? "Phil, we'll take you off, we'll move you over to the side, we'll darken out the side of the stage." Whatever. No, they kept the fucking spotlight on him the whole time.

And he really couldn't play piano anymore, because of the damage to his nerves. He was hoping that he was going to be regaining all of these things. But he's in his 70s. It's not happening. He's critically sick, you know, for the rest of his life. And it was sad to see that happen. It was a weird tour.

And what's also weird is that "The Carpet Crawlers" was the last song. There's "Dancing with the Moonlit Knight," "Tonight, Tonight,

Tonight" and a snippet of "Stagnation." It leaves a lot to be desired. You're playing "Fading Lights" early in the set, and you're only playing the first three-and-a-half minutes of it.

Martin: At least Peter and Steve are there.

Doug: True, but they sat in the crowd. They didn't go up on stage. They said, no, this is their baby; they've carried this on. They put the work in to finish this. We're just here as support to let this chapter close out in our lives. I think if Phil hadn't gotten as ill as he did, Genesis would have been the perfect candidate for a Vegas residency. Elton John was able to pull that off, as did Rod Stewart, all of those guys, every night. Phil's a showman, so he could have done that. It's a real shame. He got so fucking robbed in so many ways in his personal life. But then again, we don't know how much of it was self-inflicted, and we don't know how much of it is just because of who he is.

Martin: Well, like you alluded to way back near the beginning of this book, he's basically Albert, and we're not quite sure how much we're supposed to like Albert.

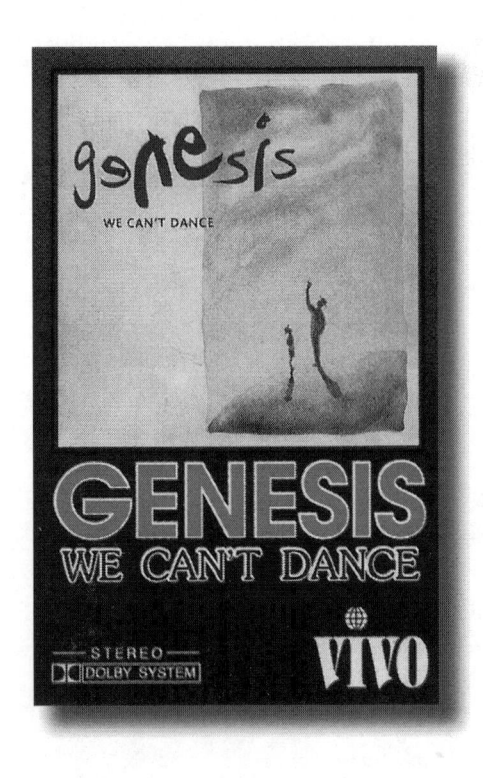

We Can't Dance

...THE NEW ALBUM...
GENESIS
...CALLING ALL STATIONS...
...CALLING ALL STATIONS...
...CALLING ALL STATIONS...
...CALLING ALL STATIONS...
OFFICIAL GENESIS WEBSITE: WWW.GENESIS-WEB.COM

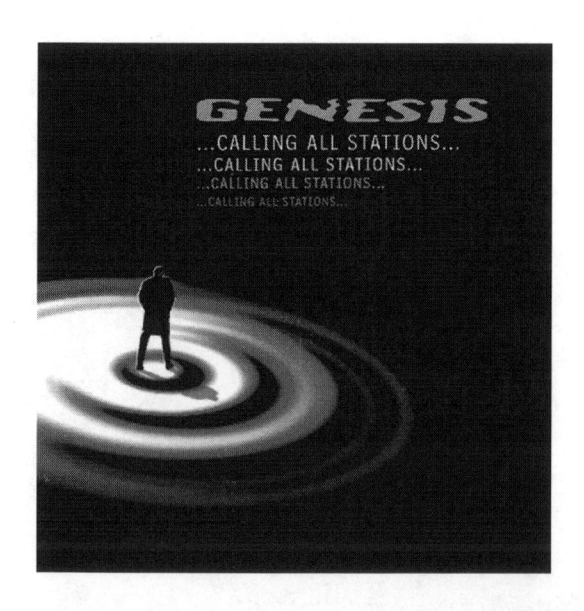

CALLING ALL STATIONS

September 1, 1997
Virgin GENCD6
Produced by Nick Davis, Tony Banks and Mike Rutherford
Engineered by Nick Davis; assisted by Ian Huffam
Recorded at The Farm, Chiddingfold, Surrey, UK
Personnel: Ray Wilson – vocals; Tony Banks – keyboards; Mike Rutherford – guitars
Additional musicians: Nir Zidkyahu, Nick D'Virgilio - drums

1. Calling All Stations (Banks, Rutherford) 5:43
2. Congo (Banks, Rutherford) 4:51
3. Shipwrecked (Banks, Rutherford) 4:23
4. Alien Afternoon (Banks, Rutherford) 7:51
5. Not About Us (Banks, Rutherford, Wilson) 4:38
6. If That's What You Need (Banks, Rutherford) 5:12
7. The Dividing Line (Banks, Rutherford) 7:45
8. Uncertain Weather (Banks, Rutherford) 5:29
9. Small Talk (Banks, Rutherford, Wilson) 5:02
10. There Must Be Some Other Way (Banks, Rutherford, Wilson) 7:54
11. One Man's Fool (Banks, Rutherford) 8:58

Entangled: Genesis on Record 1969-1976

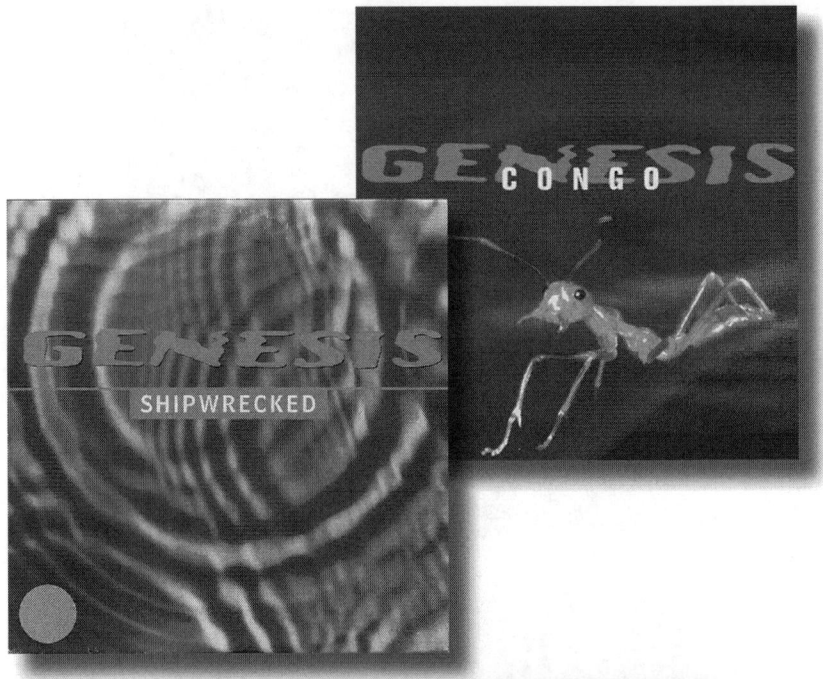

A *Calling All Stations* Timeline

June 1997. Ray Wilson is announced as the new singer for Genesis.

September 1, 1997. Genesis issue a 15th and final studio album, entitled *Calling All Stations*, featuring new vocalist Ray Wilson. It reaches No.2 on the UK charts but stalls at No.54 in the US.

September 15, 1997. "Congo" is issued as the first single from *Calling All Stations*. Used as B-sides are "Papa He Said" and "Banjo Man," both non-LP. "Congo" reaches No.29 on the UK charts.

December 1, 1997. "Shipwrecked" is issued as a single, reaching No.54 in the UK.

January 23 – May 31, 1998. The band tour Europe in support of *Calling All Stations*. A US campaign is cancelled due to poor ticket sales and the band breaks up, only to re-form in the 2000s—with Phil Collins—for additional concerts but no new albums.

February 23, 1998. "Not About Us" is issued as the third and final single from *Calling All Stations*. It stalls at No.66 on the UK charts.

May 31, 1999. Mike + The Mechanics issue a sixth album, a self-titled. Co-producing is Nick Davis, who had worked with Mike in Genesis. Ray Wilson quickly gets back on the horse, and issues, under the band name Cut_ (sic), an album called *Millionairhead*.

Behind The Lines: Genesis on Record 1978-1997

Martin talks to Daniel Bosch, Ralph Chapman and Todd Evans about *Calling All Stations*.

Martin Popoff: All right, we arrive at the very last studio album to bear the Genesis name. It's obviously a messy end to the catalogue, analogous to the likes of Pink Floyd and Rainbow, two bands I've done panel books on, actually. What are your views on *Calling All Stations*?

Daniel Bosch: Fans of this bands hate this album, critics panned it at the time and large amounts of people in both those camps feel it isn't a real Genesis album because neither Peter or Phil is singing. It's certainly not top-shelf Genesis, but it's also quite salvageable. This album gets a bad rap.

Interesting choice for new lead vocalist in Ray Wilson. He was in this band called Stiltskin, who had a hit in 1994 called "Inside" that had been used in a Levi's jeans commercial and then it became a hit on its own. They auditioned a bunch of singers. Kevin Gilbert was in line for the job until he sadly passed away. David Longdon, who later would be in Big Big Train, was almost up for the job. I'm a big fan of that band and I do wonder if things might have worked out differently had he been chosen. May he rest in peace as well; we lost him in 2021. They ended up going with Ray Wilson, who was a good choice because there's a bit of Phil and a bit of Peter to his voice. In that way he was quite versatile, for covering all aspects of the band's catalogue at this stage.

Ralph Chapman: I'm a tremendous fan of *Calling All Stations* because I'm a tremendous fan of Tony Banks and Mike Rutherford. I've told you this before, Martin. I am resentful of fans who cannot contextualise a band's career. Or who somehow think that the guy on *Trespass* is somehow not the guy on *Calling All Stations* and *From Genesis to Revelation* right through to *Calling All Stations*. I hear Tony Banks, because he's always been the force of the band. So just on that level, the fact that Tony Banks is on that record, it's justified in its creation. And I regret the sad fact that they ended there. Although I understand why they did. I think there are songs here, like "The Dividing Line" and "There Must Be Some Other Way," where Ray Wilson is really the sound of that era of Genesis.

And it was a really shrewd move on Banks' and Rutherford's

part that they picked these really inventive, aggressive, imaginative drummers to play on *Calling All Stations*, so you don't listen to *Calling All Stations* and go, "Wow, that drumming sucks." You might say it's not Phil, but you never say the drumming sucks. The drumming is superlative.

Todd Evans: Well, I always had the impression that Phil quitting Genesis in 1996 was completely unnecessary. Because they always broke and did other things anyway. I think that him doing that put too much pressure on him for *Dance into the Light*, which I think is part of the reason why it didn't do as well as they thought it would. People were like, okay, well, this is your full-time gig. Let's see what you've got.

And then *Calling All Stations* was just Tony and Mike not wanting to stop. You could say a lot about what they decided to do. There's a lot of information out there. Supposedly, they spent a weekend with Francis Dunnery from It Bites and offered him the job. And he thought about it and decided not to take it. I've never heard that this was concrete or not, but I've also heard rumours of it and I think it's probably true, that they considered giving it to Jack Hues from Wang Chung, which I think would have been a great idea.

I don't know if they ever considered Fish. I think that would have been good for Genesis to continue with Fish as their lead singer, but I don't think that Fish would have been happy doing that and I think it would have dissolved. But Jack Hues would have been a great choice, because he's got a great vocal range. And then Francis, he's got a kind of a Gabriel-esque thing going with his voice. But Francis Dunnery is kind of a flaky dude. He doesn't stick with anything for very long. There probably would have been only one album with him and he'd be like, I don't want to do this anymore; I don't want to be Phil II.

But when they announced Ray Wilson, they were really cheeky about it. I don't know if you remember this from the press, but they said a couple of things. They said, well, it's somebody famous, but not too famous. But the problem with that is Ray Wilson was only famous in the UK. His band, Stiltskin, basically had this corporate rock song that went to No.1. It was big in other countries too, but nobody had heard it in the US. So he really wasn't famous. That's one of the things that I think slows this album down, is that nobody knows who he is. And he's not ever properly introduced. He doesn't have a strong enough personality to introduce himself.

Martin: When they lose Phil, they lose way more than a third of the band. They lose probably slightly over half of the band. You're asking a lot of your fans here, because the two guys who are left aren't exactly robust and known personalities.

Todd: Well, I'm looking at what was going on at the time. I mean, a band whose centrepiece is a keyboardist, basically, most known as a synth player, this is not the time for that. Grunge has just happened, and we're getting into this whole alternative thing. You've got all this stuff that is so un-Genesis happening in the marketplace. But they also said in the press release when they announced Ray Wilson, something like, "Genesis, after all these years, have finally decided to replace Peter Gabriel." And I thought that was clever. Because Ray Wilson probably has more in common with Peter Gabriel than he does Phil, as far as the sound of his voice goes. I think he's light years away as far as having Peter's flamboyant personality, if indeed anybody could remember that to make the comparison.

But I was excited about this album. I saw the pictures and I can remember thinking—which is funny now as an older man looking back on it—that, well, he's only like 28 and they're in their 40s. How is this gonna work? So *Calling All Stations*, I've always liked it. I think it's a good album. I don't necessarily think it's a misstep. But there are some big problems with a couple of the tracks.

Martin: Over to the graphics, the writer in me is instantly stressed because long time ago we had *...and then there were three...*, which we're calling *And Then There Were Three*. Now we have *...CALLING ALL STATIONS...*, which we're going to go ahead and render as *Calling All Stations*. In fact, you might have to say it four times to get it technically correct as far as the front cover is concerned. And then of course the title track leaves off both sets of ellipses anyway. Okay, that rant out of the way, what do you think of the cover?

Daniel: It's not a great album cover, but it's not a terrible one either. The thing that I do like about it, which I think relates to the album, is it's quite dark, certainly more so than *Invisible Touch* or *We Can't Dance* or *Genesis*. It's perhaps an attempt to go back to the tone of some of their earliest stuff that they'd been doing, both musically and graphically although musically it's still very modern.

Todd: I've always really liked the cover. Atlantic did some really cool things with merchandising. They had these little stand-ups that went in the CD rack. They had this little guy and it was like 3D. I think the design of it is really great. But then they just stopped promoting it. It feels like they put it out and then just didn't do anything.

Martin: Do you like the production? Nick Davis certainly gets them a bold and strident sound.

Daniel: Yeah, and they picked a couple of really good drummers to replace Phil, in Nir Zidkyahu and Nick D'Virgilio from Spock's Beard, who's one of my favourite drummers in the world. I think he's brilliant. But yeah, he takes that walloping Hugh Padgham drum sound and then goes a step further. It can actually get a little distracting.

Martin: Amusingly, the album opens with the heaviest guitar ever on a Genesis album, although unsurprisingly, it doesn't last. But "Calling All Stations" is still a really cool, heavy, moody track, almost in that "Kashmir" and "Squonk" zone.

Daniel: Yes, I really like this as an opening track. It's got that crunchy, barking, growling opening guitar that's almost metal but not quite. And then the synthesizers have that really magical, wonderful Tony Banks feel to them. Ray's vocal is spot-on for this song. The only thing I don't like about it is that it feels like it's building to a climax towards the end of the song and then it just fades out, and in a really weird place. You're expecting them to burst through with some new elevated part and then it peters away. It's like, why? It's really anticlimactic. But it's a great, dark opening track.

Todd: "Calling All Stations" I think is 100%, A+. I love everything about it. And I even don't mind the fade-out, which a lot of people don't like, including, evidently, Daniel (laughs). They said that the first track was going to be something dark and heavy and it is definitely something dark and heavy. The melody's beautiful. I like everything about it. It's thick and lush and starts off the album with a bang, along with much more guitar than you usually hear from a Genesis album. Now if they thought that that was going to help them in the particular rock climate of the late '90s, they probably gave too much thought to that. Because I don't think it did. In any event, it's good with an album like this, where they're trying to re-introduce themselves, that the title track starts the album off in a big and imposing way.

Martin: I think the power and the drama of the first song carries over to "Congo" as well. There's a consistency there of loud arrangement, maybe even too much consistency.

Daniel: "Congo" was the first song I heard off this album, because it was the lead single. And I was really apprehensive when this came out. Because I was like, oh, who's this new guy? What's it going to be like? Is it going to be any good without Phil? Ray Wilson has a smokiness to his voice, which I really like. This song is really catchy and it's got a cool synth solo. It's not exactly poppy, but it's definitely radio-friendly. For me, it's better than any of the singles off the previous two albums, with the sole exception of "No Son of Mine" because I think that is an absolute classic. But I think it's a better single than any of the other singles off *We Can't Dance* and it's certainly better than the song "Invisible Touch," which is horrible. I like it, but it also has a bit of a weird fade-out, although it's not quite as jarring as the one on "Calling All Stations."

Todd: I don't think "Congo" should be on the album. I think it's a terrible first single. The lyrics are difficult to understand and, again, oddly specific. My biggest problem with "Congo" is the structure of it; it's just a mess. It's got a bridge that goes into nothing. It's got a bridge that happens and then they just do the chorus again. It's like, why is there not a guitar solo there or something or some kind of transition? And then it goes into this part just before the end that's new, and then the song just fades out. That's one of the only Genesis songs that is actually helped by the single edit because it's so weird structurally. But yeah, I think "Congo" just totally falls on its face.

Martin: Like the first song, it's got the big, lumbering drums.

Todd: To me, that's a positive. Apparently, Phil Collins was asked after it came out if he'd listened to it, and he said yes. And somebody said, "What do you think?" And he said, "Great drums" (laughs). Yeah, Nir Z did a fantastic job. I think they recreated that sound really well.

Ralph: When I first heard "Congo," I liked it. Again, I hear Tony Banks in it. For another non-Genesis album without Phil, take *The Fugitive*, which is a solo album from '83. I love that record and it's the same kind of thing. The guy just knew his way around a melody. The lyrics are, again, enigmatic. They're not obvious or overt. It's a really great melody line and some of the lyric lines are strong.

It's interesting, because it's 1997 and, again, you have to contextualise these things and take a look at what's going on in 1997. For lack of a better word, prog is dead. Even modern Genesis-style prog is dead. Without Phil in the band, I'm sure Atlantic Records didn't know what to make of it, of that single. For those of us who just wanted interesting music, who never had hopped on the grunge thing, it was refreshing. By that point grunge had given way to things like rap metal, and it was the rise of hip-hop music and everything had become that much more fractured.

I don't want to get into whether that was a good or a bad thing, but for a band like Genesis, who were already sort of grandfathers in late '91 when *We Can't Dance* came out, there was a whole generation gone by now. Who was gonna buy that record? Who's left? And it's funny, because *Calling All Stations* is sitting there in an interesting period in the life of this band. If you look at that period, *Both Sides* comes out in '93 and it's Phil's... well, it's not his *Calling All Stations*, but despite the presence of that single, "Both Sides of the Story," it's not a commercial record. The songs are all done by him. The songs stretch five, six minutes long and the tempos are so achingly slow. So it's not a commercial record. It's an exploration of him busting up his second marriage. And it's a commercial flop comparatively, the black mark on his career. It changes Phil, and he doesn't gain cred from that. It just makes him seem like he's even more out-of-touch.

So that's '93. And then, while he's making that record, he's forced to do some Genesis charity gig. He's busted up his marriage, so he's in a full midlife crisis, and he's gone back to his old girlfriend from school, and he's in the throes of something, so he quits Genesis. The mind boggles. He quits Genesis; he doesn't feel he can get up and sing these lyrics anymore.

And that royally pissed me off even more as I got older, although who am I to get pissed off? Anyway, the next time we hear from Phil, he's got a 20-something girlfriend and he's putting out *Dance into the Light*, which reflects his newfound domestic bliss. He's mining some of the roads that Paul Simon had mined. So he's very influenced by African music, specifically South African but also East African music.

And it falls flat on its bloody face. For some reason, I remember it was released October 21, 1996 and it was profound because now at this point, Genesis has lost a generation of fans. They've all moved on or been disenchanted by the whole aftermath of *We Can't Dance*. There's no real audience left beyond diehards like me. So the failure of *Calling All Stations*, and in tandem, "Congo" as a single, is wrapped up in its timing.

Martin: Interesting; all right, next is "Shipwrecked," which sounds like a cross between *Disintegration*-era The Cure and Peter Cetera or Air Supply, not that Genesis themselves haven't trafficked in squarely AOR ballads.

Daniel: Yeah, "Shipwrecked" is a so-so ballad. I'm not a big fan of these sappy Genesis ballads from the '80s and '90s. I like a good ballad as much as the next guy, but I'm really not into these ones with the maudlin or expected lyrics and chord changes. Although I will say again, this is better than a song like "Hold on My Heart" from *We Can't Dance*. That song is just dreadful. But it is what it is.

Ralph: "Shipwrecked" is another song about lost love and regret and isolation. And, you know, using the metaphor of being a wrecked ship, you watch a ship sink and it's an oddly emotional moment, to see it overturn. And maybe that starts with Titanic. Because ships and boats represented humanity's first ability to travel in any kind of meaningful way. I don't know, I always thought that using the metaphor of a ship going down to signify the tragedy of the end of a relationship, or the uncertainty of a relationship, was valid. I was hooked by that.

I'd disagree that Ray Wilson sounded like Peter Gabriel. He had a thicker voice. And he couldn't do the same flights of fancy, or wasn't asked to do the same flights of fancy that Phil could easily do. But on "Shipwrecked," they use his voice exactly to its strength. I'm always suspect of people who dismiss that song. All you have to do is listen to later Mike + The Mechanics records, because that's a much harder thing to get behind. With Tony Banks there, the combination of Rutherford and Banks, that's what makes it work. In interviews, one of those guys said that without Phil there, there was no mediator and that they found it harder to write songs. But it's like they'd forgotten that they'd written songs like "Squonk" together. But that's where the synergy of those two writers works so beautifully, is on "Shipwrecked."

Todd: This album, if it had gone from "Calling All Stations" into "Shipwrecked," this song could have garnered more attention. Apparently I'm in the minority, but I think "Shipwrecked" is a beautiful song and could have been a hit. It was a single but it wasn't promoted very well. I like that it's simple lyrically. Tony is doing some of his best tricks. He has that part towards the end where he delivers this dissonant chord, and it just swells and gets bigger and bigger and bigger.

But yeah, if the sequencing had gone from "Calling All Stations" to "Shipwrecked," instead of putting "Congo" in there, which I just think is weak, this album might have lived a longer life. I also like the way "Shipwrecked" sounds. It starts with that kind of AM radio sound and then they hit you with the full sound a couple of seconds later. That's really effective. Sure, it's kind of trite, but I like it.

Martin: As a bit of a criticism of Ray, do you find his vocals kind of sleepy, like he's not pushing much air? I've always found that when singers operate so within the comfortable part of their range, there's an energy that's lacking.

Todd: Yes, I do, and that's one of the reasons this project didn't work. It's not that I don't like it—I like it a lot. But there's no personality there. Phil Collins was almost a clown. He would get up in front of that band and just tell dumb jokes. And not in a way where you're thinking, like, oh, somebody shot Phil up, but in a very concise way. He was very animated. He had a particular look that was unique and you either love it or hate it. Then you get this good-looking guy with a pretty decent voice who comes on and he sings all of these pretty good songs, but not in a remarkably interesting way (laughs). And then forget Phil—this is light years away from Peter Gabriel.

Martin: With "Alien Afternoon," we're back in that zone where Genesis present an interesting enough percussive palette, and then place atmospherics on top of it. That naturally comes from Tony and his synth washes, but I actually think Ray's dreamy, drifting voice is really nice on a chill track like this.

Daniel: Yeah, he doesn't have the projection that Phil or Peter had, but I still like his vocals. I like the timbre of his voice. He's more laid-back than Phil or Peter. Although Phil was a bit like that in the early days too, and then he found a more projecting and sometimes harsh vocal approach, if you like. But you listen to the vocals on *A Trick of the Tail* and *Wind & Wuthering* in particular, he's quite whispery and quiet. I wonder if they'd stuck with Ray and done a couple more albums, if he might have come out of his shell as a singer.

As for "Alien Afternoon," if it's possible for a melody to plod, this one does, especially in the early part. But I like the lyrics of this song. There's this guy talking about this alien afternoon. He's sort of weirded-out about where he is at the moment. I like this kind of presentation, where somebody's in a place that's making them deeply uncomfortable. And I love the middle section, which is really atmospheric and builds up nicely. This is one of the longer tracks on the album, at eight minutes, and thankfully it doesn't fade too early, although again, oddly, Ray is still singing as it fades. But it's a song in two parts, and the first part I'm not so keen on.

Todd: "Alien Afternoon" is kind of "Tonight, Tonight, Tonight" Part C (laughs). I personally think the lyrics are kind of dumb, although not too bad. Put it this way: the lyrics are a solid effort addressing what is not a great idea. The problem is that Ray Wilson doesn't sell it. This guy is telling you a story about how he had this supernatural experience. The second part gets a bit more intense, with that "We are home/We are your home/We are all your home" part. That's a really great musical moment, and I think he sells it better there. But this whole, "Gotta get out/Pack my bags before I go insane/Gotta get away in time," it doesn't build properly. Tony and Mike wrote that song and Phil probably could have sold it. I don't think Ray sells it.

Martin: Do you find that with this record, we're really getting a graphic picture of Mike and Tony being of the same mind as far as songwriting goes? Like there's a shared vision that's always been there, certainly since Peter left, but I feel like with *Calling All Stations*, there's a confirmation that yes, they both love slow, atmospheric ballads with big drums where nothing much happens. I mean, There's a lot of the last two albums in this album.

Todd: Yeah, I think to Genesis' credit, they never tried to put Tony and Mike so far in the background that you didn't know who they were. If you look at any of the videos from their most successful period, all three of them are always in them. So they never just took Phil out and separated him, which I think is a good thing. Because then when you transition into this, people are used to seeing Tony and Mike and they know who they are.

But it's difficult for people who aren't fans of the band to define what they did. Phil Collins, when asked in interviews if Genesis was ever one person who would it be, he always says Tony. And I agree with that. I think Tony is the main architect, with Mike bringing some pop sensibilities and some really interesting playing that is not very guitarist-like. But as far as this album really helping you get to know the personalities, I don't think it does. I think that Tony should have sang a song on it. That might have helped. He's not that bad; he's a John Lennon kind of a vocalist. Whenever he sings a song on one of his solo albums, like on *The Fugitive*, it's surprisingly not terrible. That may have helped introduce him a little bit more.

Martin: Next is "Not About Us," another ballad that uses this consistent palette of sounds.

Daniel: "Not About Us" is the exception I was talking about with ballads. I really like "Not About Us." It was a single. The lyrics are not great, a bit wishy-washy, but the melody is absolutely gorgeous and Ray's vocal is superb; he actually puts some lift into the chorus, some energy.

Martin: The chord changes are majestic and kind of sad. Again, there's so much of Mike's and Tony's complicated personalities in this song.

Daniel: Yeah, absolutely. I feel like some of the moody atmosphere from those '70s albums is present here, although not in the production, because the sound picture is very modern, especially at the drum end of things. I think some of that was lost on *Invisible Touch* and *We Can't Dance*, which offered a higher amount of pop material.

Todd: "Not About Us" is pretty effective at what it is, at its role. They were giving Ray Wilson an opportunity to help them write something, and I think for its time it fits in. They do a really good job of sounding like the kind of mainstream rock and pop music that was happening at that time. There's not too much flash and it's kind of acoustic-based.

But maybe they should have leaned on this track more. It could have been the lead-off single. They were trying to be unique about how they presented themselves in this new configuration, and I feel like they should have gone safe with it. They should have led with a song that introduces you to this guy's voice and they could have done that with "Not About Us."

Martin: Interesting. And on cue, here comes another ballad, "If That's What You Need," awash in keyboards, again with Ray singing slow and steady, as if in a trance.

Daniel: Yeah, this one's a bit ho-hum. It doesn't do a lot for me. It sounds like a second-rate Mike + The Mechanics song. Don't get me wrong; I like Mike + The Mechanics, when they are good. But this is like a B-side of theirs; it wouldn't have made the album.

Todd: I like it because I'm a sucker for Tony Banks' thick orchestration. Otherwise, I don't think there's a lot happening in this song. The album is 68 minutes long and I feel like this could have gone. I don't think it brings anything particularly unique to the table. It's not crucial. You've got "Shipwrecked," you've got "Not About Us" and you've got "Uncertain Weather," and I think all three of those are better. This is just kind of "there."

Martin: "The Dividing Line" is more blustery, again, dominated by Phil Collins- or Jerry Marotta-like drums, and—fortunately for you, Todd—perennial torrents of Tony synths as well as a riff from him.

Todd: Yeah, "The Dividing Line" is spectacular. Had there been anything beyond the European tour, this could have become the centrepiece song from them. I looked this up last week. I thought that the American tour got cancelled before the European tour happened, but the American tour was first. It was scheduled in arenas, cancelled for arenas and then scheduled in theatres and cancelled for theatres. I was looking at some of the dates and, like, Chicago was supposed to be the Rosemont Horizon which is not that big of a venue, maybe 11,000, 12,000. And then they moved to the Rosemont Theatre which is small. I saw Dennis DeYoung there once and if they couldn't sell tickets to that, then they were really in trouble.

But "The Dividing Line" might have been the centrepiece of the live show at that point. Tony's sounds are really cool and very progressive. There's a drum solo and it's fantastic; Nir Z is just killing it on this song. The fact that it's mainly an instrumental with just a small lyrical part to it, that's pretty cool too; it makes it unique. I don't think they've done anything quite like this. When I hear it, I don't think oh, this is supposed to be like "Home by the Sea" or whatever; it's its own thing.

Ralph: The big thing about this album is the same thing that affects "The Dividing Line." It's like people arguing about whether Rush would come back and who the drummer would be, and I'm always saying, "But who would be the lyricist?" With *Calling All Stations*, the effect of the absence of Phil's voice was acute. But he was also an extraordinary drummer. Not just technically, but he had spent all these years with these two guys. So they knew each other inside and out and they knew how to play off each other.

And even if in the later era of Genesis with Collins, they largely based their recordings on writing together on drum machines that Phil would add onto. He still knew how to play off Banks and Rutherford. Again, I go to "In the Glow of the Night" as a classic example of something where he was probably playing to a rhythm track. But instinctively, he knew what Genesis was as much as anybody. As much as he even would deny it or distance himself or apologise for all those so-called wretched things he does, he was Genesis.

And now they're hiring Nir Z and they're hiring Nick D'Virgilio from Spock's Beard. They're both great drummers. In fact, "The Dividing Line" is one of those songs where you forget for a second that Phil's not there. It's a very invigorating drum track. Take a listen to the recordings of them from Poland, and you'll hear that it was a showcase moment for Nir.

But I talked about the humanity that runs through all their lyrics, going right back to "The Conqueror" and going right back to "Looking for Someone." You listen to the lyric on "Calling All Stations" or "Shipwrecked," which is another great Rutherford lyric, or "The Dividing Line," and that's still there, all the way to the last album.

Daniel: I love the synth bass intro to this song and there's some cool guitar in the intro as well. Those drums, I wonder if it was, "Hey, can you give us a little Phil Collins?" or whether it just came naturally to him. This is a really good, energetic, latter-day Genesis song and close to my favourite from the last three or four albums.

Martin: Another thing I noticed about this record is after being very turned off by the production on the first song, as the songs move on, you hear a lot of interesting production ideas constantly being added. Like, "Oh, there's a new sound" and "What is that effect Tony's using?"

Daniel: Yeah, absolutely. It's not a one-note record by any stretch of the imagination. It's funny, going back to *Genesis*, except for "That's All," that's a bit of a one-note production album, isn't it? It has the same sound the whole way through. This doesn't, which is credit to Nick Davis and his work for those guys.

Martin: "Uncertain Weather" is a nice addition to the Genesis canon, in that it also contributes to the band's identity, this time combining ballad with a soft tribal percussion backdrop. I don't know, Ray's misty, laconic tone on some of these makes me think of The Alan Parsons Project and Porcupine Tree, Steven Wilson, or even Kevin Moore from Chroma Key. He sort of lulls you into a dream state.

Daniel: Yeah, good stuff; you're right. "Uncertain Weather" is in that ballad zone but it's moody and atmospheric rather than sappy. It's not bad, but it's not great either. It's definitely not a "Not About Us" but it's better than "Shipwrecked." As I said earlier, these latter-period Genesis ballads, for the most part, aren't really my cup of tea. It's not what I want to hear from Genesis.

Todd: I feel like this is an example of Tony trying to write something similar in structure to "Undertow" from *And Then There Were Three* and really succeeding. Nick D'Virgilio plays the drums on the song and he plays them beautifully. It's not a big, fat, gated drum sound, but more conventional. Tony's doing a lot of his tricks, and I love the chords that swell and then quiet down again. The chorus sort of has two parts to it, with the second part more intense than the first. It's a strong song. I don't know how good of a single it could have been, because it doesn't seem like it's a particularly accessible ballad.

Martin: Now that I'm so won over by the production, I can listen to "Small Talk" and just revel in the tones. This is a thumping pop rock song, I suppose, with some arpeggiated guitar in there as sort of a riff. I don't want to compare to this album to Peter Gabriel all the time, but there's a bit of a funk pulse to this one, like "Sledgehammer," "Big Time" and "Steam."

Daniel: Yes, all of this is really shared by both Peter Gabriel and Genesis, isn't it? Since pretty much the third Peter Gabriel album and *Duke* into *Abacab*. It's sort of a mid-paced rocker, and there's a lot of those on this album. There's some really nice keys and synth work from Tony and just a good atmosphere.

Todd: "Small Talk" is a really effective track, and probably the closest that Ray Wilson gets to showing some kind of a personality that is recognisable. The album needed something like that for sure, something lighter towards the end. A lot of folks who don't like this album look at "Small Talk" as a reason why. I don't think it was a bad idea for them to try something like this. I've always looked at it favourably and it sits in the right spot in the album.

Martin: "There Must Be Some Other Way" returns the listener to his unsettled, pensive mood. This really is a sort of rain and clouds album, isn't it? Although, again, it's fun or at least rewarding to listen to just for the audiophile experience.

Daniel: Yeah, I like how this song sort of builds from quiet verses to loud chorus and then back again. Rush did that a lot. They'll go from quiet to loud to quiet and they'll go from half time to double time to half time and that sort of thing. I'm a sucker for that sort of arrangement. There's a really great middle section with Tony, yet again, doing a bit of a synth solo. Tony and Mike, it's funny. I know you've been grappling to describe their personalities. I would say that Tony does have personality, but it's in his music. He was never a great media guy or interviewee. Mike was a little better with that, but he was still a quiet guy, relative to other rock stars, certainly.

Todd: "There Must Be Some Other Way" is too long, although I think it's Ray Wilson's best vocal track; it's really soulful. He takes the opportunity to really open up towards the end and it's quite effective. There's also an interesting keyboard solo spot about two-thirds of the way through. I don't think I would have taken this song out of the sequence, but I feel like having it at the end right next to "One Man's Fool" is difficult for the casual fan not to think that they might want to turn it off. Getting those two songs back-to-back at their lengths is a lot to ask of somebody who already might not be comfortable with Phil Collins not being present.

Martin: Is this one a bit like "Home by the Sea?"

Todd: Yes, I'd say so. It's maybe a lot like "Home by the Sea." Lyrically, it's just okay. All three of them are responsible for this one; so Ray Wilson had something to do with it. But it's long at almost eight minutes. "One Man's Fool" is a better Genesis song. So having something as thick and long as "There Must Be Some Other Way" right before it might make you kind of tired (laughs).

Martin: Man, I'm definitely agreeing with you guys about the end of the album here. Mike and Tony are steadfast in their belief that what they are doing is right. They are creating this massive sculpture of sound, this ecosystem, that is not in the least about excitement. It's a construction that takes its time. It's like a lush forest of sound, but ultimately just sort of peaceful or ponderous, not in the least action-packed.

Ralph: *Calling All Stations* has two sins. One big sin, which is a product of the CD age, it's too long a record. What they should have done is make it a double album. They should have done what Blue Rodeo did with *The Things We Left Behind* and acknowledge that there's a fatigue that sets in. It happened with *We Can't Dance* as well, so it's not exclusive to the post-Collins era. If they had included the interesting B-sides, like "The Banjo Man" and "7/8," and if they had thoughtfully sequenced it as a double album statement and not attempted to hide the fact that their big commercial goldmine was gone, it might have looked completely different. Or if they just put it out as two 40-minute single discs, I think it'd be a very, very different conversation. So I think that's the biggest sin.

And the other big sin is that they didn't follow it up. It's a one-off to the point where it feels like a half-finished project. We celebrate *Trespass* because in many ways it bore *Nursery Cryme* and *Foxtrot* and *Selling England* and *Lamb*, right up until, in my mind, again, *Invisible Touch*. But we're left in a lurch with *Calling All Stations*. We're left with the idea that they lost confidence in it. And for people who are susceptible to influence, who don't know what to feel, that just ruins the legacy of the record.

And I feel for Ray Wilson, who kind of got screwed in some

way. Although, would we even be knowing the name Ray Wilson if he hadn't been picked? You think about some of the people like Kevin Gilbert, who were suggested. Kevin Gilbert, the guy from Toy Matinee, is a brilliant, brilliant instrumentalist and Genesis fanatic who died before he could audition. That's another story all together.

Martin: And Francis Dunnery.

Ralph: But Francis Dunnery, I think, was too big a personality even at that stage. So I don't know. And I don't think they would have ever hired someone like him. But an obscure Scotsman in a band called Stiltskin that really hadn't gone anywhere? Or Kevin Gilbert, who had done an album called *Thud* that went nowhere and was in a band called Giraffe, which used to cover Genesis, I think, as encores? But I could be wrong. These guys were waiting to be discovered, much like one could say about Phil, in that he was an unknown quantity when he took over the lead vocals. There were a few people who knew about Flaming Youth and knew about those select Genesis tracks, but vocally, they had no idea if that would work. Francis Dunnery would have changed the dynamic in a way that I don't think would have been preferred. I don't yearn for Dunnery. But I do wish they had done a follow-up. I wish they'd come to North America and just fucking sucked it up and played smaller theatres.

I also think the massive shadow that was cast by *Invisible Touch* affected *We Can't Dance* and then really affected *Calling All Stations*. There was nothing left for them to do. They had explored everything. So I think *Calling All Stations* was also a reflection of, well, what's our identity? Oh, I guess we make records. I guess we own Genesis, so let's do it. And then it was snuffed out by a lot of poor planning and bad luck, and not, in my opinion, by the record itself. Beyond, as I said, they should have made it a double album statement, representing a new chapter in their career.

Daniel: "One Man's Fool" is the closest thing to an epic on the album. It's nine minutes long, there's a lot of atmospherics, and atmospherics that are similar to those across the rest of the album. This is the thing about *Calling All Stations*. It's so atmospheric to the point of being soundtrack music. You've got this odd, quiet keyboard solo in the middle. And again, I was talking about that half time/ double time thing. It goes to double time at the end of the song, where the drums are suddenly playing twice as fast as they were in the rest of the song, which I think is a great way to close the song out, with lots of energy. Therefore, despite its length, that structure makes it a more than sensible choice to close out the album.

Todd: "One Man's Fool" is very well done as far as having a structure that is unique to Genesis. It has that part where it goes, "There are only dreams one like any other/ What means the earth to one or few means nothing to another," and when he gets to that part, it kind of slows down and strips back. I think that's pretty effective. The lyrics are good, but not great, but good enough. But I like the way they structured it, because it doesn't go where you expect it to go.

Martin: Nice. So what happened after this?

Todd: They did a theatre tour in Europe. It was bigger venues in the UK, but it worked. They were able to sell enough tickets in the bigger venues. And then after that tour was over, they did a couple festival shows in late May of '98.

Daniel: Like Ralph says, it's a real shame that they didn't make another album with Ray. This was a good start, and had they persisted, it could have become something better. But I think the problem was that they just didn't want to go as far down the food chain as they would have had to, in order to keep doing it. They were having to go down from playing stadiums to playing arenas to playing 2000- or 3000-seater rock clubs. I don't think they wanted that at this stage of their career. I don't think they wanted to go back down to that level and have to build their way up again. And that's a shame.

And the thing is, Tony Banks didn't just give up on Genesis after this. He basically gave up on rock and pop music after this. It's the last rock-based album Tony's been involved with. The only things he's done since then have been these classical, orchestral albums. And I like those fine, but I like Tony Banks, the songwriter. I miss that; that's sad to me.

So yeah, I would have loved to have seen where this lineup had gone if they'd done a couple more albums and had integrated Ray more into the band. Because he only gets a couple of writing credits on this album. Most of the songs are written by Mike and Tony, and then Ray just comes in and sings them. It would have been nice to see him do more lyrically but also musically, with the band maybe jamming the songs into existence like they'd occasionally but successfully done before.

Overall, I like *Calling All Stations* more than the previous two. Those fade-outs still bother me, and they could have dropped two or three tracks, maybe "Shipwrecked" and "If That's What You Need." It's a long album; it's three sides on vinyl. But I like the darkness and atmosphere of the album. All the way back to *Abacab*, they are all quite upbeat and bright-sounding, poppy. This album is not the dumpster fire people say it is. Because let's face it, the fans loathed it and the critics wouldn't have anything to do with it. By 1997, they'd deemed Genesis irrelevant. This album never stood a chance.

Martin: A new singer was just too much to ask of the fans, especially as one-third of a trio.

Daniel: Yes, that's exactly it. It was a bridge too far.

Ralph: There was no place in the marketplace for them anymore. Which is why they should have done another record. Because they should have said, fuck it, we're artists and we're a band. Tony should have said to Mike and Mike should have said to Tony that there's something fundamentally unique and legitimate and extraordinary about what we bring to the table musically. And just because we've got a flop album, it doesn't mean we should stop. But they did. They were 46, 47 years old.

Martin: But of course, it's not nearly the end of Genesis.

Ralph: No, it's not, although there are reasons to frame it as such, if you don't buy *We Can't Dance* or even *Invisible Touch* as the end. They get together ten years after that and they do this lame-ass reunion tour. And really, I adore Genesis, but if I'm honest with myself, the decisions they made infuriated me because they soiled their own legacy. And again, that's why *Invisible Touch* is really the last great moment.

By 2006, there was activity again as they were anxious to remarket the catalogue. The remix campaign started because, all of a sudden, they didn't like the mixes of their past catalogue and there was new technology and Super Audio discs, SACD, had come out. There was a chance to remix in 5.1 So they had to do these new interviews that came with these reissues.

So Gabriel was back and Hackett was back. It was a real love-in, and through that, my understanding of it was—and a lot of it is in Phil's book—that the idea of finally doing a *Lamb* tour was back on the table. And there's a great moment in Phil's book where they were all supposed to meet, I think, in Scotland. So maybe it's a couple of years before. I'm not really sure the timeline because I think Phil's on tour. Someone's on tour in Scotland and they all meet there. And in Phil's book, he says, I went to this meeting thinking we were going to finalise the tour. Because we'd already talked about it and agreed to it. And Gabriel showed up with the mindset of, I don't know if I want to do this tour; let's talk about it. And Phil said Peter had resumed his role of the guy who couldn't make decisions, which was kind of like a throwback to the *Lamb* thing. Are you in? Are you out? Because he left during *The Lamb* and he came back. And it was kind of a reprise of that thing.

So Gabriel was all of a sudden off the table. And they never really seemed to have a relationship with Hackett after Hackett left, because it was an acrimonious departure, no matter how you want to dress it up. But there was never a question that they were going to do a four-man tour. So they were just sitting around, and Phil, I believe, was in marital discord. He had personal issues.

And so it came almost from the management side. I think Tony Smith could see dollar signs. It's like, I'm gonna get the Collins/Banks/Rutherford band back together. That means I can have them play "Invisible Touch," I can have them play "Mama," I can have them play all those staples that people were feeling nostalgic for, truly, by 2005, 2006, 2007. Those songs that were missed again, no pun intended.

And there's a tour documentary that is surprisingly candid, if a bit evasive, which is a contradiction in terms (laughs). But there's a moment there. I went to see the first show in Toronto. And in my opinion, Phil was done. He was phoning it in. He had been so undone by the criticism, in my opinion. It's in his book. He had believed all the headlines. So by the time you got to 2006, 2007, he's 56 years old. He's not Phil anymore. Even when he does the whole bit about the other world, which was the preface to "Home by the Sea" and "Domino," it's like he's making fun.

See, the interesting thing about Phil, in his desire not to be a parody of himself, he became a parody of himself. He's saying to himself, I'm not going to be that guy you love from the '80s. But we legitimately love that guy because he was a force. This guy he presented in '07 was not a force.

And for a guy like me, a Genesis fan like me, all you had to do was listen to the section where they do "Duke's Travels." And I remember sitting with my very pregnant wife, listening to him at BMO Field doing "Duke's Travels" as part of a larger medley, and there's a whole section of "Duke's Travels" that's really driving, with really fast bass pedals. I can't sing it (laughs). And for whatever reason, the song was rearranged to halftime, not to mention the keys were changed and lowered. The guy was older so I didn't mind the key changes and whatnot.

But when you fuck with the drive of that band, that's sacrilege. We touched on this with "Just a Job to Do," "Anything She Does" and the instrumental part on "Fading Lights." Phil Collins drove that band. So to see him get on the drums in a live Genesis setting and be the slow man, to be the guy who was being dragged, that was a seismic disturbance in my life.

And then when you watch the *When in Rome* video that came out after that, they actually show—which I find extraordinary—him trying to play that, not being able to play it, and giving up and throwing his drumsticks and saying, "I'll work it out." But he never does work it out. By the time I saw it, which had happened after the tour rehearsals, he never did work it out. And I, from my lofty perch, was dismayed. He was like, I'm not going to work it out. I'm not going to rehearse; I'm not going to do this. Because I don't have to.

He said so many other things that enraged me. And I say this as someone who adores Phil, otherwise I wouldn't be writing a book about him. In the run-up to that 2007 tour, someone asked Phil how Genesis' music could change. And he made a point of saying, "I'm going to drag my drumming into the 21st century" or something like that. I'm paraphrasing. And my immediate thought on that was, "They've beaten you." The critics have beaten you. Everyone has beaten you, Phil. That's the last thing you should be doing. Because that was such a part of Genesis, of what made them great. He was chilling out by '91, but there were still great moments.

But that's like McCartney saying, in a fantasy land where Lennon hadn't been murdered and Harrison hadn't died and they reunite, "You know what? I'm gonna lay back on my bass lines. That whole thing on 'Paperback Writer' or 'Rain,' I'm gonna simplify. Because you know what? That's too '60s, man." That's what Phil was doing. It's like, you don't get it. You're so close and inside, but also so battered by the criticism that you've lost your way. Phil was my hero. But the effect of that was this: I watched him walk through that show in Toronto. Doesn't mean the songs weren't great. But there was something entirely absent. I had first detected it on the *We Can't Dance* tour, but it was profound on the 2007 tour.

And then on the final tour, The Last Domino? Tour in 2021, 2022 where he's obviously infirmed and on so many levels he's a shadow of himself, it was his humour, and his reason for doing it, knowing that he wasn't going to play, that made that tour plausible. There's a lot of reasons, but those are two reasons why that tour was valid. To be sure, you had Nic Collins drumming, and Phil wasn't there at all in terms of his vocal range and his ability to project, but he seemed to want to be there.

It was shocking to see Phil that way, but it had made up for 2007, and as a story or as a narrative about a band aging itself into retirement, it definitely made for a poetic and really deliberate and precise end to the band's career. It's a symbiotic thing because you're paying hundreds of dollars. But in the end, as a hardcore Genesis fan, it felt like a celebration of the friendship and the accomplishments of those three guys, as much as it felt like a gift to us, the fans.

GENESIS

Behind The Lines: Genesis on Record 1978-1997

Contributor Biographies

Grant Arthur
Grant is a podcaster and airs his music discussion channel, *Grant's Rock Warehaus* (with over 1000 episodes to date) on YouTube. He is a principal co-owner of *The Contrarians* as well. Grant is an avid rock CD and vinyl record collector with over 10,000+ titles in his own personal "warehaus." He began loving music at age ten when he heard The Beatles' "I Want to Hold Your Hand" and states "his life was changed forever" when he heard The Cure's 1985 album, *The Head on the Door*. These days however, he thinks way too much about Cheap Trick and April Wine.

Daniel Bosch
Daniel grew up in a musical family, with a father who was a professional double bass player in a folk band and a mother who played piano, guitar and sang. Listening to everything from classical, jazz, folk and rock from a very early age, he started collecting records at age ten. He now runs a small music-themed YouTube channel called *bicyclelegs*.

Ralph Chapman
Ralph's most recent project is scripting the very first official feature documentary on that "little ol' band from Texas," ZZ Top, in collaboration with Banger Films. Previously, he served as writer and associate producer on the VH1 series *Rock Icons*. Prior to that, he served the same roles on the critically acclaimed 11-part series on heavy metal, *Metal Evolution*. Ralph was also part of the creative team behind the Juno award-winning documentary, *Rush: Beyond the Lighted Stage* which took the Audience Award at the Tribeca Film Festival in 2010. Ralph also continues to work with Iconoclassic Records as a project producer notably overseeing the reissue campaign of The Guess Who catalogue. He continues to develop projects with Banger Films, and on his own with his production company, Wesbrage Productions, while contributing to various music-related websites in his spare time.

Tate Davis
Tate really got into music after he heard Led Zeppelin's "Heartbreaker" on the radio for the first time at age 13. After he graduated high school, Tate spent time as an on-air personality at 88.3 WMTS in Murfreesboro, Tennessee for two years before becoming a part-time member of *The Contrarians* YouTube show. His favourite musician of all time is Keith Moon.

Todd Evans
Todd used to sit in front of the stereo in Buffalo, NY and watch the records spin. After moving to Atlanta, Todd was active in his high school band and attended the University of Georgia to study Music Education. Changing majors to Journalism, his DJ shift at UGA's WUOG 90.5 FM kept the music alive. Todd contributes to the YouTube channels *The Contrarians* and *Rushfans*, where he discusses classic rock, progressive, symphonic and classic alternative rock music.

David Gallagher
David was, like most musos, bitten at a young age and made a nuisance of himself long enough to work in a record store in Scotland through the 2000s. While he always maintained the passion, overly sharing his (sometimes) informed opinions via his YouTube channel *@flicksnpicks*, the pandemic gave him licence to unleash his almost impossibly lo-fi channel onto others.

Rand Kelly
Rand has been immersed in music since he can remember, going back to the mid-1950s. He has acquired quite a collection of recordings and musical instruments over the years including guitars synthesizers as well as a Mellotron. He was born in Eureka, California in 1952 and was raised on radio hearing Elvis Presley and The Beatles, which made a huge impression towards his goal of becoming a musician. Today he performs improvised music live on YouTube for anyone interested, recording on a cellphone and sometimes overdubbing using YouTube and his TV as a studio. Favourite bands include Yes, King Crimson, ELP, Gentle Giant, Pink Floyd and, of course, Genesis.

Jamie Laszlo
Jamie was raised in Pittsburgh, Pennsylvania and listened to the local radio station, WDVE, which helped teach him a lot about popular music. Even though the facts he learned at school faded from memory just days after each exam, the facts he learned about rock music seemed to stay embedded in his head. These days, Jamie is a YouTube music commentator and moderator, regularly contributing to *The Contrarians* and *Sea of Tranquility* music review channels. He's recently been awarded his own show on *Sea of Tranquility* called *The Review Crew* and he also commandeers a thriving Facebook page called *Let's Get Physical*, singing the praises of physical music media.

Douglas Maher
Douglas is a well-known and highly regarded music historian and archivist who also spent nearly two decades working as a music columnist for Yahoo! Entertainment and journalist for *The Lakeland Ledger*, *Naples Daily News*, *All Headline News* as well as stints working at WSHE-FM in Fort Lauderdale, WJNO-AM in Palm Beach and WAMI-TV in Miami. His history includes contributing to numerous publications and documentaries including *Rush: Beyond the Lighted Stage*, *Rush: Album by Album* and *Rush: Merely Players*. Doug has amassed an inventory of over one million items in radio, music and film-related advertising pieces dating back from 1890 to 2023. He is repeatedly sought after for help by artists filling in gaps for biography and documentary projects with his arsenal of entertainment history.

Pontus Norshammar
Pontus is a Swedish journalist based in Stockholm. A music geek and a major record collector since childhood, Norshammar contributes regularly to the YouTube channel *The Contrarians*, is a regular panel member on Scot Lade's Prog Corner live streams and has appeared on the British music podcast *The Epileptic Gibbon Music Show*. He is also involved with the Swedish concert scene. The first Genesis-related music he heard was "Sussudio" by Phil Collins. When Peter Gabriel's *So* was released a year later, he embarked on a journey that had him hooked on the Genesis back catalogue.

Pete Pardo
Pete is a writer and on-air personality from the Hudson Valley in New York, and has served as the Editor-in-Chief of the *Sea of Tranquility* webzine since 2001 and the Host and Program Director of the *Sea of Tranquility* YouTube channel since 2014. With over 24,000 reviews and articles on the webzine, and over 5100 videos, 98,000 subscribers and over 60 million views on the YouTube channel, *Sea of Tranquility* has been a constant source of information and entertainment on all things hard rock and heavy metal, progressive rock, classic rock, and jazz fusion for over 22 years. Visit *Sea of Traquility* at seaoftranquility.org and youtube.com/@seaoftranquilityprog/.

Bill Schuster
Also going by the name of Howler Monkey (founder of infamous music forums, *The Monkey House* and *CryNet*), Bill is a regular contributor to *The Contrarians* (co-commandeered by the author of this book), *Rock Daydream Nation*, *Grant's Rock Warehaus* and *Ryan's Vinyl Destination* among others.

Special Thanks

A hearty appreciation goes out to Agustin Garcia de Paredes who applied his eagle eye to a copy edit of this book. Agustin is also the moderator of the *History in Five Songs with Martin Popoff* podcast Facebook page.

About the Author

At approximately 7900 (with over 7000 appearing in his books), Martin has unofficially written more record reviews than anybody in the history of music writing across all genres. Additionally, Martin has penned approximately 130 books on hard rock, heavy metal, classic rock, prog, punk and record collecting. He was Editor-in-Chief of the now retired *Brave Words & Bloody Knuckles*, Canada's foremost heavy metal publication for 14 years, and has also contributed to *Revolver*, *Guitar World*, *Goldmine*, *Record Collector*, bravewords.com, lollipop.com and hardradio.com, with many record label band bios and liner notes to his credit as well.

Additionally, Martin has been a regular contractor to Banger Films, having worked for two years as researcher on the award-winning documentary *Rush: Beyond the Lighted Stage*, on the writing and research team for the 11-episode *Metal Evolution* and on the ten-episode *Rock Icons*, both for VH1 Classic. Additionally, Martin is the writer of the original metal genre chart used in *Metal: A Headbanger's Journey* and throughout the *Metal Evolution* episodes.

Then there's his audio podcast, *History in Five Songs with Martin Popoff* and the YouTube channel he runs with Marco D'Auria and Grant Arthur, called *The Contrarians*. The community of guest analysts seen on *The Contrarians* has provided the pool of speakers used across the pages of this very book. Martin currently resides in Toronto and can be reached through martinp@inforamp.net or martinpopoff.com.

A Complete Martin Popoff Bibliography

2024: Behind the Lines: Genesis on Record: 1978 – 1997, Entangled: Genesis on Record 1969 - 1976, Run with the Wolf: Rainbow on Record, Van Halen at 50, Honesty Is No Excuse: Thin Lizzy on Record, Pictures at Eleven: Robert Plant Album by Album, Perfect Water: The Rebel Imaginos

2023: Kiss at 50, The Electric Church: The Biography, Dominance and Submission: The Blue Öyster Cult Canon, The Who and Quadrophenia, Wild Mood Swings: Disintegrating The Cure Album by Album, AC/DC at 50

2022: Pink Floyd and The Dark Side of the Moon: 50 Years, Killing the Dragon: Dio in the '90s and 2000s, Feed My Frankenstein: Alice Cooper, the Solo Years, Easy Action: The Original Alice Cooper Band, Lively Arts: The Damned Deconstructed, Yes: A Visual Biography II: 1982 – 2022, Bowie @ 75, Dream Evil: Dio in the '80s, Judas Priest: A Visual Biography, UFO: A Visual Biography

2021: Hawkwind: A Visual Biography, Loud 'n' Proud: Fifty Years of Nazareth, Yes: A Visual Biography, Uriah Heep: A Visual Biography, Driven: Rush in the '90s and "In the End," Flaming Telepaths: Imaginos Expanded and Specified, Rebel Rouser: A Sweet User Manual

2020: The Fortune: On the Rocks with Angel, Van Halen: A Visual Biography, Limelight: Rush in the '80s, Thin Lizzy: A Visual Biography, Empire of the Clouds: Iron Maiden in the 2000s, Blue Öyster Cult: A Visual Biography, Anthem: Rush in the '70s, Denim and Leather: Saxon's First Ten Years, Black Funeral: Into the Coven with Mercyful Fate

2019: Satisfaction: 10 Albums That Changed My Life, Holy Smoke: Iron Maiden in the '90s, Sensitive to Light: The Rainbow Story, Where Eagles Dare: Iron Maiden in the '80s, Aces High: The Top 250 Heavy Metal Songs of the '80s, Judas Priest: Turbo 'til Now, Born Again! Black Sabbath in the Eighties and Nineties

2018: Riff Raff: The Top 250 Heavy Metal Songs of the '70s, Lettin' Go: UFO in the '80s and '90s, Queen: Album by Album, Unchained: A Van Halen User Manual, Iron Maiden: Album by Album, Sabotage! Black Sabbath in the Seventies, Welcome to My Nightmare: 50 Years of Alice Cooper, Judas Priest: Decade of Domination, Popoff Archive – 6: American Power Metal, Popoff Archive – 5: European Power Metal, The Clash: All the Albums, All the Songs

2017: Led Zeppelin: All the Albums, All the Songs, AC/DC: Album by Album, Lights Out: Surviving the '70s with UFO, Tornado of Souls: Thrash's Titanic Clash, Caught in a Mosh: The Golden Era of Thrash, Rush: Album by Album, Beer Drinkers and Hell Raisers: The Rise of Motörhead, Metal Collector: Gathered Tales from Headbangers, Hit the Lights: The Birth of Thrash, Popoff Archive – 4: Classic Rock, Popoff Archive – 3: Hair Metal

2016: Popoff Archive – 2: Progressive Rock, Popoff Archive – 1: Doom Metal, Rock the Nation: Montrose, Gamma and Ronnie Redefined, Punk Tees: The Punk Revolution in 125 T-Shirts, Metal Heart: Aiming High with Accept, Ramones at 40, Time and a Word: The Yes Story

2015: Kickstart My Heart: A Mötley Crüe Day-by-Day, This Means War: The Sunset Years of the NWOBHM, Wheels of Steel: The Explosive Early Years of the NWOBHM, Swords and Tequila: Riot's Classic First Decade, Who Invented Heavy Metal?, Sail Away: Whitesnake's Fantastic Voyage

2014: Live Magnetic Air: The Unlikely Saga of the Superlative Max Webster, Steal Away the Night: An Ozzy Osbourne Day-by-Day, The Big Book of Hair Metal, Sweating Bullets: The Deth and Rebirth of Megadeth, Smokin' Valves: A Headbanger's Guide to 900 NWOBHM Records

2013: The Art of Metal (co-edit with Malcolm Dome), 2 Minutes to Midnight: An Iron Maiden Day-by-Day, Metallica: The Complete Illustrated History, Rush: The Illustrated History, Ye Olde Metal: 1979, Scorpions: Top of the Bill - updated and reissued as Wind of Change: The Scorpions Story in 2016

2012: Epic Ted Nugent, Fade To Black: Hard Rock Cover Art of the Vinyl Age, It's Getting Dangerous: Thin Lizzy 81-12, We Will Be Strong: Thin Lizzy 76-81, Fighting My Way Back: Thin Lizzy 69-76, The Deep Purple Royal Family: Chain of Events '80 – '11, The Deep Purple Royal Family: Chain of Events Through '79 - reissued as The Deep Purple Family Year by Year books

Behind The Lines: Genesis on Record 1978-1997

2011: Black Sabbath FAQ, The Collector's Guide to Heavy Metal: Volume 4: The '00s (co-authored with David Perri)

2010: Goldmine Standard Catalog of American Records 1948 – 1991, 7th Edition

2009: Goldmine Record Album Price Guide, 6th Edition, Goldmine 45 RPM Price Guide, 7th Edition, A Castle Full of Rascals: Deep Purple '83 – '09, Worlds Away: Voivod and the Art of Michel Langevin, Ye Olde Metal: 1978

2008: Gettin' Tighter: Deep Purple '68 – '76, All Access: The Art of the Backstage Pass, Ye Olde Metal: 1977, Ye Olde Metal: 1976

2007: Judas Priest: Heavy Metal Painkillers, Ye Olde Metal: 1973 to 1975, The Collector's Guide to Heavy Metal: Volume 3: The Nineties, Ye Olde Metal: 1968 to 1972

2006: Run for Cover: The Art of Derek Riggs, Black Sabbath: Doom Let Loose, Dio: Light Beyond the Black

2005: The Collector's Guide to Heavy Metal: Volume 2: The Eighties, Rainbow: English Castle Magic, UFO: Shoot Out the Lights, The New Wave of British Heavy Metal Singles

2004: Blue Öyster Cult: Secrets Revealed! (updated and reissued in 2009 with the same title; updated and reissued as Agents of Fortune: The Blue Öyster Cult Story in 2016), Contents Under Pressure: 30 Years of Rush at Home & Away, The Top 500 Heavy Metal Albums of All Time

2003: The Collector's Guide to Heavy Metal: Volume 1: The Seventies, The Top 500 Heavy Metal Songs of All Time

2001: Southern Rock Review

2000: Heavy Metal: 20th Century Rock and Roll, The Goldmine Price Guide to Heavy Metal Records

1997: The Collector's Guide to Heavy Metal

1993: Riff Kills Man! 25 Years of Recorded Hard Rock & Heavy Metal

See martinpopoff.com for complete details and ordering information.

Entangled: Genesis on Record 1969 – 1976

ISBN: 978-1-915246-62-6

Did Genesis represent the best and most classic definition of a progressive rock band? Were they the most British? What kind of personalities and sensibilities did we get out of Peter Gabriel, Phil Collins, Steve Hackett, Tony Banks and Mike Rutherford and where did all these 12-string guitars come from? What's a "Giant Hogweed" and who is "Harold the Barrel?" Finally, what the heck is *The Lamb Lies Down on Broadway* about, anyway?!

These are some of the questions grappled with, as Martin Popoff assembles a crack team of art rock analysts to examine the early-days records of this legendary band, namely:

From Genesis to Revelation
Trespass
Nursery Cryme
Foxtrot
Selling England by the Pound
The Lamb Lies Down on Broadway
A Trick of the Tail and finally...
Wind & Wuthering.

Indeed, each of the above is dissected track by track with side-trips into the album covers, the productions, lyrical narratives and individual performances of note. It is the hope of the author that by the end of this fantastical excursion, the reader will have discovered multiple new layers to this intensely cerebral band, prompting a reacquaintance and subsequent richness of experience when confronted with this—let's face it—often daunting catalogue.